D1325724

ENHANCING EDUCATIONAL EXCELLENCE, EQUITY AND EFFICIENCY

Evidence from evaluations of systems and schools in change

Enhancing Educational Excellence, Equity and Efficiency

Evidence from evaluations of systems and schools in change

Edited by

Roel J. Bosker
University of Twente,
The Netherlands

Bert P.M. Creemers
University of Groningen,
The Netherlands

and

Sam Stringfield
Johns Hopkins University,
Baltimore, U.S.A.

In collaboration with Interuniversitair Centrum voor
Onderwijskundig Onderzoek (ICO)

KLUWER ACADEMIC PUBLISHERS
DORDRECHT / BOSTON / LONDON

Library of Congress Cataloging-in-Publication Data

ISBN 0-7923-6138-5

Published by Kluwer Academic Publishers,
P.O. Box 17, 3300 AA Dordrecht, The Netherlands.

Sold and distributed in North, Central and South America
by Kluwer Academic Publishers,
101 Philip Drive, Norwell, MA 02061, U.S.A.

In all other countries, sold and distributed
by Kluwer Academic Publishers,
P.O. Box 322, 3300 AH Dordrecht, The Netherlands.

Printed on acid-free paper

Printed in the Netherlands.

Contents

6. Quality and Opportunities in Secondary Education: Implementation and Effects of the Common Core Curriculum   113

Greetje P. C. van der Werf, Hennie P. Brandsma, Lidwien M. C. M. Cremers-van Wees & Miranda J. Lubbers

7. Evaluating the Impact of a Raising School Standards Initiative   137

Brenda Taggart & Pam Sammons

8. Systemic, Whole-school Reform of the Middle Years of Schooling

167

Peter W. Hill & V. Jean Russell

9. Review and Prospects of Educational Effectiveness Research in the Netherlands 197
Jaap Scheerens & Bert P. M. Creemers

10. The Future Agenda of Studies into the Effectiveness of Schools 223
David Reynolds & Charles Teddlie

Preface

Promoting high standards while striving for equal opportunities under the budget constraints, these are the new global objectives of education systems. This book brings together research based evidence on the effectiveness of major Australian, Dutch and UK improvement efforts in education at both primary and secondary level, whilst making comparisons with similar US initiatives. The book addresses several major questions in this new environment. Those questions include: how to combat educational disadvantages, how to integrate pupils with special educational needs in regular education, how to implement educational standards initiatives, how to restructure secondary education, how to implement decentralized policy making, and how to implement a class size reduction initiative? Finally, the authors suggest directions for future research in order to increase our understanding of what works in education, and why?

The authors of this book are either regular members or were guest lecturers for the Dutch Interuniversity Educational Research School ICO. ICO is a centre of excellence that brings together the best educational researchers in the Netherlands and their Ph.D. students. One of the divisions of ICO focuses on the evaluation of large-scale innovations in education, and the study of educational effectiveness. The reason for this combination is of course that the school is an important lever in bringing about systemic, enduring change in education. The research school organizes summer school sessions and master classes for its Ph.D. students, where colleagues from all over the world come to teach. After a decade we felt that we had to share what brought us together with others. We decided to do so by presenting exemplary studies in this field.

We would like to thank Lisenka Alblas, Tim de Jong, Annemarie Mak and Carolien Post for their unfailing assistance in completing the manuscript.

Enschede/Groningen/Baltimore

Roel J. Bosker
Bert P.M. Creemers
Sam Stringfield

1. ENDURING PROBLEMS AND CHANGING CONCEPTIONS

Roel J. Bosker[1], Bert P.M. Creemers[2] & Sam Stringfield[3]
[1]*Faculty of Educational Science & Technology, University of Twente, the Netherlands*
[2]*GION, University of Groningen, the Netherlands*
[3]*Johns Hopkins University, Baltimore, USA*

This introductory chapters highlights some of the common issues of concern in education systems in western, industrialized societies. Changes in both the basic steering model in education as well as structural changes are being sought to find solutions to old problems and new challenges. Key features are increased local decision making, and more autonomy for schools. This latter implies that it is important to know how schools can shape their own organization so as to meet the demands imposed upon them. This chapter closes with a brief outline of the various chapters contained in this book and an explanation of nomenclature.

1.1 Enduring problems

Whatever the structural change, some problems in education seem never to disappear. The strive for higher, increasing performance levels of youngsters in education and in the economic competition between countries on the global market will probably never cease. It is the intrinsic upward drive that keeps each system up and going. But whilst trying to shape systems for this purpose, two other conditional objectives have to be met as well. These are the democratization of education according to meritocratic principles, implying equal educational opportunity to each and everyone in society regardless of socio-ethnic origin and gender. This is not only considered fair, it is also seen as an economic necessity in the societal search for 'manpower'. But next to that, it is also viewed as preventing unacceptable forms of segregation, in which the creation of a new group of 'have nots' should be avoided. The excellence of an education system is not only measured by average levels of achievement or by the percentage of extremely high performing pupils, but also by the gap that exists within the system both between privileged and underprivileged pupils, as well as between 'regular' and special needs pupils. The objectives of excellence and equity in education are often conflicting, if only because of the existence of a third objective: to increase efficiency in education systems. The contributions to this book cover these enduring themes, although each contribution has a different focus. But let us first of all attempt to describe some common themes.

1.2   A changing conception of steering

What is common to education systems in western, industrialized countries is that over the last two decades a different conception of steering has evolved. From a centralized, highly regulating type of steering, a more decentralized one has emerged. The general principles underlying this new conception of steering are that there should be less central rules, devolution of decision making powers to lower levels in the administrative hierarchy (from state to local, from local to school), and increased autonomy for schools. The philosophy is that schools seeking solutions to the problems they face depend on local circumstances, and that central steering will hinder schools both in addressing these problems as well as in finding and implementing solutions. Responsiveness is a key word here. Setting appropriate (high) standards, introducing market mechanisms (like public choice), and creating new accountability systems (like publishing school results) are the minimal steering mechanisms in such a new policy conception. And of course, finding new ways to fund schools, in which budget maximization should be prohibited and good practices stimulated, is an additional element of this conception. In one of the chapters it states that certain schools are not even aware of the fact that they receive extra funding, let alone that they know for what purpose. What will come up in the Netherlands, that we already know about from the United States with its school districts and from the United Kingdom with its local education authorities, is an intermediate level in the educational administration hierarchy. This is quite natural where a national policy intends to devolve decision making powers to municipalities or networks of schools. It remains to be seen, however, whether these intermediate levels are indeed in a position to formulate and implement adequate educational policies. As a new trend in policymaking we see an increasing interest in education and a growing political will to invest in it. This issue will be taken up in the next section.

1.3   A changing conception of the effective school

Having stated that there is an increased willingness to invest in education, we might consider one of the criticisms of school effectiveness research, namely that this research tradition serves to justify a *"refusal to respond to teachers' anxieties about increasing size of the classes they teach, the use of traditional teaching methods, such as whole class instruction, and a tendency to blame the headteachers for 'failing schools'"* (as Reynolds and Teddlie cite Elliot in their chapter). Elliot is right in some respects: Edmonds' often cited five-factor model of effective schooling (Edmonds, 1979) is a case in point. According to this model strong educational leadership, an emphasis on the core subjects, a safe and orderly school climate, high expectations of pupil performance levels, and regular evaluation of pupil progress make up an effective school. But if one is willing to undertake the effort of going back to this often cited article, one will detect that Edmonds also mentions a sixth important characteristic of an effective school: resourcing! How indeed can schools, as the most important lever of change, manage to implement the centrally stated policies successfully if they are not provided with the proper conditions and a just amount of resources? But even given the provision of ample resources, the conception of what makes a school effective is changing. It is partly in need of change because our conception of learning and instruction has radically changed over the last decades from a traditional model rooted in behaviourism and consequently direct instruction, towards a constructivistic approach of learning, in which the situatedness of learning, independent learning, and scaffolding are prominent. Moreover, as will be readily demonstrated throughout this book, isolated school and instruction factors will probably be less powerful than an integral, systemic well-designed school restructuring approach to enhance this 'new learning'.

1.4   A changing conception of evaluation

Throughout this book it will become clear that the evaluations described heavily rely on monitoring systems. This implies a couple of things. First of all the idea is that through monitoring and describing the development of pupil performance systematically, education policy might be circumscribed as informed policy. That is something quite different from evidence based policymaking. The old debate between Campbell (1969) and Cronbach (1982) now and then seems to be having a revival. In 'reforms as experiments' Campbell argues that our knowledge of social systems can only grow if we are in a position to derive clear conclusions about causal attribution: did programme X cause effect Y? According to this point of view only true experiments, most notably randomized controlled trials, can guarantee a sufficient degree of internal validity of the evaluation design to be employed. Cronbach on the other hand, states that evaluation should take into account the interests of policymakers and other stakeholders. Information should have maximum utility for decision making purposes given the political circumstances, prevailing conditions under which the programme or policy should function, and resources available. Given this set of desiderata Cronbach contends that evaluation research can virtually never meet the criteria of pure scientific research. It is this latter view that clearly prevails throughout the chapters of this book. It is inevitably so, because the object of study is either a complete school system or at least a school. And even in the one chapter in which classes are of focal interest, it is argued that experiments even in the study of class size are of limited (albeit of some) value. One can easily imagine why: double blind as a guiding principle cannot be pursued consequently here, and the external validity (the generalizability of the results) of such an experiment would be questionable (for other objections see: Goldstein and Blatchford, 1998). Thus, instead, repetitive large scale cohort studies, where both pupils and schools are studied longitudinally, are used as being more informative, especially in the case where innovations are 'full coverage' (meaning that a control group does not exist). That still leaves the opportunity for quasi-experiments, namely in the case where experiments occur quite naturally. But as will be shown throughout this book, such naturally occurring experiments almost never exist. Practices and school reform quite often seem not to be well designed. The policy conception may have changed; schools have not yet developed the capacity to pursue what we might call 'total design' approaches. One thing is quite clear from the various chapters in this book: studying isolated phenomena will not increase our understanding much of what works why in education. It is the ideal mix of things that is more likely 'to do the trick'.

1.5   About this book

As was stated above, the basic steering model underlying educational policy has drastically changed during the last two decades from a centralized highly regulating one to a decentralized less regulating one providing more autonomy at local and school level. The chapter by Hetty Dekkers, Sjoerd Karsten and Fons van Wieringen shows how different concepts of governmental steering relevant to the Dutch context are related to different political views. A critical appraisal of the recent developments is being made, informed by empirical studies in this domain. As a case in point a study is presented on the new decentralized policy on educational disadvantaged pupils, in which municipalities will play an important role.

In the next chapter, written by Geert Driessen and Lia Mulder, the issue of equity in education is addressed. As from the 1960s various local and national programme in the Netherlands aimed at improving the educational opportunities of disadvantaged children were implemented in the Netherlands. In 1985 these initiatives were integrated into the Educational Priority Policy programme (EPP). This chapter describes the inception, aims, content, underlying theories, evaluation and effects of the EPP. The focus is on the results of the quantitative longitudinal studies in primary education between 1986 and 1992.

Integration of regular and special education is the topic of Felicity Fletcher-Campbell, Cor Meijer and Sip Jan Pijl's chapter. Dutch special education has developed a wide-ranging system, and maybe because of that it has gradually grown. In 1990 a new national policy was implemented in which clusters of special and mainstream schools were seen as a way to stop the inflow of pupils in special education. The policy and its evaluation is described in this chapter, showing that some progress has been made, but that the final objective, namely more adaptive instruction for all pupils, has not yet been achieved. The situation as well as evaluation research are considered and comparisons made between the situation in the United Kingdom and the Netherlands.

One of the oldest discussions in education pertains to the potential benefits of smaller classes for pupil achievement. In the chapter of Roel Bosker, Peter Blatchford and Wim Meijnen the research is reviewed, including some recently conducted studies in the Netherlands, conceptual issues are addressed, and plausible intermediate causal mechanisms are explored. It is contended that the issue of smaller class size should be embedded both in broader national educational policy as well as in a well designed school policy, will pupils indeed benefit from a more favourable teacherpupil ratio in the early schoolyears.

Greetje van der Werf, Hennie Brandsma, Lidwien Cremers-van Wees and Miranda Lubbers focus in their chapter on a nationwide innovation in the early years of secondary schooling. In august 1993 every Dutch secondary school implemented the Common Core Curriculum [Basisvorming]. Through modernization and harmonization of the curriculum as well as a statement of minimal standards to be achieved by (almost) all pupils, the aim was to achieve three objectives: increased levels of excellence, providing pupils with skills and knowledge for future technological and socio-cultural developments, and postponing the selection of pupils into one of the main four curricular tracks in secondary education until the age of 15. In this chapter the evaluation conducted, using a series of repetitive large scale pupil cohorts to see whether the objectives were attained, is described. The results indicate that the objectives of the innovation have hardly been reached yet: schools are still organized and still working as if the implementation had not taken place.

In the next chapter Brenda Taggart and Pam Sammons show that concern about the quality of schooling in disadvantaged urban areas has been especially marked throughout the United Kingdom during the 1990s. This led to a major school improvement project in Northern Ireland, known as the Raising School Standards Initiative, that was intended to help schools address significant disadvantage and under achievement amongst their pupils. The project, based on the knowledge base of the school effectiveness tradition, was designed to target a small number of secondary schools and their main contributory primary schools. The project therefore seeks to improve the quality of school management, the standards of literacy and numeracy, the levels of qualifications, links with local industry, parental involvement in schools, attendance and punctuality, and to deal with problems of discipline in class. The improvement strategy selected is an attempt to integrate a 'top down' external approach with a 'bottom up' strategy developed within individual schools. The evaluation conducted is described in this chapter, and the main findings are: schools developed their capacity to plan, monitor and evaluate school improvement; primary schools had less difficulties implementing the improvement strategy than secondary schools; there are substantial gains for individual children, especially poor readers, in some schools, but gains in mathematics were weaker. In the discussion section it is argued that the findings from the evaluation may have consequences for developing ways to contextualize school performance and setting results in context to facilitate policies of target setting and strategies to raise standards.

Peter Hill and Jean Russell in the next chapter describe a large scale longitudinal study into the cognitive and affective development of pupils in Australian schools between kindergarten and grade 11, that shows stagnation both in maths and language in the middle years of schooling. Moreover, attitudes towards schools are rapidly declining during this stage. Building on the educational effectiveness knowledge bases guiding principles for reforming the middle years are outlined, and it is advocated that a whole school design instead of an incremental approach is needed to bring about the desired changes.

In the chapter written by Jaap Scheerens and Bert Creemers a review is presented of recent Dutch research into educational effectiveness and a link is made with evaluations of school improvement projects. The synthesis of the findings of the Dutch educational effectiveness studies show that the foundational studies into questions pertaining to the stability and consistency of educational effects are more promising than the search for single effectiveness enhancing conditions. The critical review of the school improvement projects brings some encouraging findings to the light as well, favouring integral approaches to restructuring schools that 'penetrate' the classroom. Nevertheless new routes are envisioned that bring the educational effectiveness paradigm more in line with the prevailing, constructivistic conception of (independent) learning and (indirect) instruction and with a more economically inspired research tradition.

The concluding chapter, by Dave Reynolds and Charles Teddlie briefly summarizes some of the common findings and major criticisms of school effectiveness research. Eleven 'cutting edge' areas are identified where it is argued that the future of the discipline lies in terms of a research agenda to continue disciplinary advance. These areas are: the need to use multiple outcome measures; the need to use the third, relational dimension of school; the need to expand the study of context variables; the need to analyze range within schools and classrooms; the need to study the possibly additive nature of school and family effects; the need to explore the interface between levels of schooling; the need to study naturally occurring experiments; the need to expand variation at school level; the need to study school failure or dysfunctionality; the need to use multilevel structural models; and the need to recognize the salience of issues on curriculum and assessment.

A piece of nomenclature to end this introductory chapter. The system descriptions in the chapters of this book that focus on the changes going on in Dutch education have been synchronized with the Anglo-Saxon system by the editors. Especially to those that know the Dutch system this may be a bit confusing, but if we would not have done so those with insufficient knowledge of this peculiar system might have misunderstand certain things. The nomenclature used throughout this book is shown in table 1.

A further explanation of nomenclature relates to the use of the word 'private'. In the Dutch case 70 percent of all schools might be labelled 'private', since these - mostly religious - schools are both founded and governed by parents. Nevertheless these schools are completely state funded as are the state maintained schools governed by the municipalities (the latter are called 'public schools' but the use of the word 'public' may be a bit confusing for those familiar with the English system).

Table 1. Correspondence between Anglo-Saxon and Dutch grade names, with ages of pupils included

name	age	Dutch equivalent	
pre-school	0-3	voorschools	
pre-kindergarten	4	jaargroep 1	(primary 1)
kindergarten	5	jaargroep 2	(primary 2)
grade 1	6	jaargroep 3	(primary 3)
grade 2	7	jaargroep 4	(primary 4)
grade 3	8	jaargroep 5	(primary 5)
grade 4	9	jaargroep 6	(primary 6)
grade 5	10	jaargroep 7	(primary 7)
grade 6	11	jaargroep 8	(primary 8)
grade 7	12	leerjaar 1	(secondary 1)
grade 8	13	leerjaar 2	(secondary 2)
grade 9	14	leerjaar 3	(secondary 3)
grade 10	15	leerjaar 4	(secondary 4)
grade 11	16	leerjaar 5	(secondary 5)
grade 12	17	leerjaar 6	(secondary 6)

1.6   References

Campbell, D.T. (1969). Reforms as experiments. *American Psychologist, 24*, 409-429.

Cronbach, L.J. (1982). *Designing evaluations of educational and social programs.* San Francisco: Jossey-Bass.

Edmonds, R. (1979). Effective schools for the urban poor. *Educational Leadership, 37*, 15-24.

Goldstein, H., & Blatchford, P. (1998). Class size and educational achievement: a review of methodology with particular reference to study design. *British Educational Research Journal,* 3(24), 255-268.

2. CHANGING RELATIONSHIPS BETWEEN CENTRE AND LOCALITY IN EDUCATION

Hetty P.J.M. Dekkers[1], Sjoerd Karsten[2] & Fons M.L. van Wieringen[3]
[1] *Department of Education/ITS, University of Nijmegen, the Netherlands*
[2] *Department of Education/SCO-Kohnstamm Institute, University of Amsterdam, the Netherlands*
[3] *Department of Education, University of Amsterdam, the Netherlands*

The basic steering model underlying educational policy has drastically changed during the last two decades from a centralized highly regulating one to a decentralized less regulating one providing for more autonomy at the local and school level. In this chapter it is shown how different concepts of governmental steering relevant in the Dutch context are related to different political views. A critical appraisal of the recent developments is being made, informed by empirical studies in this domain. As a case in point a study is presented on the new decentralized policy on educational disadvantaged pupils, in which municipalities will play an important role.

2.1 Introduction

The main factor that led policy makers in the Netherlands to rethink the relationship between government and society was the economic crisis at the beginning of the 80s. Three large-scale operations were set in motion at this time, which affected all areas of government including education. They are known by the terms deregulation, privatization and decentralization. In education the deregulation process started around 1985 and began to have an effect from the beginning of the 90s. Decentralization only started at the beginning of the 90s and its effects began to be seen in 1997. Privatization is, in some senses, still in the development phase.

Deregulation, privatization and decentralization are defined differently in different national contexts. In the Dutch context 'deregulation' means reducing the number of rules from national government. The idea is that schools and school governing bodies in both state and state-funded private education will be able to function with greater autonomy as a result of this. The term 'privatization' is used to mean both the hiving off of government tasks to private bodies and the encouragement of increased private contributions to the funding of schools. The word 'decentralization' is used to designate the transfer of power and funds from the national government to local authorities. There are interactions between these three types of operation. In the Dutch context they also have different supporters: deregulation is popular among Christian Democrats in the main, privatization among Liberal Conservatives and decentralization among Social Democrats.

This chapter describes the most important changes in central and local relationships. First, we will examine the nature and content of the three operations mentioned above, which have each had an effect on central and local relationships in their own way. We will then go on to focus on one of those operations, that is decentralization, pausing first of all to consider the motives behind decentralization. After that, we will discuss the most important decentralization measures and, finally, report on the effects of one of these measures, that is policies to combat educational disadvantages.

2.2   Deregulation

Deregulation is a radical policy programme, which has been dominating education for over ten years. The beginning of this process can be pinned down quite accurately to 25 March 1985, when a draft policy document containing proposals to reform the management of higher education was sent to the advisory bodies (MOW, 1985). The subtitle of this document was "A new way to manage" and it has determined thinking and action on education policy in the Netherlands, as few other policy documents have done. It is still being used and is referred to by the acronym 'HOAK', which stands for 'Hoger Onderwijs: Autonomie en Kwaliteit', meaning: Higher Education: autonomy and quality. The HOAK document has spawned various epigones, the most important of which was 'The school on route to the year 2000' (MOW, 1988), which was directed at primary and secondary education. These policy documents have given rise to a considerable number of changes in education, some of which can be traced back quite easily to the policy documents, while others have only gradually become clear.

Deregulation has boasted a real reduction and simplification of regulations and a more liberal framework for administrative activities. Deregulation is not a movement with direct roots in education, as it started elsewhere, in the field of economic activities (Stone, 1982), and fanned out gradually so that education also came within its reach. This means that deregulation cannot really be compared with changes that sprang from education itself in the first instance. It is all the more remarkable that the impetus came from outside, because deregulation connects almost seamlessly with the official ideas of the various parties with an interest in education policy. Self-rule, autonomy for the school, the school to be accountable to the parents and local community and so on, all belong to the body of ideas which welcomes deregulation of national structures, although in practice education policy has often failed to take these ideas seriously. However, deregulation could very well have been spurred on from within the education world. This is because the degree of refinement of regulations had reached its limit in the view of committees, which have since been discontinued, such as the Committee for the Reduction and Simplification of Government Regulations, known as the Geelhoed Committee (Commissie, 1984). However, in the eyes of representatives of the education world, the regulations which were the outcomes of 80 years of rule making were mostly quite easy to live with. Only opponents, which means those who were poorly represented, raised objections, as they were hardly involved in the rule-making process if at all.

2.2.1   Deregulation and autonomy

Deregulation is a government activity, which may affect the autonomy of schools. However, implementing deregulation does not directly bring about (more) autonomous schools. If we want to say something more concrete about this relationship, we need to gain some insight into the empirical interplay between the domains in which national deregulation can take place and the domains in which schools take decisions. For this reason it would be useful to have a standardized classification of types of autonomy, which we could use to investigate whether autonomy is increasing by each type. It would probably be best to use a school perspective for an analysis of autonomy. Our classification in broad terms is as follows (Leune, 1994; Davies & Hentschke, 1994):

- *community-oriented autonomy*. Which groups is the school targeting, what means and resources are being acquired to enable the school to serve these groups well?
- *normative autonomy*. What mission does the school want to accomplish? What normative-educational framework does it want to use or develop?

- *autonomy in relation to the educational product.* What powers does the school have and what decisions can the school take about goals?
- *autonomy in relation to the educational process.* What decisions can the school take about how to organize the educational process at school and class level?
- *administrative-organizational autonomy.* Which organizational and management concept does the school have?
- *financial-material autonomy.* How is the freedom to allocate resources being used by schools?
- *autonomy in relation to employment conditions.* How is the legal status, employment conditions and quality of the teaching staff being covered?

An analysis of the various policy programmes aiming to increase autonomy produces a mixed picture (Hooge, 1995; Teelken, 1995; Boerman, 1995). The effects of policy programmes in practice are seldom confined to a single area of autonomy and, taken as a whole, they have effects that serve to reduce autonomy as well as to increase it. This is partly due to the fact that, alongside explicit deregulation policies, such as the introduction of block-grant funding and the transfer of the in-service training budget to the schools, other policies with other objectives are being implemented at the same time and these have interfering side-effects. What has become clear is that regulation of the educational process has decreased, while regulation in the area of educational output has increased.

Certain matters, which used to be carried out at a national level, are being shifted to a different level, for example school level, and this changes the relationship between the two levels. Altering the relationship between schools and the national level means that one also alters the relationship between the quality of schools and the quality of the school system as a whole. Under the old view of quality, the quality of individual schools and the quality of the system as a whole were assumed to be the same. In the new interpretation, school quality can be very diverse within a band at the level of the school system. The combination of local factors that have an effect upon school results becomes more important, or to use the jargon of the field, the role of local production increases in importance.

Arguments can be advanced both for and against increasing the autonomy of schools (Leune, 1994) and all these arguments are interesting in their own right. Even more interesting though, is how the mix of arguments for and against looks at certain periods of time and for certain social groups, organizations, or even countries, and whether these arguments come to be modified under the influence of developments both within and outside education. The broad arguments *in favour* are:

- schools have to be free to find their own solutions (pragmatic);
- it is easier to improve quality at school level;
- it is easier to effect savings if autonomy is granted at the same time;
- autonomous schools are closer to parents, parents have more opportunities to have a say on real issues;
- new clients from ethnic-cultural groups can be better served by autonomous schools.

The arguments *against* are:
- autonomy magnifies (unacceptable) differences between schools;
- it has to remain possible for central authorities to intervene and innovate;
- schools threaten to become more socially selective, government intervention has a leveling effect;
- schools are not able to function autonomously;
- autonomy is an instrument by which the state evades its responsibilities.

It is possible to summarize the mix of arguments that play a role in the national debate by period, group, organization or country. This means that it is important to identify which group or body is emphasizing which arguments, from among the government itself, political parties, trade unions, school principals' associations, associations of school governing bodies and parents' associations. As well as these political arguments, there are also important arguments that relate to specialist fields. What professional conditions are emphasized by which bodies? These often have something to do with conditions that relate primarily to the qualifications of those who are managing the autonomous schools (usually the school principals and their education/training) and to new instruments for local control, management and quality care.

2.2.2   Horizontal and vertical autonomy

Increased autonomy or self-sufficiency can be interpreted in different ways, of which the two most important for the current situation in the Netherlands are vertical assigned and horizontal acquired autonomy. Vertical assigned autonomy stems from an essentially vertically integrated system, in which the schools' powers are usually granted to them by the highest level in the system. Horizontal acquired autonomy is based on schools having access to and control over resources. This concept has been borrowed from an older, but no less interesting for that, article by Smith (1971), who argued that horizontal, or lateral, autonomy has to do with the degree to which organizations are able to take decisions without being obliged to involve others. The term lateral is used to indicate a decision-making capacity based on direct control of resources. This is a different kind of decision-making capacity from that which is derived from others in a vertically integrated hierarchy. Lateral autonomy of this kind may be limited to one function and not be extended to other functions.

The current debate on the issue of autonomy lends itself well to being organized around the following questions:

- Is autonomy confined to matters which fit into the vertical hierarchy? In other words, does the Ministry remain the higher authority? Is it simply a question of vertical assigned autonomy?
- If that is no longer the case and scope has been created for horizontal acquired autonomy, then this alters the way that vertical integration can be realized. The question of how vertical integration can be guaranteed will have to be reconsidered.

Some studies (Karsten, 1998) show that the opportunities for schools to put their own slant on things is limited by the development of a new administrative layer that takes shape between central government and the local school boards and their schools. This means that schools are not all starting from the same position, but the starting point varies according to local circumstances. Their formal vertical autonomy may be increased, but their horizontal autonomy is certainly not.

Recruiting one's own resources puts the school in a freer position within the vertical column. Opportunities exist now to seek forms of compensation for shortcomings and limits in regular funding and to spread one's wings a little further. This applies to all types of educational institutions. In the field of non-compulsory education, opportunities to recruit external resources are rather limited, but sectors such as vocational and higher education, on the other hand, are awash with non-government-funded educational activities. The problem of integration is highlighted in a situation like this because the Ministry of Education, Culture and Science does not have anything approaching a monopoly here. The Ministry can try to reach a certain accommodation between the most important parties in the education field by building up certain forms of networks. In this way a vertical 'commando structure' can be replaced by a form of network management.

Deregulation is something which, in abstract terms, is evidently applicable to the whole field of education, but to say that is to deny the (sub)sector-specific nature of the way such general policies are implemented. Each sector has a number of specific factors which means that a broadly conceived policy like 'deregulation' is still open to different interpretations by different (sub)sectors.

2.3   Privatization

Unlike deregulation and decentralization, privatization of education has never been a separate policy programme in the Netherlands. There are countries (e.g. Australia, United Kingdom) where privatization of education has been afforded an equivalent political status to deregulation and decentralization. The official line in these countries is that privatization can contribute to a new economic-political infrastructure (by, for example, reducing the burden on government spending and reducing the power of the trade unions), can increase support for education in society and improve the performance of the education system.

Privatization has never been systematically deployed in the Netherlands as a means to achieve any of these three objectives, but that is not to deny that many proposals have been drawn up which relate to privatization in some way or other, and some have been realized. Examples of these include: the introduction of vouchers in higher education, setting up of contract activities, the transfer of the University of Nijenrode to the private sector, increases in lesson, course and college fees and regulation of sponsorship. Some individual policy proposals make clear what objectives these forms of privatization were aiming to achieve, but there is little evidence of a more systematic weighing up of what purposes different forms of privatization might serve. That need not be a problem if the objectives can be realized equally well by other means, such as through the more accepted programmes like deregulation and decentralization. However, that is only likely to be possible if privatization of education is not very forceful and that depends on social trends toward privatization. If the overall trend in society is in that direction, then the education world cannot avoid engaging in an open discussion on privatization.

Education policy has traditionally been active in the area where public and private domains meet. The effect of the equal financial treatment between state and private schools introduced in 1917 has been that the 'private initiative' in education has allowed itself to be subject to government regulation in exchange for generous financial support. In this sense state-funded private education in the Netherlands cannot be compared with private education in other countries, although important gradations are found. In fact, Dutch education has for the most part become public property managed by private organizations, and it is actually 'state education'. This may be one reason why the debate about privatizing education has scarcely got off the ground in the Netherlands.

Internationally, privatization has a number of aims: firstly to cut back on government, to change funding arrangements; and, secondly, an aim which has more to do with the content of education, that is the expectation that activities which are funded externally (i.e. funding from sources other than the Ministry of Education, Culture and Science) lead to more direct contact with the consumers of education and therefore stimulate innovation in curricula and the qualifications of the teachers involved. Privatization results in greater emphasis on giving business and industry access to the ordinary education system. This change means that schools are not passive institutions that simply sit and wait.

The idea of privatization gives rise to at least two sorts of arguments or reasoning. On the one hand there is the desire to increase the private component in the funding of education and the notion that it could lead to better and more relevant education for society. On the other hand, there is the fear that it jeopardizes something which is properly the task of government, that is the funding of (compulsory) education. Policy has been confined to an attempt to tap external sources of funding and, at the same time, to regulate them. An attempt to exert control is evident from a new piece of legislation from 1998 to extend the power of consent of the parent/pupil representatives on the co-determination council to setting the level of parental contributions and to the acceptance of sponsorship. The explanatory notes state that large differences in parental contributions could affect the material equality of schools and access to those schools, and sponsorship can result in services in return for the benefit of the sponsor. If pupils are to be involved in these services in return then, the explanatory notes argue, parents must have a right to have a say on this.

The broader vision of privatization, which looks at the relationship between public and private funding of educational activities, is less important for compulsory education than for the non-compulsory education sector. However, the debate has been beset by a great deal of doubt and hesitation as far as both sectors are concerned. Of course, privatization does not necessarily mean that the government ceases to be involved with the educational service in question. At least, a distinction can be made between privatization of funding and privatization of implementation. Privatization of implementation accompanied by public funding is a familiar model in the Netherlands in the form of the state-funded private schools. Privatized implementation accompanied by private funding exists in the form of private fee-paying schools, but important elements of public funding are also involved here in the form of tax credits to participants or companies.

The dormant privatization debate raises its head when, for example, the core business of the Ministry of Education, Culture and Science, namely compulsory education, comes up for discussion. Does this mean that non-compulsory education can be privatized, and if so, in what sense, and with what combination of privatization of funding and privatization of implementation? What form of privatization would this take: payment of fees, contracting out of educational programmes or private educational institutions? What combination would be appropriate and just? What is lacking is a thorough consideration of the aims of privatization and what types of privatization could be useful in education. All three objectives of privatization mentioned earlier, which have been identified abroad, could be examined in an analysis of this kind.

2.4   Decentralization

Since the early 1980s, decentralization of national government tasks to the provinces and local authorities has been one of the policy objectives of all cabinets. However, it is immediately apparent that education tends to be among the stragglers rather than the forerunners of decentralization (Van Ojen, Vermeulen, Karstanje & Van Wieringen, 1991). It was as late as 1995 before the Minister for Education, Culture and Science came up with a policy note proposing to transfer some of the responsibilities for education policy to the local level. Until recently local authorities did not make much use of their existing freedom to make policy. This caution in the field of education is generally attributed to the consequences at local level of the

1917 Pacification and the centralism in the administration of education at national level.

Since 1917, the Dutch education system has been a rare mixture of a unified education system, regulated by central laws, with schools that are administered and managed locally. Overall responsibility for the public-private education system lies with central government. The administration and management of primary and secondary schools is organized locally. The municipal authorities are, in principle, the competent authorities for publicly run schools which are in a minority. Private school boards (foundations and associations) are the competent authorities for private schools that are attended by some 70% of all pupils. What the Netherlands had in common with other continental education systems, such as the German and French systems, was the centralized management of employment conditions based on civil servant status and the centralized allocation of staff and resources to schools. In other respects, such as freedom of parental choice and freedom to set up schools, the Netherlands is more or less the odd man out in Europe.

In many Western European countries and also in a large number of former Communist countries, administrative reforms in education in which decentralization plays an important role are currently taking place. One could argue that, with its desire to decentralize, the Netherlands is more in step with other countries than it used to be. However, this is only partly true. In some countries, in fact, the process of extending autonomy, such as the various forms of school-based management, and privatization are also considered to be part of decentralization. A classic definition provided by Rondinelli (1981) is that decentralization can be seen *as a process of transferring or devolving power and authority from large to small units of governance. The smallest unit is the individual citizen.* In the Dutch situation, this has mainly been territorial decentralization, in which powers are transferred from the national government to the municipalities. This fits in with Winkler's (1989) definition of devolution, i.e. *a transfer to autonomous and independent sub-national units of government – such as provinces, cities and districts.*

In the classic, formal, centralized interpretation, local government is, on the one hand, independent and, on the other hand, the body which executes a number of specific tasks designated by central government or initiates and executes certain tasks within a designated constitutional framework. There is no difference of opinion on the procedure for allocating tasks or on the framework for those tasks, as formal patterns exist which are tailored to these kinds of questions. Another interpretation also exists which does not (only) take formal sources of power and actions by authorities for granted, but assumes a high degree of mutual dependence in these relationships (Stoker, 1991). The relationship is one of mutual influence and interdependence involving negotiation, persuasion, pressure, mobilization of support and so on. Rather than a one-sided downward process, attention is on a relationship of negotiation within an administrative system with upward movements as well as downward ones. As Fuhrman and Elmore (1990) have argued, the conception of central state-local state relationships as a zero-sum game simply does not fit the facts. For example, it cannot accommodate evidence of increased local activity coinciding with increased central state activity.

At the local level, the administrative entities in the Netherlands are the municipalities (in total about 550). The duties of the municipalities are often divided up into assigned duties and independent duties. Duties carried out in joint authority are duties which the municipality is obliged to carry out by order of a higher administrative body, which may come via an Act, Order in Council or provincial bye-law. The municipal executive has the primary responsibility, within frameworks laid down by the municipal council of course. Autonomous duties are tasks which the municipality carries out on its own initiative, for which the municipal council has the primary responsibility.

Does redirecting a larger share of funding from central to local levels simply mean that the municipalities become a kind of serving hatch? Channeling national resources down to lower levels has become more important in recent years in areas such as education, police, public housing, health care, economic services and welfare. A great deal of the new money is destined for education, employment and the reception of newcomers. In the education field, municipalities implement projects such as: improving education in Dutch and mathematics, involving parents in education, better links between education and work, reducing absenteeism, training (continuing education and retraining) and courses in Dutch for newcomers to the country a few weeks after they arrive. The national government still has a great deal of influence in all these areas, but more substance has also been given to professional implementation and the municipality can also put its own policies into practice with assistance from central government. Traditionally, the local authorities have had two sets of duties, one geared to looking after the infrastructure, and one geared to ensuring minimum participation in education. Both these areas of responsibility have been gradually enlarged and broadened. These changes in the way central government is involved in education have affected the role of local government and the status and role of private bodies such as the governing bodies of state-funded private schools. However, the way municipalities exercise their educational role is also changing, as they are becoming more dependent upon other players. They are becoming more involved with various social and cultural services and their say over social and cultural services is increasing in some cases and decreasing in others. This means that the municipalities are increasingly taking on the roles of director, intermediary and process coordinator.

Local authorities have, as has been indicated, traditionally had two sets of duties, one geared to looking after the infrastructure, and one geared to ensuring minimum participation in education and both these areas of responsibility have been gradually enlarged and broadened. Centralization and decentralization are concepts that indicate that certain functions are being moved to or from municipal authorities or national government respectively. These concepts are less appropriate for the many circumstances in which the assignment of duties, and especially the interpretation of duties, is a two-way process. An older research study, executed in the period before the decentralization process took shape, into the policies pursued by ten municipalities in three fields (school support services, adult education and compensatory preferential treatment programmes) has shown that one can certainly speak of a vertical division of power in a certain sense without this being explicitly formulated or operated as such either within or between policy domains (Karsten, 1988). This seems to be phased, an initial phase where powers are unclear seems to be followed by a clarification phase which does not, however, always turn out favourably for the local authorities. How the municipalities act is largely up to them, but the dilemma facing them is that clarification often turns out to be to the municipality's disadvantages. In this sense the assignment of powers is not a legal but a political question. The study demonstrated variants of domain definition or material standards. In the first case one can speak of domains being constructed from within the municipalities to be curtailed later by central government education policy. In the second case one can speak of domains being constructed from national policy to be interpreted later within municipal policy. If these things are viewed in the light of a proper vertical perspective, a separate consideration per domain will probably not suffice. It seems as if there may be a kind of profit and loss account operating across the policy domains. An important facet of the vertical division is the fact that there is no question of an exclusive relationship between municipality and central government in the different domains. There are often other local and regional administrative bodies operating alongside the municipalities as independent administrative bodies, private-law local/regional services subsidized by the state (school support services), collaborative groups whether or not on a private-law or public-law basis, and so on. These coordinated administrative forms can be taken into consideration.

2.4.1   Motives and intended effects of decentralization

Weiler (1990) argued in a well-known article that the main motive behind governments' decentralization policies is conflict management, and that the recent trend toward decentralization arises out of the 'legitimacy crisis' of the modern state. Others (Lauglo, 1995) have rightly argued against this that this assumption rests on weak empirical grounds. Why should there be a legitimacy crisis right now and why is there a greater need for conflict management than there used to be? Of course, one can give examples of societies where there are clear power crises and where solutions are being sought through decentralization. This was the case in Eastern and Central Europe after the fall of Communism (Karsten & Majoor, 1995). However, the legitimacy crisis in that part of Europe cannot be compared with the situation in Western Europe and Australia, where decentralization policies are also being implemented; nor with England where, under Thatcher, partial centralization was seen to be the solution to similar problems.

In the arguments for decentralization, a distinction has to be made between general arguments and sector-specific arguments, though there is some overlap. The general arguments include political and economic lines of reasoning. The classic political argument is that the closer government is to the people, the better able it is to respond to the wishes and desires of those people. The ability to respond is the main issue here. This responsiveness ought, on the one hand, to improve how the administration handles its tasks, in other words the quality of the administration; and, on the other hand, to increase democracy in terms of participation and political control. In addition, other political functions are ascribed to decentralization. One of the oldest liberal arguments concerns the role of political education and is that closeness and the opportunity to participate educates the local citizens in democratic action. Some doubts are being expressed at the moment concerning this role and so attempts are also being made to improve local democracy in that respect. Another role is that of mediating between divergent interests. Where abstract measures prove to be inadequate, local mediation by persons in authority who are familiar with the local situation can make more progress.

The economic arguments stem from the idea that the transfer of authority and powers breaks up monopolies and promotes competition. Central planning all too often delivers a product that is too expensive and often does not meet what is required. Therefore, it is easier to balance supply and demand as close as possible to the producers and customers, but the question then is: how far do you have to go? For some people, the answer to this question is the market. Others question whether, in that case, the product or service will still be provided. They point out that the 'voices' of poorer and less self-aware groups often get less of a hearing in a market situation than under political decision-making. Where in one case (the market) the emphasis is on saving time and money, in the other case (political control) balance and social costs are emphasized. Weiler (1990) mentions three important sector-specific arguments for decentralization: (a) the 'distribution' argument, which concerns power sharing; (b) the 'efficiency' argument, which is about opportunities to save costs; and (c) the 'curriculum' (cultures of learning) argument, which emphasizes the decentralization of the content of education. The first two arguments correspond closely to the general arguments mentioned above.

The first argument has clearly been prompted by the practice of 'over-centralization' of the regulation and financing of education. The main reasons for this centralization have been standardization (to allow recognition of diplomas and mobility within the country) and equality (to prevent differences between rich and poor areas being translated into differences in the educational quality of schools). Weiler points out that the distribution argument is hardly ever applied to these 'core tasks', but tends to focus on functions which can be carried out at a local level, such as the planning or monitoring of the number of facilities; the building, maintenance and management of school buildings; and the recruitment, selection and appointment of teachers and school principals. In short, functions where the responsiveness to the local community and the participation of that community, especially the consumers of the educational product, can be increased.

The second argument, that of improving efficiency, is based on two expectations. The first is that decentralization will mobilize more resources than a more centralist system. The idea here is that the more local groups and institutions are involved, the more prepared they will be to invest local public and private funds. Given how Dutch policy works in practice, this is not an unreasonable idea. The second is that decentralized systems will make better use of the available resources. This expectation has also underpinned the funding systems that have been developed elsewhere in recent years. Greater freedom to allocate spending and the feeling of ownership are expected to provide sufficient incentives for more cost-conscious behaviour than there used to be. On the other hand, there is a risk that the economies of scale provided by a centralized system will be lost. That is why the introduction of a different method of funding has been introduced parallel to a merger operation creating larger schools in the Netherlands.

The third argument concerns the nature and context of the learning process. Decentralization of the content of educational curricula ought to make education more responsive. It ought to make the curricula more readily adaptable to local economic and cultural requirements, such as the requirements of the local labour market, or the wishes of particular language groups or ethnic communities. However, in countries where these powers exist, there has been a great deal of pressure to produce a national curriculum.

Despite a general absence of empirical evidence to support it, it is generally accepted that the effects ascribed to centralization, such the distancing of politics from the citizens, stultifying over-regulation and bureaucratization, will be reduced by decentralization. Local policy is expected to have a purging effect. The minister in question defended her decentralization plans in various papers and bills. The arguments she used are largely in line with those that are generally put forward in the discussion about conducting centralized versus decentralized policies. Fleurke (1997) developed a framework to evaluate the different forms of decentralization that are now being implemented in a number of sectors in the Netherlands. He distinguishes the following intended effects:

- *Tailor-made.* Decentralized policy would create the opportunity to take relevant characteristics and circumstances of individual cases or situations into account in the administration's policy and actions, and the opportunity for differentiation and variation in policy and actions on the basis of this;

- *An integral policy*. Decentralization would lead to policies being more closely coordinated in various sectors and this would be beneficial in dealing with complex societal issues;
- *Decisiveness*. Decentralization would make it possible for the administration to react appropriately to societal changes or to changes in the circumstances under which it has to achieve its aims in the time available;
- *Efficiency*. A decentralized administration would lead to a more efficient administration, i.e. the municipalities would be better able than central government to fine tune expenditure and they could opt for more cost-effective solutions;
- *Careful consideration of interests and priorities*. Decentralized policy will lead to the careful consideration of interests and priorities.

2.4.2   Different measures and forms of decentralization

As noted earlier, education was at first reluctant to follow the general policy of decentralization. Before the appearance of the decentralization policy note "Local education policy" in 1995, only one decentralizing measure had been taken. That was the Act regulating local school transport in 1987, which gave local authorities the power to provide transport arrangements to transport children between their homes and primary and special schools. It emerged from the final evaluation of the Act (Vermeulen, Lington & Peetsma, 1994) that the expectation of tailor-made services had only been partly realized. Only 18 % of the local authorities, for example, found that they were better able to respond to specific transport needs. Most local authorities simply adopted a national model. The feeling that the increased policy freedom had less to offer than expected came about mainly due to the financial pressure put on the whole scheme by economy measures. Access to decision-making for local interest groups did increase though.

The policy note of 1995 was a major step, proposing no less than seven measures:
1. *A greater role in combating truancy and premature school-leaving.*
   The first evaluations (Voncken & Van Eck, 1997) show that important progress has been made in this area. Cooperation between the bodies involved has improved, awareness and understanding of the problems

has increased and compulsory school attendance is being enforced better than it used to be.

2. *A greater role in planning adult education and the reception of newcomers.*
   Studies into this role (Polder & Karsten, 1998) have shown that local authorities still do not feel strong enough in their negotiations with education providers and that there are also problems in defining target groups.

3. *Greater responsibility for providing education in the languages spoken by ethnic minorities.*
   This policy is still at too early a stage of development for any indications of its effects to be given.

4. *Primary responsibility for accommodation for primary and secondary schools.*
   Here too, little can be said about policy developments at this stage.

5. *Responsibility for running a school guidance service and for some aspects of its programme.*
   Here too, the same point can be made as for the last two points.

6. *The local authority has been given the option to transfer some of its administrative responsibilities to public or private management bodies.*
   Research (Van Kessel, 1998) has shown that there has been a clear shift toward transferring responsibilities to management bodies other than the local council. It appears that the motives for doing so vary among the different actors (policy-makers, civil servant and parents).

7. *A greater role in combating educational disadvantages.*
   This will be examined in more detail in the next paragraph.

These seven decentralization measures can be distinguished according to five dimensions:

- The scope of the task to be transferred, as decentralizing measures vary in scope. Some are concerned with narrow tasks and other are broader. This dimension includes the number of local authorities involved with a particular task;
- The degree of central programming. In some cases central government's role is finished after transfer, whereas in other cases it continues to have a regulatory, supervisory or funding role;

- The nature and scope of the policy instruments. This means which policy instruments will be placed at the local authorities' disposal to enable them to intervene;
- The education sector to which the measure relates;
- The extent to which the measure touches on the organizational aspects of schools. Some measures (for example, school guidance services) do not have any direct influence on the organizational aspects of schools, but other do to a greater or lesser extent.

Considering these five dimensions, the seventh measure, combating educational disadvantages, comes out the highest taking all five dimensions together, which is why we are going to examine local policies to combat educational disadvantages in more detail in the final part of this chapter.

2.4.3   Local policies to combat educational disadvantages

The Dutch government has for a number of decades been pursuing an explicit policy aimed at combating educational disadvantages resulting from economic, social and cultural factors. The most important target groups of this policy are native Dutch pupils from lower socio-economic backgrounds and pupils from ethnic minorities. Local authorities (the municipalities) have been given a much greater role in this policy since the implementation of a new law in 1997, the so called Municipal Educational Disadvantages Act (MOCW, 1997).

The first phase of the municipal educational disadvantages policy was implemented in 1997/98. Central government has handed over a number of its powers to the municipalities under this new law, but still retains ultimate responsibility for policies on educational disadvantages. The Minister of Education, Culture and Science draws up a so-called national policy framework once every four years, in which the aims and priorities of the national policy relating to educational disadvantages are outlined in general terms. This national policy framework has to be used as a frame of reference for municipal plans on educational disadvantages which local councils have to draw up for a period of four school years. In this plan the municipality has to state how the national aims will be worked out locally, how the resources allocated for this will be used, and how the scheme will be evaluated. The local council is expected to draw up this plan based on an analysis of local problems, in consultation with the local public and private school boards.

The national aims serve as a guideline but it is up to the municipalities to decide which aims are to be given priority. The municipalities are also free to add their own aims.

At the same time an important share of the resources available for reducing educational disadvantages have been passed down to the municipalities. They are authorized to distribute these resources among the school boards and institutions in their area and they are also free to use their own resources to reduce educational disadvantages. Not all of the resources have been handed over to the municipalities with this law. The scheme introduced in 1986, by which schools with disadvantaged pupils receive additional funds directly from central government, still exists. What is new, however, is the fact that the schools are obliged to use these resources in accordance with the municipal plan relating to educational disadvantages. The municipality is responsible for supervising this.

In the run up to the decentralization of the educational disadvantages policy, those for and against presented all kinds of arguments that are related to the arguments presented above relating to decentralization in general. The Minister in question defended her policy with arguments fitting in the categories of Fleurke et al. (see par. 4.1), described earlier:

- Pursuing an integral policy: the Minister stressed that the decentralization of the educational priority policy was necessary for the benefit of a coherent approach towards the complex problems schools and young people are facing today. She argued in favor of schools working together and with other local institutions involved in the support and guidance of young people, such as welfare services, youth services, libraries and health care services. The municipality should coordinate and direct this cooperation;
- Tailor-made approaches: the Minister stated that the central government could not provide tailor-made approaches on its own: that is why the fight against educational disadvantage would benefit from an approach that has been adapted to the local situation;
- Decisiveness: As a result of the cooperation at local level between schools and other institutions, it, according to the Minister, not only becomes possible to tackle the problems in a more adequate manner but also to rapidly adapt to changes in society;
- Careful consideration of interests and priorities: The municipality is awarded a guiding role in the new Act because it is in an excellent position to integrally weigh up interests and to set priorities on the basis

of a local analysis of the situation. This not only safeguards democratic control, but also makes it possible for this to take place even more directly at local level.

Some long time observers of the educational disadvantage policy have raised objections against its decentralization. A number of critics (Tesser, 1993; Tesser, Van Dugteren & Merens, 1996) have argued that the mechanisms that lead to disadvantage are not of a local or regional nature, or even a national one. It is for this reason that a centralized approach would be far more obvious. Critics very much doubt the effectiveness of the coordination by local municipalities and argue in favour of centrally developing programmes that are of a high standard and that can be used directly in everyday school practice.

As a result of the decentralized policy on educational disadvantage, a relatively large amount of money will be lost through fragmentation across municipalities, which all have to put time and energy into developing plans to combat educational disadvantage. A particular point of concern is whether it is desirable or possible to have a local disadvantaged policy in smaller municipalities (Vermeulen, 1997), where the necessary expertise will largely be lacking, which means third parties will have to be called in and paid for from resources intended for combating disadvantage. School boards with schools in more than one municipality will also lose quite a lot of time and energy for that matter. These boards have to consult various local councils, which may all emphasize different points.

The national Education Council pointed out the danger that at local level the distinction between the target group of the educational disadvantage policy and the target group of the policy aimed at pupils with learning and behavioural problems will be lost. While the two target groups do overlap to some extent, the first group is made up of collectives (children of Dutch parents with a low-level of education or parents from ethnic minorities), the second from individuals. Finally, the risk that municipalities will be starting from different points of departure, depending on local priorities and the financial situation of the local authorities has also been identified.

2.5   A comparison of differences between areas

Earlier analyses of educational priority policies (e.g. Mulder, 1996) did not look at educational priority areas separately, but a recent study (Van Langen & Portengen, 1999) does provide an evaluation from this aspect. Using multilevel analyses the aim of the study was to establish whether there are differences in the performance and performance trends in Dutch language and mathematics between pupils in grades 2, 4, and 6 from 17 educational priority areas between 1988 and 1994, which can be ascribed to the differences between educational priority areas. The 17 educational priority areas each had about ten schools that participated in the the PRIMA-cohort study in all three school years. A number of other educational priority areas were not included because of the small number of schools participating in those areas. Significant differences between the areas were hypothesized to be related to differences in the activities they engaged in and in their cooperative arrangements.

The analyses from that study carried out up to now have been confined to data from the 1994 year that looked into whether performance differences in that year could be traced back to the areas. About 2,400 pupils per school year were involved. Three levels were distinguished in the analyses: educational priority area (EPA), school and pupil. Table 1 shows the distribution of variance over the different levels per grade level. This is the null model; no account was taken of differences in socio-ethnic background and IQ.

Table 1. Null model per year group and subject area; variance proportions on different levels

grade	2		4		6	
	language	maths	language	maths	language	maths
area	<u>6</u>	6	8	4	8	8
school	20	14	12	10	10	16
pupil	72	81	80	86	82	76

Note. Underlined means not significant.

With the exception of the area effect for Dutch language in grade 2 all effects are significant. Between 4 and 8 per cent of total variance is situated at area level. The proportion of variance situated at school level is substantially greater than the proportion situated at area level. It is difficult to arrive at far-reaching conclusions; no clear pattern of distribution of variance can be detected between grades and subject areas.

Table 2 presents the results of the analysis after correction for socio-ethnic background and IQ score of individual pupils.

Table 2. Variance proportions at different levels after correction for SES and IQ

grade	2		4		6	
	language	maths	language	maths	language	maths
SES	2.35	0.60	2.86	1.04	2.69	1.36
IQ	0.24	0.36	0.30	0.40	0.31	0.44
area	<u>3</u>	5	<u>3</u>	2	<u>3</u>	<u>4</u>
school	16	12	6	11	5	18
pupil	81	83	91	87	92	78

Note. Underlined means not significant.

The most important change was found at area level. With the exception of maths in grade 2, table 2 shows that area no longer makes a significant contribution to differences in performance. One can conclude from this that in 1994 performance differences in Dutch language and mathematics cannot be attributed to differences in activities for cooperation on the part of the coordinating areas, at least not after the obvious correction for SES and IQ of the pupils has been made.

The next step in the analyses involved a search for area differences in performance-*development* between 1988 and 1994. It is after all possible that in 1988 the performance of students from certain areas was still lagging behind that of students from other EPAs, and that this gap in performance was eliminated over the years thanks to the area activities that were introduced and/or an integral approach. This could shed a different light on the results of the analyses presented earlier.

The analyses were performed on the combined data for the years 1988, 1992 and 1994 (the measurement was incomplete in 1990). They were once again related to 17 educational priority areas with 8 to 15 schools in each. The numbers of students in the groups amounted to 7,752, 7,219 and 7,022 respectively. In short the results were as follows: the factor calendar year is – across all the EPAs-students involved together - only significant in the case of language in grade 2 and in the case of maths in grade 6. In the case of language in grade 2, students showed a slight improvement after correction for background variables between 1988 and 1994. In the case of maths in grade 6, on the other hand, it was possible to observe a slight deterioration.

Significant differences between educational priority areas are found for maths in grade 2 and language and maths in grade 6. The first difference (maths in grade 2) was also found in 1994 (table 2). The fact that we are now also finding differences in grade 6 is probably related to the far greater number of students included in these analyses, due to the data of three measurements being combined.

The central question in this study was however: have significantly different developments in terms of performance taken place among the students from the various educational priority areas? This is not the case: the effect of calendar year on performance does not vary between areas. It is also not possible to detect an interaction effect between calendar year and socio-ethnic status. This therefore means that no development differences occurred between the various categories of EPA-students.

In table 2 it was noted that (in 1994) in the case of language the amount of variance explained by the factor school becomes smaller in the top grades of school. If a similar effect were to take place in the different calendar years, and here we are particularly thinking in terms of a reduction in the between-school variance at later moments, then this could indicate that as a result of area policy the differences between schools have become smaller over the course of time. We took a closer look at this in analyses that are not reported here in any detail, but were unable to establish a systematic reduction in the between-school variance (neither in language nor maths in any grade).

We can conclude that in none of the analyses - with the exception of certain flukes - was it possible to find any significant differences caused by the factor 'area' after introducing obvious control variables such as social background, ethnicity and IQ. It is also not possible to speak of a systematic reduction in the between-school variance between 1988 and 1994, which could indicate that the differences between schools have become smaller as a result of the area policy.

Mulder (1996, 172) states that we will never know how language and maths performance would have developed if there had not been an educational priority policy: *"Perhaps the educational disadvantage of the target group students would have increased, and the stability that has come about can be attributed to the educational priority policy."* Following on from this a conclusion that can be drawn on the basis of the results is that the educational priority areas examined were all just about equally successful in stabilizing the educational disadvantage of the EPA-target groups. Taking the similarity between the EPA and the decentralized educational priority policy into account, this could mutatis mutandis become an important virtue of local municipalities.

Only the future will tell if arguments presented in favour of decentralizing compensatory policy, such as an integrated approach, tailormade approaches, decisiveness, etcetera, can improve the performance of educationally disadvantaged groups, and whether municipalities will be successful in this to varying degrees. A comparison of earlier (area) results of the former centrally regulated educational priority policy with (municipal) results of the local compensatory policy, and a comparison of results of the various municipalities could provide insight into the extent to which the objectives of decentralizing the educational disadvantage policy are being achieved.

2.6   References

Boerman, P.B. (1995). Autonomieverschuivingen in het beroepsonderwijs. *Nederlands Tijdschrift voor Onderwijsrecht en Onderwijsbeleid*, Juni, 57-68.

Commissie vermindering en vereenvoudiging van overheidsregelingen (1984*). Eindbericht van de Commissie vermindering en vereenvoudiging van overheidsregelingen. Deregulering van overheidsregelingen*. 's-Gravenhage (TK 17 931 no. 9)

Daviels, B., & Hentschke, G.C. (1994). School autonomy, myth or reality? *Educational Management and Administration*, 22(2), 96-103.

Fleurke, F., Hulst, R., & Vries, P. de (1997). *Decentraliseren met beleid: een heuristiek*. Den Haag: SdU.

Fuhrman, S.H., & Elmore, R.F. (1990). Understanding local control in the wake of state education reform. *Educational Evaluation and Policy Analysis*, 12(1), 82-96.

Hooge, E.H. (1995). Ruimte voor overheid, bestuurlijk middenveld en basisscholen. *Nederlands Tijschrift voor Onderwijsrecht en Onderwijsbeleid*, juni 1995, 35-44.

Karsten, S., & Majoor, D. (1995). *Education in East Central Europe. Educational Changes after the Fall of Communism*. Munster/New York: Waxmann.

Karsten, S. (1998). School Autonomy in the Netherlands: the Development of a New Administrative Layer. *Educational Management and Administration*, 26, 395-405.

Karsten, S. (1988). *Gemeentelijk onderwijsbeleid in drievoud*. De Lier: ABC.

Kessel, N. van (1998). *Alternatief bestuur openbaar onderwijs en de positie van het directiestatuut*. Nijmegen:ITS.

Langen, A. van, & Dekkers, H. (1998). *The pros and cons of a decentralised policy aiming at combating educational disadvantage*. Paper presented at AERA, San Diego, CA.

Langen, A. van, & Portengen, R. (1999). *Decentralisatie van onderwijsachterstanden: Een internationale zoektocht naar knelpunten en succesfactoren*. Nijmegen: ITS.

Lauglo, J. (1995). Forms of Decentralisation and Their Implications for Education. *Comparative Education*, 31, 5-29.

Leune, J.M.G. (1994). Onderwijskwaliteit en de autonomie van scholen. In B.P.M. Creemers (Ed.), *Deregulering en de kwaliteit van het onderwijs* (pp. 27-48). Groningen: RION.

MOCW (Ministerie van Onderwijs, Cultuur en Wetenschappen) (1997). *Wet Gemeentelijk onderwijsachterstandenbeleid.* 's-Gravenhage, SdU.

MOW (Ministerie van Onderwijs en Wetenschappen) (1985). *Hoger Onderwijs: Autonomie en Kwaliteit. Een andere besturingswijze.* 's-Gravenhage: Staatsdrukkerij.

MOW (Ministerie van Onderwijs en Wetenschappen) (1988). *De school op weg naar 2000, een besturingsfilosofie voor de negentiger jaren.* 's-Gravenhage: Staatsdrukkerij.

Mulder, L. (1996). *Meer voorrang, minder achterstand?* Nijmegen: ITS.

Ojen, Q. H. J. M. van, Vermeulen, M., Karstanje, P.N., & Wieringen, A.M.L. van (1991). *Verticaal Machtsevenwicht in het onderwijsbeleid.* De Lier: ABC.

Polder, K.J., & Karsten, S. (1998). *Educatie onder Wet Educatie en Beroepsonderwijs: ontwikkelingen in 1998.* Amsterdam: SCO-Kohnstamm Instituut.

Rondinelli, D.A. (1981). Government decentralization in comparative perspective: theory and practice in developing countries. *International Review of Administrative Sciences*, 47, 133-145

Smith, D. (1971). Power, ideology, and the transmission of knowledge: an exploratory essay. In E. Hopper (Ed.), *Readings in the theory of educational systems* (pp. 240-261). London: Hutchinson.

Stoker, G. (1991). Introduction: Trends in European Local Government. In R.Batley & G.Stoker (Eds.), *Local government in Europe* (pp. 1-20). Houndmills/London: Macmillan.

Stone, A (1982) *Regulation and its alternatives.* Washington, DC: Congressional Quarterly Press.

Teelken, C. (1995). Autonomieverschuivingen in het voortgezet onderwijs. *Nederlands Tijdschrift voor Onderwijsrecht en Onderwijsbeleid,* juni, 45-56.

Tesser, P. (1993). *Rapportage minderheden 1993.* Rijswijk: SCP.

Tesser, P., Dugteren, F. van, & Merens, A. (1996). *Rapportage minderheden 1996.* Rijswijk: SCP.

Vermeulen, B.P. (1997). Gemeentelijk onderwijsbeleid. In B.P. Vermeulen, G.J. Redert & P.W. Doop (Eds.), *Lokaal onderwijsbeleid: theorie en praktijk.* 's-Gravenhage: VOR.

Vermeulen, M., Lington, H., & Peetsma, T.T.D. (1994). *Gemeentelijk beleid voor het leerlingenvervoer.* De Lier: ABC.

Voncken, E., & Eck, E. van (1997). *Evaluatie van de regionale meld- en coordinatiefunctie voortijdig schoolverlaten.* Amsterdam: SCO-Kohnstamm Instituut.

Weiler, H. (1990). Comparative Perspectives on Educational Decentralization: An exercise in contradiction?, *Educational Evaluation and Policy Analysis*, 12(4), 433-448.

Wieringen, A. M. L. van (1996). *Onderwijsbeleid in Nederland.* Alphen aan de Rijn: Samsom H. D. Tjeenk Willink.

Winkler, D. (1989). *Decentralization in Education: An economic perspective.* Washington, D.C.: World Bank.

3. THE ENHANCEMENT OF EDUCATIONAL OPPORTUNITIES OF DISADVANTAGED CHILDREN

Geert W.J.M. Driessen & Lia W.J. Mulder
ITS, University of Nijmegen, the Netherlands

As from the 1960s various local and national programmes aimed at improving the educational opportunities of disadvantaged children were implemented in the Netherlands. In 1985 these initiatives were integrated into the Educational Priority Policy programme (EPP). This chapter describes the coming about, the aims, contents, underlying theories, evaluation and effects of the EPP. The focus is on the results of the quantitative longitudinal studies in primary education in the period 1986-1992.

3.1 Prologue

In the 1960s and 1970s several compensatory education programmes and programmes aimed at enhancing the involvement of parents in their children's school career were implemented in a number of large cities in the Netherlands. These were set up to improve the educational opportunities of children from working-class neighbourhoods. Despite the disappointing results in the Netherlands and abroad (cf. Scheerens, 1987), these local initiatives were adopted in the national Social Priority Policy [Onderwijsstimuleringsbeleid] in 1974. The aim of this, too, was to combat the disadvantages of native working-class children by providing schools with additional resources. At around the same time the number of immigrant children entering education started to gather momentum. Because it soon became clear that many of these children were experiencing major problems when they entered Dutch education, the government started to make additional resources available to schools within the framework of the Cultural Minority Policy [Culturele Minderhedenbeleid]. The allocation of these resources was among other things dependent on how long the children in question had been in the Netherlands.

In the years that followed there was a growing conviction that the problems which the immigrant children were experiencing in education were the same as those being experienced by Dutch working-class children. The policies aimed at improving their position, however, were fragmented, incoherent and adhockery. Above that, the evaluations of several large Dutch priority and compensation projects showed that they could do very little to enhance the opportunities of the disadvantaged children. All in all the future for an educational policy for disadvantaged children did not look very promising. At the same time, however, more and more studies regarding these children's weak educational position became available, indicating that something more structural and aimed at the long term should be done. To secure the existing provisions, to guarantee the continuity of the policy and to simplify the regulations, in 1985 the two policy tracks, i.e. the Social Priority Policy and the Cultural Minority Policy, were eventually integrated into the Educational Priority Policy [Onderwijsvoorrangsbeleid: OVB]. This policy is currently still in force, although a few amendments have been made over time and in the 1998/99 school year some major changes have been implemented.

3.2   The educational priority policy

3.2.1   Aims and components

The central goal of the Educational Priority Policy (EPP) was to reduce or eliminate the educational disadvantage of children insofar as they are a consequence of social, economical and cultural circumstances. The main target groups were non-indigenous and indigenous children whose parents have a low educational and occupational level.

The efforts of the EPP were first of all directed at raising the Dutch language and arithmetic achievement levels in primary schools. From several studies it had become clear that it are especially these achievements which form the main inhibiting factor with regard to the disadvantaged children's school careers. The principles, goals and instruments of the EPP were described in an Educational Priority Plan. The first plan, for the period 1985-1989, contained the following aspects:

- the organization of activities aimed at improving the educational achievements and attainments of disadvantaged children;
- regulations concerning the allocation of facilities to primary schools;
- the Educational Priority Areas policy;
- the policy with regard to Minority Language and Culture Teaching;
- policy intentions regarding Intercultural Education;

- regulations concerning the provision of facilities for ethnic minority children in secondary education.

Although most of these aspects are directly related to improving the disadvantaged children's opportunities, Minority Language and Culture Teaching [Onderwijs in Eigen Taal en Cultuur] and Intercultural Education [Intercultureel Onderwijs] were in part developed with other intentions.

Minority Language and Culture Teaching

Minority Language and Culture Teaching (MLCT) has been the subject of fierce controversy ever since its inception around 1970, predominantly due to the objectives that were formulated for it (and not only in the Netherlands, for that matter; cf. Lam, 1992; Driessen, 1996b). Official, subsidized MLCT was open to immigrant pupils, mainly from the Mediterranean area (notably Turkey and Morocco). They could attend MLCT classes up to 2.5 hours per week during school hours and 2.5 hours after school hours.

In the course of its history, MLCT has, among other things, been aimed at facilitating the reintegration of migrant children upon their return to their native countries, advancing their integration in Dutch society, developing a positive self-concept, diminishing the gap between the school and home environment, and making a contribution to intercultural education. In the second half of the 1980s MLCT was increasingly viewed as a means of improving the educational success of immigrant children. Meanwhile, however, several studies showed that the practice of MLCT was a very problematic one. In addition, it became clear that the goals of MLCT were not being achieved (Driessen & Van der Grinten, 1994). In that period the idea that command of the mother tongue is conducive to the learning of Dutch gained considerably ground. In the process of emphasizing the linguistic side of things the cultural component was dropped entirely from MLCT, which henceforth was called MLT.

In the beginning of the 1990s the climate with respect to ethnic minorities changed. Before that time it was a rather permissive one. However, more and more studies showed that the educational position of most of the minorities had hardly improved and that their prospects on the labour market were still very unfavourable. Under these conditions it no longer was taboo to make demands on them. It was in this climate that another change with regard to MLT was implemented. In the lower grades of primary education, the mother tongue was to function mainly as an auxiliary language for the learning of Dutch and the other school subjects. In the upper grades, the languages of the immigrant countries could be learned as a separate subject and part of the cultural policy.

As from the school year 1998/99 some other changes have taken effect. As from that date MLT is called Non-Indigenous Living Languages Teaching [Onderwijs in Allochtone Levende Talen]. The government has opted for a decentralized approach, devolving responsibilities predominantly onto municipal councils and schools. In addition MLT as a subject is provided as an extracurricular activity, that is, after school hours (cf. Driessen, 1997).

Intercultural education

Within the Dutch context the term Intercultural Education (ICE) has been used by the government since the beginning of the 1980s. It is generally not very clear just what it stands for. It can probably best be taken to mean a kind of differentiation of what in the UK or the US is referred to as Multicultural Education (cf. Banks, 1993).

The Dutch government at that time saw ICE as an important means of giving effect to acculturation, i.e. a multi-sided process of getting to know each other, accepting and appreciating each other and opening oneself up to each other's cultures. The government started out from the assumption that the pupils grow up in a multi-cultural society. That was something that needed to be expressed in all school subjects that were suitable for this. It would however not have to be something to which only isolated attention was paid, but something that was going to serve as a starting point for all subjects.

For a short time the importance of the development of the self-image was emphasized. Later on this aspect was transferred to MLCT. The following were added: combating and preventing stigmatization/stereo-typing, discrimination and racism on the basis of ethnic and cultural differences. Over the years the knowledge aspect has however been increasingly emphasized: the acquisition of knowledge with respect to each other's backgrounds, circumstances and cultures, by the indigenous population group as well as by the ethnic minority groups, and the acquisition of insight into the way in which values, norms, customs and circumstances determine the behaviour of people. In addition to affective and socio-psychologically oriented objectives such as respect, acceptance and self-image, a number of cognitive objectives were incorporated in the policy. Furthermore, ICE was considered useful in combating structural inequality, in so far that this was being fuelled by ethnic prejudice and discrimination (cf. Fase, Kole, Van Paridon & Vlug, 1990).

As far as the concrete implementation was concerned, the government had the following resources and instruments in mind: public information, guidelines and brochures, subsidizing educational resource development, in-service training courses for teachers, making it compulsory for teacher training institutions to pay attention to life in a multi-ethnic and multi-cultural society in their work plans. Furthermore a project policy was pursued, which meant that some schools were offered the possibility to experiment with the design of ICE. The role-model function was of essential importance in this, because other schools might wish to implement these projects.

Only a few studies have been carried out into the coming about and design of ICE and hardly any into the effects of ICE on pupils. Halfway the 1980s, Fase and Van den Berg (1985) concluded that very little had been undertaken: ICE had a low priority at schools compared with other activities. Furthermore, there was no evidence that ICE had any effects. A few years later, Fase, Kole, Paridon and Vlug (1990) on the basis of new research added that the results as far as the project policy was concerned were not very encouraging either. ICE simply was a topic that only a very limited amount of attention was being paid to. Moreover, the implementation of ICE was restricted to multi-ethnic schools.

In later EPP policy documents ICE was not mentioned anymore; apparently it was decided to unlink the compensatory policy and ICE completely.

The staffing and areas components

Specifically aimed at improving the educational opportunities of the EPP target groups were the 'staffing' and the 'areas' component. Within *the areas component* primary and secondary schools and welfare institutions, such as libraries and day nurseries, worked together at local or regional level in an effort to combat disadvantages. 'Areas' are Educational Priority Areas (EPAs) [Onderwijsvoorrangsgebieden], in which a cumulation of disadvantaging factors produces a high rate of educational deprivation. The idea behind the area approach was that it was assumed that some causes of educational disadvantage lie outside school and should therefore be dealt with outside school. At the start in 1986 there were 70 priority areas. On the basis of an area plan, these areas were awarded a sum of money each year for the coordination of priority activities and for the implementation of specific projects. Their activities included: preschool activities with parents and their children; reading promotion projects, in collaboration with libraries; homework projects; registration and guidance projects for truants and early school leavers.

Under *the staffing component* primary schools were given additional staff on the basis of the socio-economic and ethnic composition of their pupil population. (For that matter, the staffing component currently still is in effect.) In the allocation of these resources various categories of disadvantaged pupils were distinguished by means of a so-called weighting factor, which is based on the parents' educational and occupational level and country of origin. Roughly speaking, this means that:

- ethnic minority children count as 1.90;
- children of caravan dwellers count as 1.70;
- barge's' children count as 1.40;
- Dutch working-class children count as 1.25;
- other children 'simply' count as 1.00.

The first four categories made up the EPP target groups, the last was the non-disadvantaged category. In its definition of a minority child, the Ministry of Education started out from the country of birth of the parents. When at least one of the parents was born in a Mediterranean country or former colony, or was a refugee the child was considered to be a minority child. At the start of the EPP in the 1986/87 school year, 51.9% of the primary school pupils fell in the 1.00-category, 38.8% in the 1.25-category and 8.9% in the 1.90-category; only 0.1 and 0.3% of the pupils were in the 1.40- and 1.70-category. In the 1993/94 school year these percentages were 55.3, 33.0, 11.3, 0.1 and 0.3, respectively. This means that almost half of the primary school pupils were considered to be disadvantaged. In practice, the number of extra EPP-teachers varied considerably. In the 1993/94 school year 42.3% of the schools did not receive any extra staffing at all. Another 40.7% did receive less than one extra teacher. For instance, schools with more than 75% of 1.25-pupils on average did not receive more than one extra teacher. On the other hand, schools with more than 50% of 1.90-pupils on average received more than three extra teachers. It is therefore legitimate to conclude that the staffing component of the EPP in essence was an ethnic minority policy.

The assigning of the weighting factors has come about on the basis of the assumed extent of educational disadvantage in combination with the amount of available financial resources. The EPP in essence was a facilities policy. The average weighting of pupils at a school determined the number of teachers allocated. The schools in the priority areas benefited from the staffing component as well as from the area component.

The schools and EPA's were to a large extent free to decide how they wished to use the allocated resources and to adapt the EPP to their own specific situation. The objective nevertheless always remained the same: to reduce the educational disadvantages of the EPP-target groups. Examples of school activities include improving contacts between teachers and parents, extra instruction via the child's home language, extra lessons Dutch as a Second Language (DSL), and remedial teaching (cf. Tesser, 1994). However, research findings showed that most schools used the resources for forming smaller classes, which means that all the pupils in a class profited from the extra funding, and not the EPP target groups exclusively. As in the allocation of teachers there was no distinction made between the regular staff and the additional staff based on the number of disadvantaged pupils, schools often were not even aware of the fact that they received extra funding.

In secondary education there were no resource schemes similar to the one in primary education, although minority children might nevertheless be temporarily entitled to resources within the framework of programmes aimed at facilitating their entry into the Dutch education system, e.g. DSL classes or International Transition Classes (cf. Fase, 1994).

Related topics

Preschool and early school programmes
One of the findings of the research that has been carried out into the educational position of disadvantaged groups is that ethnic minority pupils are already considerably behind when they start primary education, and that they do not catch up over the years. It is for this reason that in attempts to combat, respectively prevent disadvantages the emphasis is increasingly being put on the first years at school and the preschool period. All kinds of home and center-based intervention programmes have been developed at national as well as local level for children between 0 and 6/7 years of age. In these efforts the emphasis is largely on the linguistic and cognitive development of the children, which may be combined with providing educational support to the parents. These programmes are often based on or derived from compensatory (education) programmes and strategies similar to the ones developed in the USA (cf. Blok & Leseman, 1996; Combes, 1995). In the second part of the 1980s this approach towards educational disadvantage was given an important impetus by the introduction of a series of so-called 'Hippy'-projects (cf. Eldering & Vedder, 1993; Kook, 1996).

Dutch as a second language
At the start in kindergarten ethnic minority children often already lag far behind as regards their Dutch language proficiency level, according to a study by Driessen (1996b) at the age of 6 even 13 to 21 months. The problems of these

children essentially are a language problem. But not only at the start of their school career, also in later years of primary and secondary education Dutch language proficiency often forms an almost insurmountable obstacle (Driessen, 1992, 1995). For this reason special teaching methods and material adapted to the specific situation of immigrants have been developed. Special attention is given to vocabulary training as it is becoming more and more clear that these children just do not know enough Dutch words, which has negative effects on all school subjects (cf. Appel & Vermeer, 1996).

Transfer from school to work

The transfer from school to work very often poses a problem for ethnic minority and working class youth, especially for boys. Truancy, early school leaving and drop-out are rather common phenomena in this category (cf. Dekkers & Driessen, 1997). Which end in temporary low-paid jobs, unemployment or social security dependence. Within the framework of the EPP special attention was paid to these youngsters, they were monitored and various projects were implemented (Tesser & Veenman, 1997).

3.2.2   Theoretical basis

The question as to whether or not the EPP yielded the desired result, is preceded by the question as to whether or not, on the basis of the starting points, strategies and instruments used in the policy, it is in fact realistic to expect any kind of effect at all. These questions form the main topic of a study by Mulder (1996), of which a summary will be given below. Mulder discerns two kinds of theories, viz. the policy theory and the instruments theory.

The policy theory

By policy theory is meant the causal (cause-effect), final (aim-means) and the normative suppositions that underlie the policy (cf. Van de Graaf & Hoppe, 1992). Mulder (1996) studied various policy documents to reconstruct the policy theory underlying the EPP. The final judgement is that the policy theory behind the EPP has a lot of weak points. The most important of these are the vague formulation of the objective and the contradictions contained therein, the lack of a sound analysis of the problem and the fact that the suppositions in the policy theory are in general not supported by social science research or theories. In particular within the staff establishment policy the supposed relationships are based on quicksand. The policy theory underlying the area policy is a stronger and more well-founded one.

The vagueness of the policy theory, and with this the non-committal nature of the policy, can for a large part be explained by the normative framework within which the policy came about. Within that framework two aspects are of crucial importance. In the first place, the ambiguity with regard to the objective. Since World War II the government has seen it as one of its task to contribute towards reducing social inequality. Initially, this was founded on economic motives, later largely on ideological ones. From the moment the ideological motives got the upper hand, there has been a lack of clarity about the question as to what one really hopes to achieve with the policy. Does one hope to achieve a reduction of social inequality or achieve as high an educational level for *all* pupils as possible? Is one aiming for maximum individual development or for equal social opportunities? And connected to this: should education be labour market-oriented, with the emphasis on achievements and cognitive subjects or should it be child-oriented in which case non-cognitive and cognitive subjects have the same priority? Within the EPP these choices are not made. The result of this is that it is only possible to speak in vague and general terms about what one hopes to achieve and how one wants to go about this.

The second aspect within the normative framework that is also partly responsible for the vagueness of the policy theory is the Dutch constitutional 'freedom of education'. This principle restricts the government in its possibilities to place demands on how the resources to combat disadvantage are to be used, because if it were to do so it would be interfering with the schools' freedom to determine the content of instruction. Statements about how to act in order to achieve certain policy goals are therefore only sporadically made in policy texts and when they are made they are not very concrete. This in particular applies in relation to the use of the additional staff, because in this case the government has to address itself directly to the individual schools. In the case of requirements and recommendations for the use of the area resources the government is less directly involved with the schools. This is probably also (one of) the reason(s) that the policy theory underlying the area policy is clearer and more concrete than the one underlying the staff establishment policy.

The instruments theory

According to the instruments theory the fact as to whether or not the policy instruments are used correctly in practice, is in the first place determined by the interactions between those implementing the policy (government officials) and the members of the target group (cf. Bressers & Klok, 1991). In the EPP the target group was made up of the individual schools and the priority areas. From the analysis of the implementation phase of the EPP it is possible to conclude that this in general went well (Verhaak & Brandsma, 1991). In so far that it is possible to check this, the policy instruments were used correctly from an administrative point of view. The interaction between the government officials on the one hand and the schools and areas on the other can be characterized as 'constructive co-operation'. As far as the staffing component is concerned, it has been established that this yields relatively few additional staffing places for most schools, including many schools with a high percentage of EPP-pupils.

Whether or not the policy instruments have an effect on the behaviour of the target group depends on the availability of behaviour alternatives and behaviour motives. It is possible to establish how the effectuation phase of the EPP went on the basis of data obtained from teachers and headteachers with regard to their familiarity with the EPP, their attitude in relation to that policy, the way in which the resources were used at their school, if applicable, their experiences with the area co-operation. From the answers it is possible to conclude that in 1992, after six years of EPP, the effect of the policy on the schools that were only receiving additional staff (staff establishment schools) still had not really come about as yet. These schools lacked the necessary knowledge about the policy, about the resources awarded to them and, possibly as a result of this, about how these resources are to be used. The schools within the EPA's (area schools) came out better on all of these points.

In order to be able to answer the question as to why the effect of the policy was better in area schools than in staff establishment schools, the effect of the behaviour motives of the various school types was looked into. Three kinds of motives were distinguished: individual behaviour motives, social behaviour motives and behaviour motives pertaining to legal standards (Bressers & Klok, 1991). *Individual* behaviour motives are related to someone personally weighing up the cost and effect of something. What kind of investment does one need to make in terms of time, money and effort, and what does one get in return? In short: what are the personal consequences of a behaviour alternative? *Social* behaviour motives are derived from the importance that one attaches to belonging to a group or being appreciated by this group. Whether or not one opts for a behaviour alternative is in this case dictated by one's environment. Behaviour motives pertaining to *legal standards* are related to consequences in terms of deviance and conformity. The target group is or is not expected to stick to the rules that have been laid down.

The conclusion is that in the case of the staff establishment schools the individual behaviour motives have a (strong) negative effect on the kind of behaviour the government would like to see and that the social behaviour and behaviour motives pertaining to legal standards have a neutral effect. In the area schools individual behaviour motives, social behaviour motives and motives pertaining to legal standards all have a positive influence. It is possible to conclude from this that the chances of the behaviour the government would like to see being chosen are very small at the staff establishment schools and very big at the area schools. The resources that are awarded to individual schools could therefore not be expected to have much of any effect from the outset. The limited amount of resources and the total lack of rules and (social) control are responsible for the fact that the policy merely existed on paper at most staff establishment schools. As a result of the greater amount of additional resources and the joint and thereby less non-committal approach, the staffing as well as the area component of the policy got far better off the ground at the area schools.

On the basis of the above findings, Mulder (1996) expected that the chances of any element of the policy objective being achieved are greater at schools within the priority areas than outside. In view of the fact that the policy hardly got off the ground at schools that were only assigned additional staff, it was not considered likely that any part of the objective would have been achieved at those schools as yet.

3.2.3   An international comparison

Programmes

The position of disadvantaged children in the US, Australia, Canada and West European countries like the UK, Belgium, France, Germany and the Netherlands is very much alike in many respects. Despite these similarities, however, the way national governments have tried to tackle the educational problems of low socio-economic and minority ethnic groups may differ significantly depending on the political and institutional contexts and the broader socio-economic structures (Fase, 1994; Day, Van Veen & Walraven, 1997; Reid, 1997).

The early Dutch local compensatory projects were largely based on the ideas behind the US compensatory and enrichment programmes like Head Start, Follow Through and Title 1. Head Start is a preschool programme that provides educational and medical services for poor children. Head Start operates via local centres, which differ greatly in the way they work. Follow Through is a follow-up to Head Start for kindergarten and the early of primary schoolyears. Its aim is to retain and build on academic progress made in the preschool programmes. The programme is organized as a planned-variation experiment in which different models for educating disadvantaged children were tested. The purpose of Title 1 (or Chapter I) is to strengthen and improve the educational quality and educational opportunities of primary and secondary school children who are poor, handicapped, neglected, delinquent, migrant or American Indian. The main approach is to provide extra financial support on the basis of acceptable submitted plans. The so-called 'pull-out' model is the most common activity. Here children leave their class 30 to 40 minutes every day for remedial language and arithmetic teaching. Most of the Title I teachers are deployed to reduce the size of regular classes. Other programmes include Success for All (cf. Slavin, Karweit & Madden, 1989), Upward Bound, and the Summer Training and Education Program (STEP).

In Australia the so-called whole school approach is a prominent underlying philosophy, which includes improving the curriculum, school organization, relations with out-of-school institutions and pedagogical approaches. An important programme is the anti-poverty Disadvantaged Schools Programme (DSP), which was set up in 1975. This aims to stimulate literacy and numeracy, enhance life experience and self confidence and improve interaction between schools and neighbourhood. The National Equity Programme for Schools (NEPS) is directed at creating equal opportunities for disadvantaged children. A specific programme is Students at Risk (STAR), aimed at early school leavers.

In West European countries various initiatives have been taken to improve the educational position of disadvantaged children. Since 1981, in *France*, for instance, so-called ZEPs (Zônes d'Education Prioritaires [Educational Priority Areas]) have been in operation. In ZEPs professionals and volunteers from such different areas as teaching, social services, health care and the police force work together. Activities include reading programmes, promoting citizenship, and extra school help. Since 1991 *Belgium* has an Educational Priority Policy [OnderwijsVoorrangsBeleid] aimed at improving the opportunities of ethnic minorities in nursery, primary and lower secondary schools. Schools with an approved action plan and at least 20 pupils of the target group are entitled to extra teaching staff. Special attention is given to the learning of Dutch and to bridging the gap between school and home environment. Since 1995 nursery and primary schools with large numbers of socially disadvantaged children also receive extra teachers. In *Germany* no special national regulations for disadvantaged children exist, although there are local projects, i.e. mother tongue teaching for migrant children. Although the *UK* has had its Educational Priority Areas, since the introduction of the National Curriculum in 1989, which is meant for *all* children, national provisions for children at risk are missing. The solving of specific problems depends on the efforts at local level, e.g. local education authorities, schools, and individual teachers. Provisions for ethnic minorities with language problems are available under the Section 11 programme. However, this programme was recently subject to cutbacks (main sources: Scheerens, 1987; Fase, 1994; De Geus, Buis, Jacobs & Mulder, 1997; De Geus, Jacobs, Buis & Mulder, 1997).

Evaluation

Many of the programmes for disadvantaged children are accompanied by some sort of evaluation. However, the scope and quality of the studies differ greatly. Much research is done on the implementation of the programmes, which often leads to the conclusion that the programmes are successful, although no study into actual effectiveness was involved. Most studies are qualitative oriented and focus on small local projects. The United States and the Netherlands seem to be the only countries with large-scale, nationwide longitudinal evaluation results available, although in Belgium, France and Australia such studies have recently been started.

In general it is probably safe to conclude that the results of the evaluation studies are often inconsistent, that insofar positive effects are found these are rather small, and that these effects only occur in the first years after the 'treatment' and then gradually fade out. However, in some cases long-term effects were found. For instance, the evaluations of the US programmes initially showed that the influence of the children's home environment outweighed that of the school programme by far, and that the compensatory programmes were doomed to be, and in fact were, ineffective (Scheerens, 1987; Vermeulen, Breemans, Mulder & Tesser, 1987). However, there was a lot of criticism regarding the methodology used in the evaluations. Later, more sophisticated studies indicated that there were positive effects of compensatory programmes - however small and if only in the early years (Rossi & Montgomery, 1994; Borman & D'Agostino, 1996).

3.3   The evaluation of the EPP

3.3.1   Design

In order to evaluate the Educational Priority Policy, within the framework of the National Evaluation of the EPP a number of large-scale cohort studies were started since 1986 in both primary and secondary education, supplemented by specific related research projects and in-depth studies (Kloprogge, 1989). This chapter focuses on the cohort studies in primary education, as they form the core of the EPP evaluation. For an account of other studies, see among others Meijnen and Kloprogge (1993), Van der Werf (1993, 1995), Van der Werf and Bosker (1993), Mulder and Van der Werf (1997), Driessen (1993, 1995), Driessen and Dekkers (1997), Driessen, Mulder and Jungbluth (1999), and Wolbers and Driessen (1996). The cohort studies were started in the school year 1988/89 in grades 2, 4 and 6 of primary education. A second and third round of measurements took place in 1990/91 and 1992/93. Some 700 schools and 35,000 pupils took part in each round. In 1994/95 the EPP evaluation cohorts at primary schools were incorporated in a newly started study, the Primary Education cohort study (PRIMA). Its first round of measurements took place in 1994/95, the second in 1996/97, and the third in 1998/99. An important modification was the fact that now also kindergarten was included.

In the studies in primary education the performance of the pupils was related to:
• the disadvantaged category they belonged to;
• the amount of additional resources the school received.

Regarding the former, the focus was on the three main categories: 1.00-, 1.25- and 1.90-pupils; regarding the latter, three categories were distinguished: area schools, staff establishment schools, and non-EPP schools. In this way an attempt was made to get an insight into the effects of the policy pursued. The evaluation design can be viewed as a combination of a quasi-experimental and longitudinal cohort study. The pupils at non-EPP schools can be viewed as the control group, the pupils at the area and staff establishment schools as the experimental groups. The criterion variables in the evaluation are the language and arithmetic achievement levels. The degree of disadvantage is established by contrasting the achievement levels of the target group pupils with the scores of a national representative sample of all the pupils in the same year. The further the mean scores of the target group pupils lie below the mean scores of the national sample, the bigger the educational arrears. It is possible to speak of an EPP effect if between two measurements the difference in achievement levels between the target groups and the reference group, i.e. the 1.00-category, become smaller. Since the language and arithmetic tests for each of the years differed both in level of difficulty and number of items, the raw test scores were transformed into so-called T-scores, with a mean of 50 and a standard deviation of 10.

As from 1989/90 5,000 pupils of the primary education cohorts were also followed in secondary education. In 1989/90 another large-scale cohort study was started in the first year of secondary education (VOCL). Almost 400 schools and 20,000 pupils took part in this study. In 1991/92 the pupils that were in the third year participated again. In 1993/94 and 1995/96 this scheme was repeated for a newly started cohort. Because no additional resources are allocated in secondary education, bar a few exceptions, the cohorts that were started in that phase of education have a different purpose than the primary education cohorts. The main emphasis here was on monitoring the educational progress of the various categories of pupils.

As regards the effectiveness study, this chapter focuses on the question as to whether or not, in the period 1988-1992, the EPP led to a reduction in the educational disadvantage of the target groups, in particular in relation to primary education.

3.3.2   Results

The main effectiveness study

In order to determine the effectiveness of the EPP in primary education, one opted for a bi-annual measurement of the language and arithmetic achievement levels of pupils in grades 2, 4 and 6. Data were furthermore collected on the social and ethnic background of the pupils, their intelligence and relevant school, class and parent characteristics. A 'reference sample' was used as a criterion for establishing the degree of disadvantage. This involved a randomly selected 3.5% sample of all Dutch primary schools. In order to be able to trace area effects the reference sample was supplemented with schools from half the EPA's. The scores of the pupils in the reference group acted as the norm against which the achievement levels of the EPP target groups were measured. If the policy were effective, the achievement levels of the target group pupils would in time stay less far behind the reference mean.

The question as to whether in 1992, six years after the start of the EPP, any part of the EPP objective had been achieved, was examined in two ways:

- By means of a cross-sectional comparison: are the target group pupils who were in grades 2, 4 and 6 in 1992 performing better than those who were in the same form in 1988 and 1990?
- By means of a longitudinal comparison: how are the target group pupils who were in grade 2 in 1988 performing in grade 6, four years on? And how are

the target group pupils who were in grade 2 in 1990 performing in grade 4, two years on?

From the *cross-sectional* comparison it appears that since 1988 the achievements of pupils at schools in EPA's have in general improved more than the achievements of pupils at schools that are only awarded the EPP staff establishment or that are not entitled to additional resources. In particular the 1.90-pupils at area schools have caught up somewhat. The differences involved are only minor ones, but they are big enough for them not to just be coincidental.

This (limited) improvement in achievement can however not simply be attributed to the EPP. This is because the group of 1.90-pupils tested in 1992 differs from the group that took part in the study in 1988 on one important point: in 1992 the pupils had on average already been in the Netherlands for a longer period of time and the percentage of older immigrant children entering the Dutch school system was considerably smaller. This was in particular the case for the Turkish and Moroccan pupils, the pupils who largely attend area schools. The fact that pupils perform better the longer they have been in the Netherlands has already been shown on several occasions (cf. Driessen, 1993, 1995). And this time too, it appears from the analyses that the longer period of stay in the Netherlands is largely responsible for the improved achievements at area schools.

The results from the *longitudinal* comparison show that the achievements of the 1.25-pupils get further behind those of the 1.00-pupils as they make their way through primary education. This applies for all pupils, regardless of whether they attend a non-EPP, a staff establishment or an area school. The fact that pupils from the lower social classes get more and more behind has already been established years ago. Striking is that the disadvantage of the 1.90-pupils does not get any worse in the course of their primary education, but remains constant. But here we are only talking about the 'better' 1.90-pupils. Compared with the two indigenous groups, i.e. the 1.00- and the 1.25-category, a relatively large proportion of the 1.90-pupils that were tested in grade 2, repeated a year or were referred to special education.

3.3.3   Effectiveness and policy reconsidered

In short, it is possible to draw the following conclusions from the research results:
- The aims of the EPP were vaguely formulated by the government and contain a number of contradictions. There is no sound analysis of the problem;

- The staffing component is a very weak part of the policy. The supposed effect of the EPP staff establishment is totally unfounded. As a result of the relatively limited amount of resources per school, and the total lack of rules and (social) control the EPP only exists on paper at most of the schools that only get additional staff. Indeed, as long as policy makers do not require 'true' implementation, the supposed effect will remain absent;
- The area component of the policy is considerably stronger than the staffing component. The suppositions, on which the area policy is based, are reasonably well founded and are (partly) supported by social science research. As a result of the larger amounts of additional resources and the joint, and consequently, less non-committal approach, the staffing as well as the area component of the policy got off the ground much better at area schools than at staff establishment schools;
- In the period 1988-1992 the EPP did not lead to a reduction in the language and arithmetic arrears of the target group pupils at schools only receiving additional staff and at schools in EPA's.

The question now is what is the relationship between the findings with respect to the policy (the first three conclusions) and the concrete results which failed to materialize in the shape of a reduction in the language and arithmetic delay of the target group pupils (the last conclusion).

Causal relationship versus conditional relationship

The reason for reconstructing the policy theory underlying the EPP was that policy research shows that the effectiveness of a policy among other things depends on the quality of the policy theory (Hoogerwerf, 1984). This means that one supposes that there is a direct link between the quality of the policy theory and the objective being achieved. This relationship is not necessarily a causal one. It is not true to say that as long as the policy theory is all right, the objective will automatically be achieved. It is also not true to say that when the objective is not achieved, this is due to a bad policy theory. One can only speak of a conditional relationship. The policy theory has to be qualitatively sound, in order to give the policy any chance of success. In other words, a weak policy theory makes the chances of the policy being a success, rather small. The same conditional relationship exists between the implementation phase of the policy and the objective being achieved. A policy can only lead to the desired results, when the decisions taken by those pursuing the policy are actually put into practice. But if no results are being achieved, this does not necessarily have to be caused by a poor effect.

This conditional relationship limits the possibilities of the research at hand to lay the link between the findings with respect to the policy aspects and the results of the empirical research. The fact that in 1992, after six years of EPP, there were still no concrete signs of the objective being achieved (to a greater or lesser extent), cannot just simply be attributed to the weak policy theory or an unsuccessful implementation phase. There are after all other factors that can be responsible for the objective (not) being achieved, even when this has been clearly described, and there is a detailed analysis of the problem, and the supposed relationships are supported by scientific research and there was a successful implementation phase.

One of these relevant factors is, for example, the *amount* of resources that are made available. It has appeared that the majority of the schools that qualify for EPP-additional staffing have to make do with one or one half of one additional establishment place. Often more than fifty percent of the pupils attending these schools are target group pupils. Is it then realistic to expect any effects from this limited amount of additional staff? If it is not, then it does not make any difference what the policy theory looks like, or whether the effectuation phase went well or not.

The *time* aspect also plays a role: history shows that educational disadvantage is a very persistent problem. The policy possibly needs more time and perhaps we can only expect to see tangible results in ten years time, even in the case of a well thought out policy theory and successful effectuation phase. Or perhaps the EPP objective is not feasible at all.

One conclusion that can be drawn for sure is that in the case of the staff establishment policy the conditions needed to make the policy a success, i.e. a qualitatively sound policy theory and a successful effectuation phase, have not been met. One can therefore not expect to see any effects from this policy component if the policy remains unchanged. The area policy clearly had more chances of success. Despite this, no real concrete results have been achieved, at least not in the form of improved achievements.

Effectiveness study versus effect study

Whether or not the EPP has led to anything over the past years has in this chapter been established on the basis of the development of the language and arithmetic achievements of the target group pupils. This involved an effectiveness study: the degree to which the policy contributed to the objective being achieved was looked into. Policy can however also have effects that are not directly visible from the degree to which the objective has been achieved. In this case we are not talking about policy effectiveness, but about policy effects: *any* kind of effect of the policy. At area schools for instance, increasing emphasis has in recent years been placed on improving the achievement levels of the target group pupils. In addition the results of school effectiveness studies into many areas have started to receive more and more attention in the planning of EPP activities. Furthermore it is possible to note a slight improvement, since 1988, in the attention that immigrant pupils receive in the form of extra tuition, specific exercises and special methods. In view of the fact that we in particular see these improved working methods at area schools, one could possibly speak in terms of a policy effect here. It is in any case true to say that the areas are paying more and more attention to the disadvantage issue. A complete network was set up within which research was carried out, methods and materials were developed and support was offered, an effect of the EPP that should most certainly not be underestimated.

Related issues

In addition to the problematic points raised until now, some other issues are of relevance in considering the findings of the EPP evaluation.

One shortcoming of the effect measurement is the restriction to language and arithmetic, which do not cover the complete curriculum area and the EPP goals. Partly this has been met with in-depth studies and additional measurements (Mulder, 1996).

Another problem could be the fact that there is no clear control group in the design as is the case in an experimental situation. Actually there is a rather rude classification in nine categories (the combination of school category and EPP pupil category; see par. 3.1), while it probably would have been more appropriate to work with a continuous scale implying more or less EPP facilities.

In the longitudinal analyses there is the problem that there is a 'loss' of pupils because they had to repeat a year, were referred to special education, were absent or had left to another school. Because it is a well established fact that it are especially the EPP target groups, notably the 1.90-category, that make up this category of pupils, one can speak of differential loss (attrition bias). As a consequence the results of the target groups will be flattered.

One problem is that the staffing component is not based on the actual educational arrears of individual children, but on the average achievement levels of the category as a whole. Whether the facilitated children were educationally disadvantaged is unclear. On the one hand this means that part of the targeted children were in reality not at risk, while on the other hand another part of the children were wrongly not categorized as at risk. Of course this is of consequence to the categories used in the EPP evaluation. This points to the need for further refinements to be made to the definition of disadvantaged categories (cf. Evans, 1995).

Another problem is that the additional staffing that was allocated with respect to individual disadvantage was awarded to the school as a whole, which in most cases means that the school population profits from the extra staff and not necessarily the individual children.

3.4   Recent developments

At the beginning of the 1990s there were more and more signs indicating that policy in the field of disadvantaged children in education was not having the desired effects. (Which, however, does not mean that no progress had been made!) These observations among others based on the numerous EPP evaluation study reports made the national government reconsider the policy that was being pursued. The government set up a number of committees and project groups with the aim of arriving at new ideas for a more effective approach. Three committees in particular should be mentioned in this context: the Committee Non-Indigenous Pupils in Education (CALO, 1992), the Committee (Pre)school Education (Leseman & Cordus, 1994) and the Committee Evaluation of Primary Education (CEB, 1994). The observations and recommendations of the committees have led to various adjustments of the educational policy pursued until then. One was the drastic reorganization of Minority Language Teaching, another the fact that Intercultural Education was no longer seen as a separate policy track, but more as part of the general educational policy (see above). In addition much more attention was paid to preschool and early school programmes, to Dutch as a Second Language education, now explicitly as a policy track, and reducing absenteeism and unqualified school leaving (cf. Tesser, Van Dugteren & Mertens, 1996).

Three other developments should be mentioned. In 1993 the new Act governing EPA's was accepted by the Upper and Lower Houses of Parliament. This act among other things states that a National Policy Framework will be issued once every four years. This is a document in which the area activities that qualify for funding are mentioned, that forms the basis for ministerial decisions with regard to the distribution of funds. The National Policy Framework 1993-1997 mentions the following objectives:

- to improve the learning achievements in language and arithmetic at primary schools;
- to improve the proficiency level in Dutch of immigrant pupils as well as of Dutch pupils with another native language;
- a more proportional transfer to the various forms of secondary education in comparison with the non-target group pupils;
- to improve the initial reception of newcomers;
- to reduce absenteeism;
- to reduce the number of pupils leaving school without qualification in the first phase of secondary education.

These objectives reflect the direction of the policy. They link up with the policy designed to see to it that everyone leaves school with a basic vocational qualification. With this a clear choice has been made for labour market-oriented education with the emphasis on the cognitive subjects.

The areas are obliged to undertake activities in line with these objectives. They have to formulate concrete objectives, complete with target figures and they need to draw up a report every year on the results achieved. The weak points of the area policy in the period 1986-1992 in particular concerned the vague objectives and the contradictions contained therein, and the fact that aspects of the policy were not put into practice. In the new set-up it are precisely these points that are tackled, as a result of which the area policy is clearly gaining power.

The staff establishment policy has also been amended, but for the time being only from an administrative point of view. The criteria for qualifying for the 1.25- weighting, i.e. the Dutch working class children, have been sharpened up since 1993 for pupils enrolling at a school. Before 1993 only one of the parents needed to have a low level of education; after that year this criterion applied to both parents. Eventually this will lead to halving the 1.25-category. This is, in itself, a good development, because as a result of the broad definition of the indigenous target group of the EPP one has incorrectly been given the impression that things are not too bad as far as the disadvantage of the 1.25-pupils is concerned. Apart from this sharpening up of the criteria no other changes have been made in the staff establishment policy for the time being. The proposed improvements that are mentioned in EPP papers, reports and policy documents every year again, such as a broad public information campaign, ear-marking of the EPP staff establishment, specification of the intention of this staff establishment, implementation examples, output-control, etcetera, still fail to get off the ground.

It still very much remains to be seen whether the staff establishment policy would in fact succeed if the proposed plans were actually implemented. Research into subsidies carried out in recent years shows that when subsidies are awarded to individual institutions, they frequently have a 'gift-effect', i.e. the subsidy is collected but nothing is done with it. Subsidies can be far more effective when they are awarded to promote co-operation. In particular when that co-operation subsequently leads to 'networks' being formed within which new developments start to take place that have a positive effect on other participants. These findings reflect the differences in the way the subsidies are awarded to staff establishment schools and to area schools. To the staff establishment schools, which are awarded the subsidy on an individual basis, the additional staff is generally no more than a gift and a welcome supplement to their tight regular staff establishment. The aim of the area facilities on the other hand is to promote co-operation. The evaluation results indicate that this way of awarding subsidies does indeed have a greater impact. In light of the results discussed here there is also a great deal to be said for taking a closer look at the possibilities for 'individual' schools to link up with a cooperative network. Subsidies can also be much more effective if they are coupled to some sort of accountability. There are, however, a number of specific problems in relation to the EPP. As mentioned earlier, because of the Dutch constitutional freedom of education the subsidies cannot be earmarked. Each school has the freedom to use them. Moreover, most schools only receive a very limited amount of subsidy. It is, indeed, highly questionably whether it can be expected that these schools on an individual basis can accomplish much with these extra resources as regards improving educational achievements.

The last development is the result of the idea that central government is not the proper body to give shape to the content of the policy tracks, that these would be dependent on local circumstances. The concrete design of the policy therefore needed to be determined at a decentralized level and should fall under the local authorities responsibility. This also links up with the government's efforts to reinforce local educational policy. The main idea behind this is that the school will be better equipped to fulfil its primary task if it links up more closely with the broader societal context. At local level there would be more possibilities for education to be given a place in an integrated minority policy. With effect from the 1998/99 school year the EPP was transformed into the so-called Local Educational Disadvantage Policy in which financial resources are paid in a combined form to the local authorities. These authorities will use funding in accordance with a local compensatory plan authorities drawn up for the purpose. The plan will among other things elaborate on objectives formulated in the National Policy Framework and will indicate the way in which a school will have to use the resources given by the local municipality. In addition to these resources schools also receive certain direct EPP funding. However, they also have to stick to the local compensatory plan when it comes to using this funding.

3.5   Epilogue

In the second half of the 1970s and especially the 1980s a large number of policies were developed and introduced with respect to the position of disadvantaged children in education. These were aimed at preventing and reducing educational disadvantage and also had a number of cultural, socio-psychological and emancipatory objectives. At the beginning of the 1990s an assessment was made of the situation. It would appear that the disadvantages suffered by working class and ethnic minority children had not got any less over the years: they were already considerably behind when they entered primary school, and did not catch up throughout their school career. Thus the aim of the Educational Priority Policy appears not to have been achieved. Only one element seems to have been relatively successful: the Educational Priority Areas.

As far as bilingual education is concerned it has to be noted that the so-called reception models hardly managed to get a foot off the ground and have only been used at a small number of schools. Opinions vary on the effect of these experiments. This also applies to minority language and culture teaching. Furthermore there is a great deal of discussion about the extent to which this kind of education is (still) useful and whether it does not in fact reduce educational opportunities and result in segregation instead of integration. It has in any case not resulted in improved performance in the basic subjects, and the positive effects in terms of 'own' language and culture achievement levels for half of the minorities, in particular the Moroccan children, are practically non-existent.

Intercultural education has simply languished from the very beginning. It is a very vague concept receiving hardly any attention in schools. The government does not seem to know how to handle it either.

From the realization that disadvantages need to be tackled as early as possible, a number of preschool and early school programmes have been developed at national and local level in recent years. To what extent these are effective has often not been investigated, and when it has, the results in the main have not been really encouraging.

Finally, an aspect that has only recently been recognized as a separate policy track, Dutch as a second language. A large number of methods and materials have been developed in this area in recent years. Recent studies carried out by the Education Inspectorate however show that the results in this area are disappointing. These methods are still hardly being used, their quality leaves a great deal to be desired, and they are not being used in accordance with the aims.

When looking at the results in the various different areas, it seemed in the early 1990s that the limits of educational policy and practice with respect to disadvantaged children had been reached. Roughly speaking hardly any aspect of the policy pursued had led to the effects anticipated by the government. This disappointing observation resulted in the government opting for a radical new approach, with the key words being decentralization, deregulation and increased autonomy. The national government would in future be only providing the framework for policy. The responsibility for planning, implementation and evaluation would be given to the local municipalities. It would only be possible to arrive at an integral and effective approach at local level. The municipalities as well as the schools would be given much more autonomy with respect to how resources were spent and policy content.

To what extent Local Educational Disadvantage Policy (LEDP) will lead to the desired results will remain unclear for some time to come. At the moment it is possible to speak of a transitional period during which there is largely a lack of clarity and uncertainty. The municipalities are familiarizing themselves with the possibilities of giving shape to an adequate, tailormade policy, and what their role should be in all of this. The possibility that every municipality will try to re-invent the wheel is not inconceivable. In particular smaller municipalities are going to be faced with entirely new tasks. It remains to be seen to what extent they are adequately equipped to deal with these. The same also applies to the schools themselves who will have to develop and implement new programmes. The main disadvantages are therefore that expertise will be fragmented and that costs will rise as a result. It is possible to draw a parallel with respect to all the developmental work carried out within the framework of EPP, MLCT, DSL, ICE and the preschool and early school projects up until now. Here too an enormous amount of methods, materials, programmes and projects were developed at local level. This development, however, has generally not been efficient and effective. The Dutch Social and Cultural Planning Office is of the opinion that the improved results will have to be achieved inside and not outside the classroom. There will in particular be a need for programmes of a high standard and for detailed methods that can be used by teachers without too much difficulty in everyday educational practice. Critics of LEDP are therefore already asking whether it might be necessary to keep some sort of central coordination at national level (cf. Tesser, Van Dugteren & Merens, 1996). Other criticism, from the Education Council, is aimed at the fact that the municipalities will have too much influence on the organization of education at privately run schools. The council feels that the freedom to provide education, which is an extremely important issue in the Netherlands and which has been laid down in the Constitution, will suffer as a result. Other critics are afraid for the future position of MLT. According to the new set-up this will have to be given outside regular school hours. It also becomes strongly dependent on the municipalities. They will determine to a large extent whether or not it will be offered and to which minority groups. The municipalities also have the freedom to use the money they receive for MLT in the fight to combat educational disadvantage. In the new policy the Educational Priority Areas no longer exist. A lot of people are concerned that much of what has been achieved over the past ten years as a result of a great deal of effort will be lost. Perhaps the fact that all schools will have to work in accordance with the local compensatory plan will offer opportunities for schools, who up until now have been operating individually, to become involved in a cooperative network. Because cooperation appears to be the key word, also when it comes to combating educational disadvantage.

One important point of criticism with respect to LEDP is that a thorough analysis of the policy pursued up until now is lacking, and that the government's positive expectations with respect to the new policy cannot be backed up by facts (Penders, 1997). For the time being hardly any studies have been carried out in the Netherlands into the design and implementation of such policies abroad, such as for example in the UK, USA and Sweden. Of particular importance is the question as to what effect the policy has had, and to what extent it can be transposed to the Dutch situation (cf. Levin, 1997).

NOTE

Throughout this chapter in particular use is made of the following sources: Van der Werf (1995), Mulder (1996) and Driessen (i.p.).

3.6   References

Appel, R., & Vermeer, A. (1996). Uitbreiding van de Nederlandse woordenschat van allochtone leerlingen in het basisonderwijs. *Pedagogische Studiën*, 73(1), 82-92.

Banks, J. (1993). Multicultural education: Historical development, dimensions, and practice. *Review of Research in Education*, 19, 3-49.

Blok, H., & Leseman, P. (1996). Effecten van voorschoolse stimuleringsprogramma's: Een review van reviews. *Pedagogische Studiën*, 73(3), 184-197.

Borman, G., & D'Agostino, J. (1996). Title I and student achievement: A meta-analysis of federal evaluation results. *Educational Evaluation and Policy Analysis*, 18(4), 309-326.

Bressers, J., & Klok, P.J. (1991). Hoe valt effectiviteit van beleid te verklaren? Deel 2: Instrumententheorie. In J. Bressers & A. Hoogerwerf (Eds.), *Beleidsevaluatie* (pp. 136-154). Alphen a/d Rijn: Samson H.D. Tjeenk Willink.

CALO (1992). *Ceders in de tuin. Naar een nieuwe opzet van het onderwijsbeleid voor allochtone leerlingen,* Den Haag: Sdu/DOP.

CEB (1994). *Evaluatie van het basisonderwijs. Inhoud en opbrengsten van het basisonderwijs.* De Meern: Inspectie van het basisonderwijs.

Combes, J. (1995). Programmes and issues related to early childhood. In OECD, *Our children at risk* (pp. 51-78). Paris: OECD.

Day, C., Veen, D. van, & Walraven, G. (1997). *Children and youth at risk and urban education. Research, policy and practice.* Leuven/Apeldoorn: Garant.

De Geus, W., Buis, T., Jacobs, E., & Mulder, L. (1997). *Onderzoek naar onderwijsachterstanden: Strategieën en resultaten voor risicokinderen in internationaal perspectief.* Nijmegen/Utrecht: ITS/SAC.

De Geus, W., Jacobs, E., Buis, T., & Mulder, L. (1997). *Research on children and youth at risk in an international perspective.* Paper presented at the ECER 1997, September 24-27, Frankfurt, Germany.

Dekkers, H., & Driessen, G. (1997). An evaluation of the Educational Priority Policy in relation to early school leaving. *Studies in Educational Evaluation*, 23(3), 209-230.

Driessen, G. (1992). First and second language proficiency: Prospects for Turkish and Moroccan children in the Netherlands. *Language, Culture and Curriculum*, 5(1), 23-40.

Driessen, G. (1993). Socio-economic or ethnic determinants of educational opportunities? Results from the Educational Priority Policy programme in the Netherlands. *Studies in Educational Evaluation*, 19(3), 265-280.

Driessen, G. (1995). The educational progress of immigrant children in the Netherlands. *Language, Culture and Curriculum*, 8(3), 265-280.

Driessen, G. (1996a). Minority Language and Culture Teaching in the Netherlands: Policies, arguments, evaluation and prospects. *Compare*, 26(3), 315-332.

Driessen, G. (1996b). De taalvaardigheid Nederlands van allochtone en autochtone leerlingen. De ontwikkeling in het basisonderwijs in kaart gebracht. *Gramma/TTT - Tijdschrift voor Taalwetenschap*, 5(1), 31-40.

Driessen, G. (1997). From mother tongue to foreign language: Prospects for Minority-Language Education in the Netherlands. In T. Bongaerts & K. de Bot (Eds.), *Perspectives on foreign-language policy. Studies in honour of Theo van Els* (pp. 181-200). Amsterdam/Philadelphia: Benjamins.

Driessen, G. (i.p.). The limits of educational policy and practice? The case of ethnic minority pupils in the Netherlands. *Comparative Education.*

Driessen, G., & Dekkers, H. (1997). Educational opportunities in the Netherlands: Policy, students performance and issues. *International Review of Education,* 43(4), 299-315.

Driessen, G., & Van der Grinten, M. (1994). Home language proficiency in the Netherlands: The evaluation of Turkish and Moroccan bilingual programmes - A critical review, *Studies in Educational Evaluation,* 20(3), 365-386.

Driessen, G., Mulder, L., & Jungbluth, P. (1999). Structural and cultural determinants of educational opportunities in the Netherlands. In S. Weil (Ed.), *Roots and routes: Ethnicity and migration in global perspective* (pp. 83-104). Jerusalem: Magnes Press.

Eldering, L., & Vedder, P. (1993). Culture sensitive home intervention: The Dutch HIPPY experiment. In L. Eldering & P. Leseman (Eds.), *Early intervention and culture. Preparation for literacy. The interface between theory and practice* (pp. 231-252). S.l.: UNESCO Publishing.

Evans, P. (1995). Children and youth 'at risk'. In: OECD, *Our children at risk* (pp. 13-50). Paris: OECD.

Fase, W. (1994). *Ethnic divisions in Western European education.* Münster/New York: Waxmann.

Fase, W., & Berg, G. van den (1985). *Theorie en praktijk van Intercultureel Onderwijs.* Den Haag: SVO.

Fase, W., Kole, S., Paridon, C. van, & Vlug, V. (1990). *Vorm geven aan Intercultureel Onderwijs.* De Lier: ABC.

Graaf, H. van de, & Hoppe, R. (1992). *Beleid en politiek. Een inleiding tot de beleidswetenschap en de beleidskunde.* Muiderberg: Coutinho.

Hoogerwerf, A. (1984). Beleid berust op veronderstellingen: de beleidstheorie. *Acta Politica, 19,* 493-532.

Kloprogge, J. (1989). The evaluation of the new Dutch national Education Priority Programme. *Studies in Educational Evaluation,* 15(3), 207-218.

Kook, H. (1996). *Overstap. Effecten op mondelinge taalvaardigheid en lezen.* Zoetermeer: Hageman.

Lam, T. (1992). Review of practices and problems in the evaluation of bilingual education. *Review of Educational Research,* 62(2), 181-203.

Leseman, P., & Cordus, J. (1994). *(Allochtone) Kleuters meer aandacht. Advies van de Commissie (Voor)schoolse Educatie.* Rijswijk: Ministerie van WVC.

Levin, B. (1997). The lessons of international education reform. *Journal of Education Policy,* 12(4), 253-266.

Meijnen, G., & Kloprogge, J. (Eds.). (1993). Evaluatie Onderwijsvoorrangsbeleid. *Pedagogische Studiën,* 70(2), 82-134, & 70(4), 242-273.

Mulder, L. (1996). *Meer voorrang, minder achterstand? Het Onderwijsvoorrangsbeleid getoetst.* Nijmegen: ITS.

Mulder, L., & Werf, G. van der (1997). Implementation and effects of the Dutch Educational Priority Policy: Results of four years of evaluation studies. *Educational Research and Evaluation,* 3(4), 317-339.

Penders, T. (1997). Decentralisatie van onderwijsachterstandenbeleid. *Tijdschrift voor de Onderwijspraktijk,* 42/77(1), 8-14.

Reid, I. (1997). Inequality and education in Britain in the 1990s: A diagnosis and prescription. *Research in Education,* 57, 12-24.

Rossi, R., & Montgomery, A. (1994). *Educational reforms and students at risk. A review of the current state of the art.* Washington DC: US Department of Education.

Scheerens, J. (1987). *Enhancing educational opportunities for disadvantaged learners. A review of Dutch research on compensatory education and educational development policy.* Amsterdam/Oxford/New York: North-Holland Publishing Company.

Slavin, R., Karweit, N., & Madden, N. (1989). *Effective programs for students at risk.* Boston: Allyn and Bacon.

Tesser, P. (1994), A framework for educational priority routines. Recommendations and checklist. In G. Driessen & P. Jungbluth (Eds.), *Educational opportunities. Tackling ethnic, class and gender inequality through research* (pp. 143-184). Münster/New York: Waxmann.

Tesser, P., & Veenman, J. (1997). *Rapportage minderheden 1997. Van school naar werk; de arbeidskansen van jongeren uit de minderheden in verband met het door hen gevolgde onderwijs.* Rijswijk/Den Haag: SCP/VUGA.

Tesser, P., Dugteren, F. van, & Merens, A. (1996). *Rapportage minderheden 1996. Bevolking, arbeid, onderwijs, huisvesting.* Rijswijk/Den Haag: SCP/VUGA.

Tomlinson, S., & Graft, M. (Eds.). (1995). *Ethnic relations and schooling. Policy and practice in the 1990s.* London/Atlantic Highlands, NJ: Athlone.

Verhaak, C., & Brandsma, H. (1991). *Onderwijsvoorrangsgebieden op weg. Een beschrijving van de gebieden als organisatienetwerken en projectorganisaties.* Nijmegen/Groningen: ITS/GION.

Vermeulen, H., Breemans, A., Mulder, L., & Tesser, P. (1988). *Onderzoek naar compensatieprogramma's in de Verenigde Staten en Groot-Britannië. Een literatuurstudie ten behoeve van de evaluatie van het Onderwijsvoorrangsbeleid.* Nijmegen: ITS.

Werf , M. van der (Ed.). (1993). De andere kant van de OVB-evaluatie. *Tijdschrift voor Onderwijswetenschappen,* 23(2/3), 51-147.

Werf, M. van der (1995). *The Educational Priority Policy in the Netherlands. Content, implementation and outcomes.* Den Haag: SVO.

Werf, M., van der, & Bosker, R. (Eds.). (1993). Opportunity structures in primary schools. *Tijdschrift voor Onderwijsresearch,* 18(2), 65-129.

Wolbers, M., & Driessen, G. (1996). Social class or ethnic background? Determinants of secondary school careers of ethnic minority pupils. *The Netherlands' Journal of Social Sciences,* 23(2), 109-126.

4. INTEGRATION POLICY AND PRACTICE

Felicity Fletcher-Campbell[1], Cor J.W. Meijer[2] & Sip Jan Pijl[3]

[1]*National Foundation for Educational Research, Slough, England*
[2]*European Agency for Development in Special Needs Education, Middelfart, Denmark*
[3]*GION, University of Groningen, The Netherlands*

Dutch special education has developed a wide-ranging system, and maybe because of that it gradually has grown. In 1990 a new national policy has been implemented in which clustering of special and mainstream schools is seen as a way to stop the inflow of pupils in special education. The policy and its evaluation is described in this chapter, showing that some progress has been made, but that the final objective, namely more adaptive instruction for all pupils, has not been achieved yet. This situation and the evaluation research as well are being reflected upon, making comparisons between the situation in the United Kingdom and the Netherlands.

4.1 Special education: current situation and main problems

4.1.1 Special education system

The educational system in the Netherlands consists of regular schools and an impressive separate special school system. Since the sixties, Dutch special education has developed into a wide-ranging system for pupils with special educational needs. The Dutch educational system distinguishes nowadays 12 types of special education, mainly for every disability a separate schooltype, for instance schools for the learning disabled, the mild mentally retarded, the deaf, etcetera.

Concerning the age group of 4-19 years old about 4% of all children follow education in a separate special education setting. The large majority of children with special needs consists of the learning disabled and the mild mentally retarded. These two groups cater for about 70% of all children in special education: 2.8% of all children attend these two school types. Thus, most of the children belong to the group of learning disabled (1.5%) and the mild mentally retarded (1.3%). The other groups count for relative small percentages: severely mentally retarded (0.3%) and severely maladjusted or behavioural problems (0.3%). All the other types of disability count for 0.1% or less.

For a long time, this highly differentiated and extensive special education system was seen as an expression of the concern for pupils with special needs. Nowadays, a growing group of policy makers, educators and parents think segregation in education has gone too far. A gradually increasing number of parents want their special needs child to attend a regular school, so the child will receive as normal schooling as possible.

Recently, the government launched two policy programs, one aimed at stimulating integration of pupils with the milder forms of special needs and one separate track for pupils with the more severe needs. This article will focus on the former group of children: the milder special educational needs. It is this group that forms the target group of the so-called WSNS-innovation, where the acronym WSNS represents Together to School Again [Weer Samen Naar School]; recently an evaluation study concerning this policy has been conducted, and it is this study that will be discussed here extensively.

4.1.2   Problems in special education

Recent studies concerning the factors that have contributed to an expanding special education system revealed that these factors can be divided into three groups (Ministerie van Onderwijs en Wetenschappen, 1990 & 1991).

First, the *policy and administrative conditions* contributed to segregation. Until now there are two separate laws, one for regular education and one for special education. This in itself had a clear effect in terms of an increase of the special education system (Doornbos & Stevens, 1987). Separate legislation for regular and special education underlines the legislator's view that pupils with special educational needs should be placed in special schools.

The fact that the Dutch government policy on integration has been unsuccessful is demonstrated by the expanding special education sector. The 1985 Primary Education Act - which aimed, among other things, to take differences in pupils' abilities, interests and learning pace into account - was not enough to halt the number of children being referred to special schools. Also other efforts to stop the growth of the special education school system did not result in the desired effects.

In this context it is usually referred to as the 'paradox of legislation' (Doornbos, 1991; Van Rijswijk, 1991). Doornbos and Van Rijswijk suggest that the government was in fact rewarding the increase in special education. In other words, the government stimulated what it did not want. It was clear that the funding system contained a reward for every referral to a special school. The funding system can be characterized by stating that it contains a 'bonus' for special school placement and a disincentive for placement in the mainstream: the finances are linked to the system and not to the pupil with special educational needs. A child in a special school receives far more support than the same child within the mainstream school.

The second group concerns *educational factors*. It is generally felt that education does not sufficiently take into account the increasing differences among pupils. At the same time, there are no special facilities available for children who are 'different' in regular schools, which contributes to more referrals to special schools.

Indeed, regular schools have huge difficulties in taking differences among pupils into account. The widespread approach in Dutch schools is that all children are expected to learn the same material in precisely the same amount of time. As a result, having to repeat a year is still quite common in Dutch regular schools (Reezigt & Knuver, 1995). Teachers point out that repeating a year is a tool for creating homogeneous classes. Pupil differences seem to pose huge problems and the only way these can be reduced is by taking drastic action in the form of pupils repeating years and referrals to special schools.

The third group of factors that contributed to the firm increase of the separate special school system concerns *the strong division between the regular and special school system*. This division has a few negative consequences: the services for special education are inextricably linked to a special education setting, which largely results in pupils being placed permanently in separate schools, for special help is only available when pupils enter a school for special education. Even if temporary support could provide a solution, it is impossible in practice. Legal obstacles make it difficult for the two separate school systems to organize this support in a more flexible way. This means that the pupil with special needs has to be taken to the facilities instead of vice versa. The responsibility for the pupil is passed on to another part of the education system. It is clear that special education is an attractive alternative: it offers special provision for pupils with special needs. It is the system that deprives regular education of the possibility of helping pupils under the same conditions. In this sense, the provision enhances the need (the law of supply and demand). It is difficult to realize collaboration between regular and special education, because each school has its own financial, administrative and staff systems.

It also appears that referral to a special school is usually permanent. Only a tiny minority (less than 1%) of pupils with special needs in LOM and MLK schools, the schools for the learning disabled and the mild mentally retarded, return to regular primary education in any year (Centraal Bureau voor de Statistiek, 1993). This is rather awkward since researchers have not found huge differences between the special schools for these groups (LOM and MLK) and regular schools. Indeed, research has found many similarities concerning teaching methods, teacher behaviour and organization (Pijl & Pijl, 1993).

Special education placement does not diminish the problems and academic difficulties of the pupils referred and as such it often functions as safety-valve: i.e. as an additional means of relieving regular education of difficult-to-handle and time-consuming pupils. In this sense the high costs and side-effects of a segregated system, such as labeling or a shattered school career, are unjustified. The discussion also refers to a wider societal context. The segregation of these pupils is considered to be in conflict with widely accepted human rights, socially undesirable, and a perhaps convenient, but not necessary way to provide special services.

4.2   Dutch policymaking concerning integration

One important step towards integration was the Primary School Act of 1985. This Act stated that the major goal of primary schools is to offer appropriate instruction to all children aged 4 to 12, and to guarantee all children an uninterrupted school career. Ideally, each child would receive the instruction that fits the unique educational needs. If primary schools are able to offer this so-called adaptive instruction, the number of special needs pupils was expected to decrease more or less spontaneously. However, in the years after 1985, the expansion of special education did not stop.

In 1990 a new government policy document, 'Together to School Again' (the so-called WSNS[Weer Samen naar School]-policy), was intended to make a fresh start in integrating pupils with special needs. Under this policy, all primary schools and the special schools for learning disabled and mild mentally retarded children (LOM and MLK) have been grouped into regional clusters. Extra funding was available to set up these clusters. The money is labeled for extra staff with the specific task to offer help to pupils with special needs. As a result of this policy, regular and special schools began to work together; special needs coordinators were appointed in every regular school, training programmes were launched, new legislation passed, and regulations for new funding of regular and special schools were drawn up.

In 1995 parliament decided to change the funding for LOM and MLK-schools drastically: each of the 300 school clusters will be funded equally, based on the total enrolment in primary education. About 50% of this amount will be transferred directly to existing special provisions and the other half will be allocated to the school cluster.

As a result, regions have to adapt their special education provision to the new funding structure. Some regions may have to close special schools, especially in areas where there was a high degree of segregated provisions compared to other regions, while other areas receive additional funds as a reward for a regional effective integration policy.

For the education of the other types of special needs (pupils with sensory, physical, or mental disabilities or behavioural problems) a separate line of policy development has recently been started (Ministerie van Onderwijs, Cultuur & Wetenschappen, 1996). Until now, these pupils can only receive the support they need after admittance to a full-time special school. Recent government reports propose that the financing mechanism (funding special schools on the basis of the number of children that are placed) should be stopped in favour of linking financing of special services to the pupil involved, regardless of the type of schooling. The idea is to change from a supply-oriented financing to a demand-oriented financing. If a pupil meets the criteria for this so-called 'pupil-bound budget', parents and pupils can choose a school, special or regular, and take part in deciding how to use the funding. This development is not under discussion here.

4.3 The evaluation of the integration policy in the Netherlands

In 1992 the Minister of Education and Science installed an evaluation committee, with the task to monitor the progress as a result of the 'Together to School Again'- or the 'WSNS-policy' (Peschar & Meijer, 1997). The committee had to find an answer to the following questions:

1. Are regular schools capable of educating target group pupils (those who were until now educated in LOM-and MLK-schools), with the help of the facilities that have been provided through the school clusters?
2. What are the characteristics of the school clusters, which differences exist between them, and what are the developments within school clusters?
3. Can a new funding structure be implemented and what are the possible effects?
4. What are the developments in terms of the growth of the special school system?

The evaluation group started with an analytical evaluation study that had to reveal whether the formulated policy goals could be expected to be achieved as a result of the implemented programme. In this study the goals and means that were inherent to the WSNS-policy were carefully analyzed (Meijer, Meijnen & Scheerens, 1993).

In figure 1 the essential features of the WSNS-policy are described:

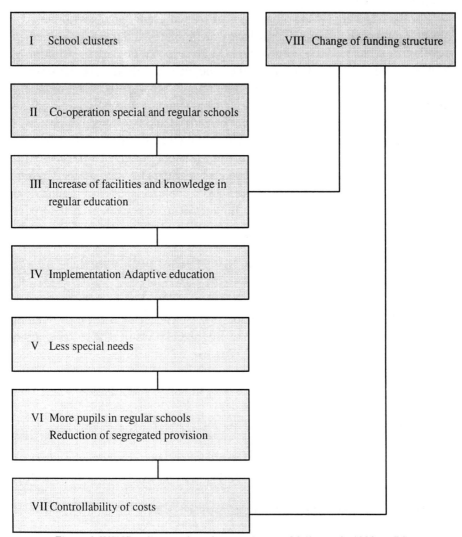

Figure 1. WSNS-policy: goals and means (source: Meijer et al., 1993, p. 76)

The assumption behind the WSNS-policy is that through the implementation of two central innovations, the development of school clusters (consisting of a network of co-operating special and mainstream schools) and the change of the funding system, more children with special needs will be educated in the mainstream school. This will lead to a decrease of the costs for segregated provision and in increase of the provision in the mainstream school.

The programme for the evaluation of the WSNS-policy is described in Bosker and Meijer (1993). They constructed an comprehensive research design for the period of 1993-1997. During the evaluation period slight changes to this programme have been made on the basis of new developments and needs for additional data.

Within the framework of the evaluation more than 20 research projects have been conducted by research groups in five different universities. The most important key-studies are listed below:

1. A study that was focused on the assessment of developments in the numbers of children referred to special education. Included was an assessment of the pupil-streams between the regular and the special school system. This statistical study was not only confined to the schooltypes that form the target of the WSNS-integration policy, but also other types of special schools were included. Furthermore, the study analyzed data from a long period of time: developments since 1975 were studied.

2. Several studies were conducted with respect to the developments in the school clusters: a few examples of good practice were described, the effects of the school cluster model was assessed, as well as the role of the special schools in the clusters and the way the special provision was re-organized on a regional level.

3. Concerning the creation of 'adaptive education' (education that is adapted to differences in the classroom) several studies have been conducted. In these studies it was assessed whether schools were able to deal effectively with larger differences in the classes. Several topics have been addressed within this thematic area: the influence of teaching materials on adaptive education, the activities that have been undertaken and the processes that are used in schools and classes concerning pupils with special educational needs, the quality of adaptive education throughout the country, the effects of school improvement activities on adaptive education and pupil achievements, and so on.

4. The position of children with special educational needs in regular education and their characteristics have been assessed by another group of studies. Here also the role of the parents and their attitudes towards integration have

been analyzed. Generally, in these studies the impact of integration on the level of pupils forms the central issue.

5. Specific studies have been conducted in order to scrutinize the chain of goals and means as given in figure 1. In these studies the different relations are analyzed between the various concepts that are central within the WSNS-philosophy. Through the use of multi-level analysis and through the synthesis of the findings in the other research projects it is tried to find empirical support for the model.

6. The last group of studies were focused on the issue of financing. Different approaches have been used here in order to develop answers to the question of the validity and feasibility of the new funding model:
   - literature studies concerning possible explanations for regional differences in the incidence of special needs;
   - empirical studies: the assessment of attitudes of different 'actor groups' (parents, teachers, headteachers, coordinators of school clusters, school boards) to possible changes in the funding system. Also empirical studies were conducted to describe the degree of the current regional variation in the incidence of special needs and the explanations for these differences;
   - comparative studies: experiences in four other countries with comparable models of funding of special needs education. Also the experiences of different funding models within the health sector have been assessed;
   - analytical studies: desk-studies in the area of alternative funding models. Here the goal was to develop alternative funding models and to analyze potential pros and cons of these models.

It is impossible to describe the designs of the different studies here at length. The interested reader is referred to the final report of the evaluation committee (Peschar & Meijer, 1997). However a few key data concerning these projects are given here. The samples for the different studies vary from very large (survey studies) to rather small (in depth studies). In some studies large groups of pupils were used in the samples (up to 18,000 pupils of regular schools and almost 2,000 in special schools). Also many hundreds of parents, principals, school teachers, coordinators of clusters and so on haven been selected for the studies within the context of the evaluation WSNS.

4.4   Evaluation

4.4.1   Introduction

In section 3, four leading questions for the evaluation of the WSNS-policy were presented. The next four sections summarize the results of evaluation studies into the capability of regular schools to educate pupils with special needs, the development of school clusters, alternative funding models and pupil attendance percentages in special education.

4.4.2   Adaptive education

One of the goals of the WSNS policy is to realize what has been called 'adaptive education' in primary schools. Adaptive education refers to the idea that pupils learn in different ways and at a different pace. Education has to provide for these differing needs by offering a variety of instructional approaches and learning methods and by allowing pupils to work in their own pace. Education has to adapt to pupils.

Research (Houtveen, 1997) has addressed various aspects of adaptive education. It shows that teachers increasingly accept that pupils differ and that these differences have to have consequences for their instruction and that teachers enhance self-confidence and feelings of competence in pupils. In a description of teachers' working according to plan five phases have been distinguished: finding a learning problem, analysis of the problem, planning instruction, instruction, and evaluation. Research has shown that teachers in third and fourth grade on average work in reasonable detail trough the first three phases, but activities of the remaining planning phases are largely missing. It seems justified to conclude that planned ways of instructing special needs pupils are to be improved. Yet compared to earlier descriptions of working according to plan considerable progress is reported in the last five years (Houtveen, 1997).

The term differentiation refers to the instructional arrangements taken in order to adapt instruction to the different needs of pupils. It can focus on several aspects of instruction, for example the goals, the working groups in the classroom, evaluation, explanation, etc. Several research projects have been addressed to the evaluation of this central theme in WSNS policy. The results are not very promising; the inspectorate concludes that only 17% of the schools do well. In general it can be stated that teachers are aware of the differences between pupils in the classroom and that they indeed have a fairly accurate idea of the problems and needs of their pupils. However, this knowledge is only limited transferred into adapting instruction to their needs. Research shows that large differences exist between teachers in realizing adaptive instruction: some teachers do take the differences between their pupils in account, while others brush these aside. Houtveen (1997) states that over a 15 year period differentiation by teachers in classrooms has grown, that teachers are more open to it and have more materials and methods available to implement this.

Taking care of pupils' special needs not only demands actions from individual teachers in classrooms. Working according to plan, teacher support, peripatetic teaching, teacher training and using materials and methods supporting adaptive instruction should be supported at school level. Results show that schools have taken actions for ongoing assessment, registration of results and the analyses of these results in teacher meetings. But only a minority of the schools ensures that during the meetings decisions are made about the education of the pupils with special needs and drawing up individual education plans.

A growing number of regular schools are involved in peripatetic teaching: a special teacher supports a regular teacher with a special needs pupil in the classroom. About 70% of the schools has appointed a special educational needs coordinator (SENCO) responsible for coordinating special needs teaching in the school. The SENCO supports colleagues with working with individual education plans, organizing teacher meetings, building a library of materials useful in special needs instruction, coordinating small group instruction, etcetera. The appointment of the SENCO's is a result of WSNS policy and as such a fairly new development in regular education.

The number of schools developing an explicit policy for teacher training is growing rapidly. The majority of these focus on assessment and effective instructional strategies for pupils with special needs, handling behaviour problems and implementing assessment systems in the school.

To sum up: A number of preconditions for adaptive instruction have been fulfilled reasonably, but in every day practice in classrooms educationally relevant differences between pupils are often neglected. Since the start of the WSNS policy a number of improvements have been described and acknowledged as, however modest, effects of the WSNS policy. Research refers particularly to growing motivation and skills of teachers and to the availability of teacher support in the school.

There are high expectancies about the contribution of adaptive instruction to pupils' performances. It has been described as benefiting pupils' cognitive and social-emotional development. However, Dutch research into the effects of adaptive education has failed to find any effect of adaptive instruction on pupils' performances or even established negative effects! These results are in contrast with American research (Wang & Walberg, 1985; Wang, 1992) showing positive effects of adaptive instruction. A number of alternative explanations for these disappointing results has been put forward. Adaptive education is taken as a complex and comprehensive concept and developing instruments to measure that concept has been difficult. A second explanation addresses the pupil samples involved in research into the effects of adaptation. Most research projects focussed on instruction for pupils with special needs: the group with difficulties in making progress. The argument is that it is hard to find effects of adaptive education in a group making less progress anyway. A third explanation is that although schools do make progress in implementing adaptive education, it will take many years to make schools adaptive and that therefore effects of this way of working in schools can not be established yet.

The evaluation of WSNS and of adaptive education also addressed the attitudes of parents towards this development. Parents in general regard with sympathy the strive for integration. Regular education has to use the utmost endeavours to prevent a pupil's referral to a special school. But, if it does not succeed, the arrears in performance are getting larger or the behaviour problems are too disturbing, placement in a special school must be possible. Parents find it hard to imagine a school system without the LOM- and MLK-schools. Research shows that a still respectable percentage of parents doubt the capabilities of regular schools to cope with pupils with special needs. As such this view is not surprising because parents see in every practice pupils being referred to special schools. That of course enhances their idea that regular education finds it hard to suit the needs of all children. When in the years to come funding of regular and special schools will change and regular schools have the resources to cater for the needs of a wider range of pupils, parents' attitudes may change.

Separate analyses focussed on the validity of the model presented in figure 1. Research showed that the functioning of school clusters, the first goal in the model, contributes to the percentage of pupils referred to special schools (VI). The contribution is fairly modest, it explains 6% of the referral differences between schools. A number of studies showed relations between the co-operation of schools (II) and an increasing knowledge in regular education (part of III) with the implementation of adaptive education on school level (part of IV). The (standardized) relation between the implementation of adaptive education on school level and adaptive education in the classroom (the remaining component of IV) is 0.38. Since no direct relation has been found between co-operation of schools and an increasing knowledge in regular education with adaptive education in the classroom, adaptive education on school level is considered an important intermediate link. Relations with the fifth goal, less special needs, were extensively researched but decisive answers are lacking.

The results briefly presented here are generally taken as a first confirmation of the model.

4.4.3   School clusters

One of the tools in WSNS policy is the organization of schools in school clusters. Since school year 1992/93 all elementary regular schools together with LOM- and MLK- schools are organized in about 300 school clusters. Basic question here is if schools actually started working together and what the effects of working in clusters are?

Recent research (Hofman, 1997) has described both the goals and the activities of the clusters. Most clusters formulated several goals and started a wide range of activities. The focus of most clusters in the first years was on the organization of the cluster, but in recent years attention shifts gradually to goals and activities on school level, like: training of teachers, working with individual education programmes, special needs support, and peripatetic teaching. The schools within all clusters were stimulated by central government to optimize the referral procedure on cluster level. In 1996 only a minority (15%) fully complied with the proposed procedure, but most other clusters were making preparations to optimize the referral procedure. The contribution from the schools for special education to development in the cluster is reported growing, especially in teacher training, peripatetic teaching and referral procedures.

To sum up: new forms of school organization, the clusters, have been established in Dutch primary education. Appointing special needs coordinators and introducing various forms of support in regular education is expected to improve the education of special needs pupils in the near future.

4.4.4   Funding

An important asset of the WSNS policy are new regulations for funding regular and special education. The idea is to fund each of the 300 school clusters equally, based on the total enrolment in primary education. Funding then is no longer based on the number of pupils declared eligible for special education, but depends on the total number of pupils in a region. About 50% of the available funding will be transferred directly to existing special provisions and the other half will be allocated to the school cluster. This will be implemented in 1998, and as a result, regions will have to adapt their special education provision to the new funding structure.

Several research projects have been conducted to evaluate the coming funding model. With literature studies, empirical studies, comparative studies and analytical studies it was attempted to address two key issues in funding: 1) The direct funding of clusters and 2) Leveling of differences between regions.

1. The question 'who to fund' has received much attention. By using information from other fields, like health care, and other countries the possible effects of directing funds to the pupil, the school, the school board, the cluster or other regionally operating organizations, like a school advisory board have empirically and analytically been investigated. The conclusions are that considering criteria like effectiveness, efficiency, legitimacy, feasibility and robustness against strategic behaviour, funding models in which resources are directed towards regionally operating organizations are to be preferred. So, the overall conclusions of these analyses tend to support the WSNS policy plans here. Investigations of the opinion of various actors revealed that actors working in special schools regarded funding special education as the best option. Actors from regular education on the other hand agreed with direct funding of clusters.

2. Analyses of statistical data have shown that the percentage of pupils attending special schools varies enormously between regions within the Netherlands. The change from pupil based funding to a funding system based on population parameters will inevitably result in smoothing out these differences. Some regions with a high degree of segregated provisions may have to close down special schools in the future, while other areas may receive additional funds as a 'reward' for a regional effective integration policy. The question is if these differences between regions can be explained by other factors than a historically grown situation in special education provisions. Is it, in other words just a difference in supply of special education facilities or do these differences correlate with a different distribution of pupils with special needs in the country? Research has failed to come up with any evidence for an unequal distribution of special needs between regions. There are differences in the incidence of pupils from low socio-economic status groups between regions, but these are compensated already by regulations about regular funding in education. The overall conclusion is that there are no contra indications to smooth out these differences over clusters of a minimum size (over 2,000 pupils).

4.4.5   Percentage of pupils referred

An important aspect of the evaluation of the WSNS policy in 1997 was the analysis of the percentage of pupils referred to schools for special education each year since the base line year (1992). In the analysis of the education statistics an overview has been prepared of developments in the last 20 years. The aim was to clarify the amount of growth of special education in general and more specific of the schools for learning disabled (LOM) and for the mildly mentally retarded (MLK). A second goal was to describe the relative contribution of regular schools to the growth. After all, changes in duration of special school placement and in the referrals from other special schools can influence overall attendance percentages in special education.

Analyses of special education attendance can be based on various indicators, for instance attendance on a specific time or attendance per cohort. Both methods result in different figures with different interpretations. In the school year 1995/96 about 4% of all 4 to 19 years old attend a school for special education. However, some of the pupils not attending special education in that particular year have attended a special school in the past or will do so in the future. Pijl and Pijl (1995) showed that from the pupils born in 1980 about 10% would attend for a shorter or a longer period a special school before the age of 19. The first percentage can be interpreted as special education turnover (pupils x length of stay), the latter as an individual's chance to enter special education during the school career.

Since 1975 the overall special education attendance has grown from 2.1% to 4.0% in 1996. The LOM- and MLK- schools make up two-thirds of this group, about 2.8% in 1996. The attendance is unevenly distributed across ages. The highest attendance percentage can be found in the age group of eleven years old pupils, namely over 7%.

The WSNS policy explicitly focuses on the elementary school age range (4 to 12). For this group the LOM- and MLK- attendance has grown from 2.82% in 1985 to 3.21% in 1993 and since then slightly declined to 3.07% in 1996. The base line attendance in the WSNS policy, the percentage in 1992, is 3.19%, which suggests that the WSNS policy has had an impact on special school referrals. Closer analysis of the data reveals that the growth of the LOM-attendance stopped in 1990 and since then gradually declined. This can be attributed fully to a decline in referrals and not to a shorter stay in special education. The percentage of pupils placed in MLK schools grew until 1994 and then stabilized. Surprising is that the inflow of LOM- schools started to reduce years before the WSNS policy was expected to have some impact. It may well be that schools anticipated the new policy-guidelines, but it is also conceivable that attendance percentages declined at least partly due to other, older policy initiatives in special education known as 'formation fixation'.

Other segments of special education, the schools for pupils with sensory, physical, mental handicaps and/or behavioural problems show a continuous growth. The growth is especially apparent in the schools for severally speech handicapped pupils, multiple handicapped and severally mentally retarded pupils. About 40% of the growth is due to a longer stay in special education, while the remainder can be contributed to an increase in inflow. There is no evidence that the decline in LOM- and MLK- schools is responsible for the increase in attendance in the other segments of special education.

To sum up: in the implementation phase of the WSNS policy the percentage of pupils in the LOM- and MLK- schools has stabilized and now seems to go down. WSNS as a policy has met the targets, but in claiming that success it may partly adorn itself with borrowed plumes.

4.4.6   Overview of findings

In the evaluation several aspects of adaptive education have been studied. A number of preconditions for adaptive instruction have been fulfilled reasonably, but in every day practice in classrooms educationally relevant differences between pupils are often neglected. Since the start of the WSNS policy a number of improvements have been described and acknowledged as, however modest, effects of the WSNS policy. Research refers particularly to growing motivation and skills of teachers and to the availability of teacher support in the school. Research into the effects of adaptive education has failed to find any effect of adaptive instruction on pupils' performances or even established negative effects.

Central element in the WSNS policy is the organization of schools in school clusters. Basic question here is if schools actually started working together and what the effects of working in clusters are. The results of several evaluation studies show that new forms of school organization, the clusters, have been established since 1992. Appointing special needs coordinators and introducing various forms of support in regular education is expected to improve the education of special needs pupils in the near future.

The new regulations for funding regular and special education are no longer based on the number of pupils declared eligible for special education, but depend on the total number of pupils in a region. Considering criteria like effectiveness, efficiency, legitimacy, feasibility and robustness against strategic behaviour it is concluded that funding models in which resources are directed towards regionally operating organizations are to be preferred. Introducing a funding system based on population parameters will inevitably result in smoothing out differences between regions in the percentage of pupils attending special schools. The overall conclusion is that there are no contra indications to smooth out these differences over clusters of a minimum size (over 2,000 pupils).

The analysis of the percentage of pupils referred each year to schools for special education since the base line year (1992) has been a central criterion in the evaluation of the WSNS policy. The analysis of education statistics has made clear that during the implementation phase of WSNS the percentage of pupils in the LOM- and MLK- schools has stabilized and now seems to go down. WSNS as a policy has met this target.

4.5   Reflections

4.5.1   Introduction

These recent innovations in the organization of special education in the Netherlands resonate with developments in the United Kingdom (UK). Common issues include the increase in the number of pupils identified as having special educational needs; the continuation of a robust segregated sector, despite legislation promoting integration; a desire to strengthen links between the special and mainstream sectors; evidence that teachers find differentiation in the classroom difficult; and the use of budget allocation mechanisms to encourage developments in practice. These have to be set against the differences: for example, in the UK, there is a more limited range of types of school which parents may choose for their child; a smaller proportion of the school-aged population attends special school; and the financing schemes are diverse. Very small differences in context may have a disproportional impact on the effectiveness on any one particular policy and there is increasing realization that international studies are instructive in revealing and analyzing issues, rather than in suggesting common solutions. However, there are some points of discussion.

4.5.2   Reflections on the policy

The current policy initiative in the Netherlands aims to revitalize efforts to integrate pupils with special educational needs. The policy has two strands relating, respectively, to organization - the grouping of schools into regional clusters; and to finance - the allocation of resources to support these clusters.

This is a wise strategy. There is evidence from the UK, first, that policies to promote a greater degree of integration are more favourably received where additional (or redirected) resources are available; and, second, that the mere allocation of resources without a clear policy can lead to 'resource drift', with money intended for pupils with special educational needs being diverted for other purposes. Furthermore, a strong aspect of the WSNS policy is that the option of maintaining the previous system is not available - provision will have to adapt to fit the new funding system. The progress of integration in the UK has sometimes been hindered by the fact that while it has been encouraged in principle (and it is, of course, enshrined in law), there has often been no direct incentive for schools to become more integrated - the option is merely there if they wish to take it. Such a model is not very strong when there are other factors persuading schools of the disadvantages of having a greater proportion of pupils with special educational needs. For example, in the current UK context, some schools fear that the presence of such pupils will lower the overall scores in national assessment and public examinations and will thus make the school less popular with parents.

Clusters

Any country aiming to reduce its special sector and give greater opportunities for adequate provision for pupils with special educational needs in mainstream schools faces a twofold challenge: first, how best to redeploy special sector staff, both to utilize their skills and expertise and to give them professional satisfaction; and, second, how to develop practice in mainstream schools so that there is a high quality of 'adaptive education'. One of the problems revealed in similar attempts in the UK to bring together special and mainstream schools is that teachers who have spent most of their careers in special schools may not be in the optimum position to advise their mainstream colleagues (Lunt, Evans, Norwich & Wedell, 1994; Evans, Lunt, Wedell & Dyson, 1999). This is not a comment on the overall efficacy of practice in special schools nor on the quality of special schoolteachers *per se*. Rather, it is about the fact that what works in a small school, with very small classes, usually with two adults permanently attached to them and largely responsible for just that one group of pupils (as in a primary school model), does not necessarily transfer to large schools, large classes, and a situation, especially in secondary schools, where a greater number of adults are presenting the curriculum to the pupil with learning difficulties. Experience in the UK suggests that staff accustomed to teaching in a special school tend to think in terms of discrete individual programmes for pupils, often requiring a high degree of one-to-one support. The skills and teaching techniques for integrating a pupil with learning difficulties into the mainstream classroom and the regular curriculum, so that the pupil is part of the larger group and learns as a member of that group, may be different. The redeployment of special school staff into peripatetic support services, for example, has often been unsuccessful unless there has been associated training both to inform them of ways of supporting pupils in mainstream schools and to equip them to work with other adults (mainstream teachers) in a consultative capacity.

Effective provision for pupils with special educational needs in mainstream schools depends considerably on the skills of the special educational needs coordinator. As in the Netherlands, this post has rapidly gained in importance in recent years in the UK, following the implementation of the Code of Practice (Department for Education, 1994) which recommended that every school should have a SENCO. There is research evidence (for example, Derrington, Evans & Lee, 1996; Lewis, Neill & Campbell, 1997) that there is a very wide range of both expertise and practice among these postholders, ranging from a situation where the title is largely nominal, to meet statutory requirements, to one where the postholder has extensive experience of providing for pupils with learning difficulties.

As regards the situation in the Netherlands, a question arises about the training which the Dutch SENCO receives and/or the standards and shape of the role. In the UK, in recognition of the changing role of special needs coordinators, the Teacher Training Agency (TTA) (the government appointed body responsible for all initial and in-service education and training of teachers) has issued a statement of the standards required of them (TTA, 1998), there is financial support available for their training and a number of institutes of higher education provide courses which aim to equip teachers with the required knowledge, skills and expertise to lead special education in their schools.

The national consultation over the draft Standards for special educational needs coordinators, highlighted the fact that the effectiveness of the coordinator depends on the way in which a school's senior management team enables him or her to do the job.

Thus the question arises of what is being done to train not only teachers to fulfil the demands of coordinating special education within a mainstream school but also headteachers and senior managers so that they are aware of the impact that having a greater number of pupils with learning difficulties on their school roll has on their managerial responsibilities.

The financial situation

While there is evidence that budgetary control acts as an incentive and, in particular, jointly held funds encourage collaboration between agencies and institutions that have not previously collaborated (see Fletcher-Campbell, 1990 and Lunt, Evans, Norwich & Wedell, 1994 for case studies), in the present scenario in the Netherlands, it would seem that there are going to be both winners and losers, according to the local context. In the UK, budgets to meet special educational needs vary according to individual local education authorities' financial schemes and formulae, and often depend on the basic *per capita* amount that schools receive (which can differ substantially across the country). The Netherlands is in a much stronger position to bring coherence to the funding of special education provision across the country. However, the situation of the two countries is similar in that there is evidence of considerable differences in identification of special educational needs not only across local areas but also across schools. This is often associated with differences in socio-economic background - what is an exceptional literacy difficulty in one area may be the norm in another.

There is evidence from some schools in the UK that moving away from conceiving additional funding as attached to particular pupils encourages schools to think about making the curriculum accessible for the total school roll - rather than offering the curriculum and then supporting the minority who find the curriculum difficult to access. Thus it may be that resources should be spent on professional development and equipping all teachers to meet pupils' needs, rather than on individual support for individual pupils identified as having learning difficulties. This approach is, perhaps, more in line with that of 'school reform' rather than of the focus on individual pupils - which pupil-led funding tends to encourage.

4.5.3   Reflections on the evaluation

There would appear to be an impressive list of research and evaluation projects relating to the new initiative in the Netherlands. The importance placed on evaluation is marked not only by the size of the budget allocated but also by the range of people involved in undertaking the research and in providing empirical data. It is to be hoped that a meta-analysis will be undertaken of the findings. It is stated above that the research samples varied; presumably, the methodologies did too. There could be either consensus or conflict within the data thus generated. Similar groups of studies in the UK have shown that any new policy initiative may have a differential effect in different circumstances. These circumstances may include, for example, size of school or administrative area, the profile of special educational needs in a school or area, the attitudes of staff and the 'ethos' of the school, the nature of the community (urban/rural, socio-economic and ethic structure). It has been pointed out that above that some aspects of the initiative have been subject only to analytic research. It may be that particular care needs to be exerted here as differential, context-dependent effects are usually revealed best, in the first instance, by empirical research.

Dutch colleagues report above that there does not seem to be any evidence to date of improved pupil outcomes and it is pointed out that it is difficult collecting data about learning outcomes for pupils with learning difficulties as they progress at a slow rate, there is a lack of readily available instruments and there is a long lead time between the enhancement of pedagogy and increases in pupil achievement. Some of these issues reflect the UK position.

In the UK there is a lack of reliable comparable data about the progress of pupils with special educational needs. Special schools tend to use highly idiosyncratic assessment instruments and schemes that often operate at pupil level (to inform individual education plans) rather than at the level of the group or institution. Pupils with learning difficulties tend not to demonstrate progress according to the national assessment schemes and scales designed for the majority of the population. In the UK, for example, all pupils are assessed on a national scale at the ages of 7, 11 and 14, and, at 16 (at the end of statutory schooling) results in public examinations are published. One of the problems inherent in the English system is that pupils with learning difficulties often do not progress up a level between assessment points (termed 'key stages'); furthermore, some will not attain even the first level available by the end of statutory education. While it is very unusual in the UK system for pupils to repeat a year (as they do not have to reach a particular standard to progress to the next key stage and a range of achievement is expected within each key stage assessment), nevertheless, pupils with learning difficulties often appear to make no progress, whether in mainstream or special school, although both progress and achievements can be significant when assessed on more appropriate and finely tuned scales.

In England, there has recently been developed a set of assessment scales (in literacy, numeracy and personal and social development) (Department for Education and Employment, 1998) which it is hoped will be nationally applicable to all pupils with special educational needs, regardless of where they receive their education, and which will be capable of showing the progress of individual pupils as well as of groups of pupils. It is hoped that these group or institutional profiles will be used as the basis for professional dialogue across schools.

Such initiatives are both broadening the scope of ways in which pupils with special educational needs can be assessed and move forward, and providing data which can be used for comparative purposes and which might, thus, ultimately be used as evidence for the most effective pupil placement - although there is a very long way to go before there are adequate and reliable data sets and the position in the UK is very much at the beginning of an evolutionary and developmental process. It may be that the evaluation in the Netherlands needs to consider what means of assessing pupil learning outcomes are available at a national level, what would be useful and what need to be developed.

It will be interesting to see if the evaluation in the Netherlands monitors what similarities and differences in practice there are between those schools and areas that are 'losers' and those that are 'winners' under the new system. There is evidence from the UK that there is the danger that the losers may feel that they cannot cope without the previous level of resources and thus be reluctant to accept pupils with learning difficulties. Experience at the local level in the UK, where is as yet no nationally applicable funding formulae, suggests that where budget allocation mechanisms are open and explained, there is less dissent and a greater will to accept what is available. The evaluation should, perhaps, not accept that a rational, nationally applicable formula for budget allocation would necessarily lead to more even provision. Differences in provision may be a result not only of the actual practice and assumptions about special education within a geographical area but also the general provision made within mainstream education. These may remain even if there is no difference in the constitution of the school-aged population in different areas as previous research in the Netherlands has suggested.

One of the problems in the UK has been that while there has been movement away from placement in special schools, there has not been a comparable shift in monies from the special sector to the mainstream sector (HMI and the Audit Commission, 1992). The Dutch decision to give areas an overall budget would seem to overcome this difficulty although evidence at the local level in the UK (where individual local education authorities have tried to reduce special school places and place more pupils in mainstream) suggests that the evaluation ought to consider the problems surrounding 'parallel funding' - where a special school costs the same amount to keep open with a reduced roll as it did on a larger roll, and where there has to be space in the system to accommodate parental preference. Evidence in the UK suggests that decision making is helped by very careful monitoring of the population so that future demands can be predicted, and rigorous unit costing of different types of provision. Generally, however, in the UK, the data on the costs of special education provision are extremely frail (Fletcher-Campbell, 1996; Coopers & Lybrand, 1998).

4.5.4   Wherein lies policy?

By way of conclusion it is, perhaps, worth raising the question of where policy for developing special education is located and what, thus, should be the breadth of any evaluation such as that being undertaken in the Netherlands. In the Netherlands, as in the UK and elsewhere, it is a relatively easy job to point to various pieces of legislation which show the path of special education policy and which can be shown to support the overall aim of integration which is widely favoured and clearly articulated in the Salamanca Agreement (UNESCO, 1994). However, the few examples from the UK cited above - such as the necessity for training for special needs coordinators and for headteachers, for adaptations to the national assessment scheme and to school target setting requirements, and greater comparability of budgets - highlight the fact that dedicated policy needs to be seen alongside main educational policy developments. If integration is to be encouraged, the whole education system within a country needs to acknowledge the presence of pupils with special educational needs and *any* policy initiative needs to be scrutinized for its effect on these pupils and the way in which they are accommodated within it. In the UK, the track record has been variable: very often, special schools and pupils with special educational needs have been tacked on the end of some policy initiatives as an after-thought while being the discrete focus of other specific legislation. If experience in the UK is anything to go by, perhaps one of the challenges which Dutch evaluators might address is to analyze the way in which there is conflict between the WSNS policy and other strands of education policy. In many cases, while there are explicit policy initiatives supporting integration, there are others that implicitly hinder it.

We are returned, once again, to the truism that special education is dependent on the general education system. If integration is to mature into inclusion (see Pijl, Meijer & Hegarty, 1997 for a discussion) then *all* education policy must be inclusive and the needs of all pupils considered within all developments. It may be that considering the effects on pupils with special educational needs should be built into the evaluation of any education policy.

4.6   References

Bosker, R.J., & Meijer, C.J.W. (1993). *Uitvoeringsplan voor de evaluatie van het Weer Samen Naar School-beleid.* De Lier: Academisch Boeken Centrum.

Centraal Bureau voor de Statistiek (1993). *Statistiek van het basisonderwijs, het speciaal onderwijs en het voortgezet speciaal onderwijs 1992/'93.* 's-Gravenhage: SDU.

Coopers & Lybrand, (1998). *Managing Budgets for Special Educational Needs*. London: CIPFA/Coopers & Lybrand.

Department for Education (1994). *Code of Practice on the Identification and Assessment of Special Educational Needs*. London: DfEE.

Department for Education and Employment/Qualifications and Curriculum Authority (1998). *Supporting the Target Setting Process: guidance for effective target setting for pupils with special educational needs*. London: DfEE.

Derrington, C., Evans, C., & Lee, B. (1996). *The Code in Practice*. Slough: NFER.

Doornbos, K. (1991). *School- en leermoeilijkheden: epidemie of systeemeffect*. In K. Doornbos et al. (Eds.), *Samen naar school. Aangepast onderwijs in gewone scholen* (pp.11-30). Nijkerk: Intro.

Doornbos, K., & Stevens, L.M. (Eds.). (1987). *De groei van het speciaal onderwijs: Analyse van historie en onderzoek*. 's-Gravenhage: Staatsuitgeverij.

Evans, J., Lunt, I., Wedell, K., & Dyson, A. (1999). *Collaborating for effectiveness: empowering schools to be inclusive*. Buckingham: Open University Press.

Fletcher-Campbell, F. (1990). *LEA Support for Special Educational Needs*. Slough: NFER.

Fletcher-Campbell, F. (1996). *The Resourcing of Special Educational Needs*. Slough: NFER.

Her Majesty's Inspectorate and the Audit Commission (1992). *Getting in on the Act. Special Educational Needs: the national picture*. London: HMSO.

Hofman, R.H. (1997). Samenwerkingsverbanden. In J.L. Peschar & C.J.W. Meijer (Eds.), *WSNS op weg* (pp 45-68). Groningen: Wolters-Noordhoff.

Houtveen, A.A.M. (1997). De werkvloer. In J.L. Peschar & C.J.W. Meijer (Eds.), *WSNS op weg* (pp 69-111). Groningen: Wolters-Noordhoff.

Lewis, A., Neill, S., & Campbell, R. (1996). *The Implementation of the Code of Practice in Primary and Secondary Schools; a National Survey of Perceptions of Special Educational Needs Coordinators*. Coventry: University of Warwick, Institute of Education.

Lunt, I., Evans, J., Norwich, B., & Wedell, K.(1994). *Working Together: Inter-school collaboration for special needs*. London: David Fulton.

Meijer, C.J.W., Meijnen, G.W., & Scheerens, J. (1993). *Over wegen, schatten en sturen. Analytische beleidsevaluatie "Weer Samen Naar School"*. De Lier: Academisch Boeken Centrum.

Ministerie van Onderwijs & Wetenschappen (1990). *Weer samen naar school. Perspectief om leerlingen ook in reguliere scholen onderwijs op maat te bieden. Hoofdlijnennotitie*. 's-Gravenhage: SDU.

Ministerie van Onderwijs & Wetenschappen (1991). *3x Akkoord*. 's-Gravenhage: SDU.

Ministerie van Onderwijs, Cultuur & Wetenschappen (1996). *De Rugzak. Beleidsplan voor het onderwijs aan leerlingen met een handicap*. 's-Gravenhage: SDU.

Peschar, J.L., & Meijer, C.J.W. (Eds.). (1997). *WSNS op weg*. Groningen: Wolters-Noordhoff.

Pijl, S.J., Meijer, C.J.W., & Hegarty, S. (1997). *Inclusive Education: a global agenda*. London: Routledge.

Pijl, Y.J., & Pijl, S.J.(1993). *Kenmerken van leerlingen en onderwijs in basis-, LOM- en MLK-onderwijs*. Groningen: RION.

Pijl, Y.J., & Pijl, S.J. (1995). Ontwikkelingen in de deelname aan het (voortgezet) speciaal onderwijs. *Pedagogische Studiën, 2*, 102-113.

Reezigt, G.J., & Knuver, A.W.M. (1995). Zittenblijven in het basisonderwijs. *Pedagogische Studiën, 72*(2), 114-133.

Rijswijk, C.M. van (1991). Bestuur en beheer van geïntegreerd primair onderwijs. In K. Doornbos et al. (Eds.), *Samen naar school. Aangepast onderwijs in gewone scholen* (pp.115-135). Nijkerk: Intro.

Teacher Training Agency (TTA) (1998). *National Standards for Special Educational Needs Coordinators*. London: Teacher Training Agency.

UNESCO (1994). *The Salamanca Statement and Framework for Action on Special Needs Education*. Paris: UNESCO.

Wang, M.C. (1992). *Adaptive education strategies: Building on diversity*. Baltimore: Brookes.

Wang, M.C., & Walberg, H.J. (Eds.). (1985). *Adapting Instruction to Individual Differences*. McCutchan: Berkeley.

5. THE FORTHCOMING CLASS SIZE REDUCTION INITIATIVE

Roel J. Bosker[1], Peter Blatchford[2] & G. Wim Meijnen[3]
[1]*Faculty of Educational Science & Technology, University of Twente, the Netherlands*
[2]*The Institute of Education, University of London, United Kingdom*
[3]*Department of Education, University of Amsterdam, the Netherlands*

One of the oldest discussions in education concerns the potential benefits of smaller classes for pupil achievement. In this chapter the research is reviewed including some recently conducted studies in the Netherlands, conceptual issues are addressed, and plausible intermediate causal mechanisms are explored. It is contended that the issue of smaller class size should be embedded both in broader national educational policy as well as in a well designed school policy, if pupils are to benefit from a more favourable pupil-to-teacher ratio in the early school years.

5.1 Introduction

"Does Money Matter?" (Hedges, Laine & Greenwald., 1994a), "Money Might Matter Somewhere" (Hanushek, 1994), "Money Does Matter Somewhere" (Hedges, Laine & Greenwald, 1994b), "When Money Matters" (Wenglinsky, 1997). Titles of recent articles and research reports that express positions in an ongoing debate on investments in education. Resourcing in education is of course affected by two major issues: teacher salaries and, most of all, by the pupil-to-teacher ratio or class size. No wonder that a parallel debate is continuously ongoing regarding the potential benefits of small classes on pupil achievement. Blatchford and Mortimore (1994, 411) traced the following statements on this issue:

'Reducing the class size to the point where student achievement would likely benefit ... is prohibitively expensive' (Tomlinson, 1990).

'The evidence ... suggests that .... reducing class size will not itself make a substantial difference in student achievement' (Slavin, 1989).

> *'The outcomes of this research effort (into the connection between class size and educational attainments) have been conflicting, inconclusive and disappointingly meagre' (Burstall, 1992).*

> *'.... drastic class-size reductions in early grades seem to offer the best hope yet advanced ... How much more evidence do leaders need before they apply these strong findings to help improve schooling?' (Achilles, Nye, Zaharias & Fulton, 1993).*

> *'Large reduction in school class size promise learning benefits of a magnitude commonly believed not within the power of education to achieve' (Glass, Cahen, Smith & Filby, 1982).*

In the Netherlands the same positions have been taken up.

> *'The committee takes the position that class size indeed has direct effects on the quality of primary education (and) judges that big classes have negative effects on pupil achievement' (CKAG, 1996).*

> *'The results reported in this contribution show that there are serious doubts whether a class size reduction in primary education would positively affect pupil achievement' (Dobbelsteen, Levin & Oosterbeek, 1999).*

Given these unreconcilable statements on potential benefits, it is surprising to note that some governments are nevertheless aiming for general class size reduction. In the United States of America the Federal initiative aims for a pupil-to-teacher ratio of 18 to 1 for the early years. In California "the billion dollar initiative" opts for a class size of 20 pupils. And in the Netherlands "a billion guilder initiative" has the same objective.

In this chapter, devoted to what looks like a very simple intended innovation in primary education, we will explore the class size issue, look into sources of variation in class sizes across and within countries, summarize the evaluation research into this topic by focusing on a recent research study conducted in the Netherlands, explore plausible causal mechanisms, and outline major research topics to be addressed when seeking further clarification in this area. We begin with some contextual information on primary education in the Netherlands, which is helpful when considering the class size issue.

5.2   Context

In understanding the issues related to the class size debate, it is relevant to give a brief outline of the Dutch situation regarding policy and class size differences within and between schools. Around the turn of the century the school funding controversy was settled when it was legally enshrined that both public schools and private religious schools should be equally funded. Moreover, it was also agreed that parents had the freedom to found schools, determine the religious or ideological basis upon which a school was founded, and that schools had more or less the freedom to determine the content of instruction. Central prescriptions were confined, amongst others, to the number of teaching hours per subject per week. Moreover the schools received separate budgets for teacher salaries, maintenance, learning materials, etc. depending on the number of pupils enrolled. Schools, for instance, were not allowed to use the budget available for teacher salaries for other purposes. Recently, lump sum financing was introduced into the system.

The Dutch education system has two types of primary schools: public and private. The latter, with some exceptions, are religiously (Roman Catholic and Protestant) based and state funded. More recently Islamic schools and schools based on other ideological bases have been founded and were state funded as well. Nowadays, these type of schools serve about seven per cent of the pupil population. More than two thirds of primary schools then are private in the sense that they are governed by private bodies. Private schools, in the sense of being virtually financed by parents, are almost non-existant.

The freedom of school founding and determining the content of instruction has the ideological basis that the state should not interfere in the pedagogical preferences of parents (and teachers). For this reason there is no national curriculum, but instead guidelines on the subject matter to be taught (to be verified by the inspectorate) and certain global goals to be achieved by the end of primary schooling. Standards of course are implicitly present by the foreshadowing effects of the tracked system of Dutch secondary education, and more explicitly by a test given to pupils in grade 6. Since 70 per cent of schools use a test developed by the national testing service CITO for this purpose, these more or less implicit standards are operationally formalized in the content of this test.

The principle of non-interference by the state, especially concerning pedagogical principles, however, dominates the education system. In the early nineties, a new governing policy was also introduced: local authorities and school boards were given more power as a consequence of decentralization and a striving for more school autonomy. Therefore, most decisions are now taken by the school board (for public schools this is the local authority). For religious or ideologically based schools the board consists mainly of parents, but in practice much of the decision making power is delegated to the school principal. This may be seen as the driving force for the enormous variation in class size within schools.

Variation between schools is caused by certain special funding arrangements for schools in rural areas, and for schools that have many disadvantaged pupils. The funding formula, originally based on a minimum pupil-to-teacher ratio for each age-group, has been made (almost) linear. As a consequence multigrade classes are a common phenomenon: 80 per cent of primary schools have at least one multigrade class, and 46 per cent of all classes are multigraded (Kral, 1997).

The actual primary school class size (operationally defined as the size of the class in which the pupils spend more than half of their time in school) was assessed by the Inspectorate in 1995. The Inspectorate reassessed this data in 1996 to gain more insight into within school variability in class size. Table 1 gives descriptive data on class sizes.

Two interesting conclusions can be derived from the figures. First, with the slight exception of grade-1, Dutch primary schools strive for equal class size: in all grades they have approximately the same size. Second, because of continuous enrollment of 4-year olds, pre-kindergarten and kindergarten class sizes increase throughout the school year, and by the end of the year are largest. This phenomenon is also true of early reception classes for 4 and 5 year olds in England and Wales (Blatchford, Goldstein & Mortimore, 1998).

Table 1. Class sizes at the start and end of the school year (1994/1995) (Source: Inspectorate of Education, 1995)

grade	beginning	end
pre-kindergarten (4-year olds)	19.4	26.1
kindergarten	24.7	26.2
pre-kindergarten and kindergarten combined	23.7	29.0
grade 1	23.3	23.7
grade 2	25.4	25.3
grade 3	25.3	25.2
grade 4	25.0	24.8
grade 5	25.2	25.0
grade 6	25.0	24.9

Table 2 contains the relevant data concerning variation in class size between and within schools.

Table 2. Variation in class size across and within schools (1994/95). Source: Inspectorate of Education (1996)

average class size per school		differences in size between largest and smallest class within schools	
≤ 15	6%	≤ 5	11%
16-20	11%	6-10	24%
21-30	71%	11-15	38%
31-35	12%	16-20	14%
> 35	3%	> 20	8%

The results presented in table 2 indicate an enormous variation in average class size. First, it can be seen that 17% of schools (mostly rural) have classes of less than 20 pupils on average, whereas at the upper end 15% of schools (in urban areas, with few disadvantaged pupils) have an average class size of over 30, with 3% even having an average of over 35. Second, the variation in class size within schools is also large. In 65% of schools the difference between the largest and smallest class within the school was more than 10 pupils.

How do the figures on class size in the Netherlands compare to those in other countries? Table 3 presents data from the IEA-study on reading literacy on class size and pupil-to-teacher ratios for 9-year olds, together with figures on spending in education.

Table 3. Class size and pupil-to-teacher ratio's per country (source: Ross & Postlethwaite, 1994, 129; OECD, 1995, 89)

country	class size for reading	pupil-to-teacher ratio	spending on education relative to GNP per capita
Belgium (French speaking)	20.3	16.9	16.1
Denmark	17.2	14.9	24.0
(West-)Germany	22.5	22.0	14.7
Finland	24.6	19.6	26.6
France	23.5	21.9	16.2
Hungary	23.4	16.0	26.6
Ireland	31.0	30.6	13.9
Italy	16.0	16.8	23.3
the Netherlands	25.7	22.5	15.1
New Zealand	29.7	24.3	14.4
Norway	17.7	12.1	25.3
Spain	28.8	24.5	17.7
Sweden	20.1	13.1	29.1
Switzerland	19.6	14.5	16.0
United States	24.6	20.6	24.5

For the United Kingdom the situation is very similar to that in the Netherlands (cf. Blatchford & Mortimore, 1994; Blatchford, Goldstein & Mortimore, 1998). The general pattern is that less spending on education is related to a more unfavorable pupil-to-teacher ratio and to a larger class size. Notice, however, in some countries the vast discrepancies between class size and pupil-to-teacher ratio. One is clearly not a practical synonym for the other. Here we find a first conceptual confusion that we will come back to later.

Variations in class sizes between countries, between schools within a country, and even within schools, may have the following causes. Variations between countries have to do with national policies regarding school funding and teacher salaries. The Netherlands score below the OECD average of 6.1% with only 5% of the gross national product being spent on education. Next to this, because of the non-interference principle, there are no restrictions on the maximum primary school class size in the Netherlands (unlike such countries as Denmark, Norway, Germany, Finland, France, Italy, Greece and Scotland (see RISE, 1994). Dutch variation in class size is a direct result of funding policy that favours small schools in rural areas, and schools with high numbers of disadvantaged pupils. Part of the variation across schools, but all of the variation within schools, is a direct consequence of school policy: does the school want to work with a year group system or with multigrade/multi-age classes, or does it want to use teachers for one-to-one tutoring or for other special activities for pupils-at-risk? Only 30% of schools (Polder & Gijtenbeek, 1995) refer to the latter two considerations (with respect to pupils-at-risk) when making policy plans for the deployment of their staff. That schools hardly make use of their policy making capacities is also shown by looking at class size in schools with many disadvantaged pupils (see table 4).

Table 4. Class size by school score, indicating the percentage of disadvantaged pupils within a school. (Source: Bosker & Hox, 1996)

grade	school score			
	100-124	125-149	150-174	≥ 175
pre-kindergarten	26.8	25.0	25.8	22.1
grade 1	24.1	21.1	19.8	18.4
grade 3	25.1	22.9	20.8	20.6
grade 5	24.9	23.1	21.6	19.7

The higher the school score the higher the percentage of disadvantaged pupils. The maximum score is 190, indicating a 100% "black" school with all pupils from ethnic-minority families with parents having low levels of formal education. The minimum score is 100% for schools in which all parents have at least average levels of education (whether these are ethnic minority or indigenous families). The most notable point about the table is that the staffing budget (money given to schools for special purposes, namely helping disadvantaged pupils) is virtually "swamped" by the schools. It is used for generally reducing class size in all grades, and this issue is addressed later.

5.3   Conceptual issues

The concept of class size is not as simple as many think. Much of the presumed evidence on spending in education and pupil achievement used to debate the "does money matter?" issue is based on pupil-to-teacher ratio and pupil achievement data at high levels of aggregation (district or school-level). This kind of evidence can only be of limited use in the class size debate. For one thing the pupil-to-teacher ratio does not have to be translated linearly into class sizes of a particular kind in each school's grades within a district. Moreover, as Blatchford, Goldstein and Mortimore (1998) have argued, class size as recorded on a school register may not actually match the day-to-day experiences of pupils and teachers. There may be a difference between the 'registered' class size and that 'experienced' by pupils. It is the experienced class size that might be expected to affect pupils' educational experiences and learning outcomes.

Secondly we run into the risk of an ecological fallacy: a relation that may exist on the level of districts or schools may not be true at the (combined) levels of classes and pupils. A big class in a school with relatively many small classes may have a different effect on teacher motivation and commitment and subsequently on pupil achievement levels, than a very big class in a school with relatively many big classes. While aggregate analyses may give a clue, they are never conclusive. Then there are observational studies into class size effects, one of which will be summarized in the sequel to this chapter, in which size is assumed to be a fixed characteristic of a class of pupils. Experimental studies make sure that this assumption is true by indeed fixing it to a certain number or range. And finally microlevel studies assess precisely the number of pupils in an instructional group receiving instruction in a particular domain within a certain time frame. The experimental and microlevel studies, of course, come closest within the range of the concept of class size as it is meant.

The conceptual confusion may be a reason for the opposite positions taken, we cited at the beginning of this chapter. Aggregate level research, as reviewed by Hanushek (1986), and later synthesized by means of statistical meta-analysis (Hedges, Laine & Greenwald, 1994a), appears to show the least convincing results. Hanushek finds in his vote count synthesis that most studies fail to demonstrate a relationship between pupil-to-teacher ratio and pupil achievement, and the small number of studies indicating positive effects are counterbalanced by a similar amount of studies showing negative effects. (Note that negative effects – the smaller the pupil-to-teacher ratio the larger the gains in achievement- indicate a possible positive effect of class size reduction).

Hedges et al. follow a different approach. First of all the application of models for statistical meta-analysis allows the authors to weigh the information available according to the precision of the estimates obtained in each study. Secondly they follow a different logic. The main aim is not to prove how much resources matter, but to investigate the hypothesis that the pupil-to-teacher ratio has negative effects, or conversely that it has positive effects on pupil achievement. The authors conclude "these results suggest that since there are positive relationships between outcome ... and teacher/pupil ratio but no negative relations .... the typical result is positive" (Hedges, Laine & Greenwald, 1994a, 10). Further analysis by these researchers led them to the finding that "the typical effects of class size are decidedly mixed", which inference is solely based on the evidence with respect to the pupil-to-teacher ratio approximation of class size. They sum up their results by stating "that resources matter, but allocation of resources to a specific area (such as reducing class size...) may not be helpful in all situations. That is, local circumstances may determine which resource inputs are most effective". The picture thus is not very clear cut.

The microlevel studies that Glass and Smith (1979) synthesize using statistical meta-analysis are more relevant to the issue. These results indicate that class size affects pupil achievement only marginally in the class size range of 20 and over, but substantially with a class size of below 20. Slavin (1989) has criticized the basic material Glass and Smith use in their meta-analysis, showing that studies were included on one-to-one tutoring and strange domains like instruction on hitting a tennis ball against a wall during 30 seconds. Slavin re-examined the material, and selected the best 14 studies, namely those that used random assignment of pupils to smaller or larger classes, studying regular education, and focusing on effects to be achieved over a longer period of time. Part of his results, namely those relating to more or less regular class sizes, are presented in table 5.

Table 5. Results from a best-evidence synthesis of class size studies. (source: Slavin, 1989, 249)

		14 – 17		20 – 23
	0.17	(14 – 30)	0.15	(20 – 28)
	0.17	(15 – 30)	0.04	(23 – 27)
	0.08	(16 – 37)	0.04	(23 – 30)
	0.04	(16 – 30)	0.00	(23 – 37)
	0.05	(16 – 23)		
	-0.29	(17 – 35)		
median effect size	0.06		0.04	

Each entry in the table represents one study. The first number is the effect size when comparing achievement levels of pupils in small classes to larger classes. Figures between brackets are the actual class size comparisons made. The effects of small classes appear to be rather modest. Robinson (1990) conducted another review of partly the same evidence. His results indicate that especially young children benefit from small classes in the early years of schooling.

This finding coincides with a turning point in class size research: the focus shifts from a general interest in class size effects to their particular impact on pupil achievement in the early years.

5.4   Studies on class size effects

5.4.1   The STAR project

The most cited study on class size effects in the nineties is the STAR (Student-Teacher Achievement Ratio) project conducted in Tennessee in the United States (Finn & Achilles, 1990; Word, 1990). 79 voluntary schools were selected for this experiment. Within the schools both teachers and pupils were randomly assigned to small (13-17) and large classes (22-25) or to a large class with a teacher aide. The pupils were followed from kindergarten entry until grade three, with later studies addressing the question of potential lasting benefits (Nye, Achilles, Zaharias, Fulton & Wallenhorst, 1993). The effect sizes reported are in the range of 0.17 (kindergarten, maths) to 0.34 (grade 1, language). Research into the long-term effects indicate that the results, although a bit smaller, indeed seemed to last until the end of primary schooling. Although generally viewed as the most pervasive study on class size, the STAR project has also been criticized on a number of grounds. First of all the schools were self-selected, which may have led to selection bias. The fact that small and large classes were created within each school does not solve this problem. Also they may have been particularly motivated by the fact that they were in the position to prove that a class size reduction would be beneficial to pupils. The Hawthorne effect in this case would mean that teachers in small classes would have been particularly motivated by the special circumstance of the experiment and the apparently favourable condition. But on the other hand a John Henry effect may have led to biased results implying that the beneficial effects of small classes over large classes may not have been as big as they could have been, since teachers in larger classes may have felt urged to prove the point that whatever the conditions of schooling, they would maintain the quality of instruction and learning. Another criticism relates to the random assignment procedure. Because of the experimental approach and randomization, the researchers did not use pre-test measures. Not only would their inclusion have increased the precision of the estimates to be obtained, but also their absence makes it impossible to test potential differential effects of class size for initially low versus high achieving pupils. For a discussion of other problems concerning the validity of the STAR findings, and a further multilevel re-analysis of the STAR data, we refer to Blatchford, Goldstein and Mortimore (1998) and to Goldstein and Blatchford (1998).

5.4.2   Class size reduction in California

Partly as a consequence of the positive results found in Tennessee, California launched a "billion dollar initiative" almost overnight: classes for the youngest pupils had to be reduced from 29 to an average 20. The decision was taken in the summer of 1996 and implementation started six weeks later with grade 1 (the focus again was to achieve a class size reduction from kindergarten to grade 3). Despite the spatial limitations and the shortage of qualified teachers which led to hiring teachers without credentials or to delayed implementation, the initiative quickly progressed. In the summer of 1999 the first results of the evaluation were presented (CSR, 1999). Third grade pupils in smaller classes outperformed pupils from larger classes even after taking pre-existing differences into account. The effect size is 0.10 - a rather modest result. But unlike the STAR experiment it could not be demonstrated that ethnic minorities, low socio-economic status pupils, or those with sub-standard English (most notably children from immigrant families) especially benefited from the initiative. The evaluation used existing data on standardized achievement tests, which were readily available. A serious drawback is that nothing could be said about the implications of class size reduction in kindergarten, simply because there was no data available. As a consequence, as was the case in the STAR-evaluation, a pre-test measure was lacking.

5.4.3   Two Dutch studies on class size effects

The same drawback applies to the study on class size effects conducted in the Netherlands by Bosker and Hox (1996). They also used a pre-existing database, containing longitudinal information on 13,500 pupils in over 400 primary schools collected in the so-called PRIMA cohort studies.

The main sample of the PRIMA cohort consisted of 416 randomly sampled primary schools. Within these schools for four groups of pupils (kindergarten, grades 2, 4, and 6) data were gathered on IQ (excluding kindergarten pupils), gender, socio-ethnic status, mathematics, and language achievement.

The tests were administered in October and November for grades 2 and up, and shortly after Christmas in kindergarten. Covariates at the teacher/classroom level were: teacher experience, single-grade or multigrade, full-time or part-time teaching job, job satisfaction and efficacy. Percentage of girls, mean IQ, and mean socio-ethnic status were included as classroom contextual characteristics serving as covariates in the analysis. The latter two contextual variables were needed as covariates in the design, since in Dutch primary schools staffing and resourcing of schools not only depends on the number of pupils, but also on their socio-ethnic status. Thus, as was demonstrated before, in schools with a high percentage of disadvantaged pupils, classes are regularly smaller, in which case one might erroneously conclude that by increasing class size achievement levels rise. Finally, class size is measured for the class the cohort pupils were in one school year before (when pupils were in pre-kindergarten, grade 1, 3 and 5 respectively). Since class size effects may not be linear in reality, the variable is made polytomous by creating as categories 5-9, 10-14, 15-19, 20-24, 25-29, 30-34, 35-39.

Although the data were observational, instead of experimental, treating the hierarchical structure of the data by using multilevel statistical models and by including the covariates mentioned in the analysis, one gets as close as one to make causal inferences on class size effects (cf. Raudenbush & Willms, 1996). The only serious drawback is that at the end of kindergarten, grade 2, 4, and 6 respectively, pupil achievement is of course an accumulation of all previous learning experiences in all earlier grades, and thus contains effects of varying class sizes. For this reason, the kindergarten results in particular are seen as most interesting (since these are less confounded, although almost all pupils attended pre-kindergarten and the criterion variable was measured half a year after the fact) concerning the estimation of class size effects.

Since there were no IQ-measures taken for the kindergarten pupils, separate multilevel regression models were estimated for kindergarten and for grade 2 and up. In order to be able to detect possible (cross-level) interactions between class size and pupil characteristics like socio-ethnic status, sex, and IQ, a series of additional multilevel statistical models was fitted to estimate the effects of the relevant cross-products (e.g. class size * IQ).

The average effect for classes of size 20-24 was taken as the base.

Table 6 contains the estimated effect sizes for mathematics achievement.

Table 6. Class size and arithmetic achievement: effect sizes

class size	kindergarten	grade 2, 4, 6
5-9	-.038	-.309
10-14	.416	-.062
15-19	-.227	-.086
20-24	.000	.000
25-29	-.252*	.006
30-34	-.185*	.094*
35-39	-.256*	-.032*
* significant at $\alpha < .10$ two-tailed		

The largest positive effect size for kindergarten (0.416) was found for classes containing 10 to 14 pupils, but since there are only a few of them this is statistically non-significant. Statistically significant effect sizes appear with classes of over 25 pupils. The effect sizes are -0.252 for class size 25-29, -0.185 for class size 30-34, and -0.256 for class size 35-39. With respect to grade 2 and up the largest (albeit statistically non-significant) effect size shows for classes containing less than 10 pupils, and it appears to be negative (-0.309). The largest positive effect size (0.094) is for classes of 30-34, and classes of 35-39 have a small (but statistically significant) negative effect size of -0.032.

Table 7 contains the estimated effect sizes for language achievement.

Table 7. Class size and language achievement: effect sizes

class size	kindergarten	grade 2, 4, 6
5-9	.394	.184
10-14	.189	-.038
15-19	.186	-.017
20-24	.000	.000
25-29	-.092*	-.052
30-34	-.044	-.007
35-39	-.265*	-.109*
* significant at α<.10 two-tailed		

Positive, but statistically non-significant, effect sizes in kindergarten show up for classes of less than twenty pupils. Class sizes of 25-29 and 35-39 have statistically significant negative effect sizes of -0.092 and -0.265 respectively. For grades 2, 4, and 6 the only statistically significant effect size is found to be -0.109 (for class size 35-39).

Of the four potential interaction effects of socio-ethnic status and class size on pupil achievement, only one turned out to be statistically significant: the effect of socio-ethnic status on arithmetic achievement in kindergarten becomes smaller with increasing class size. Put differently: when class sizes become smaller the achievement gap between disadvantaged and other pupils becomes bigger. The same pattern occurs for interaction effects of sex and IQ with class size on language achievement in grades 2, 4 and 6: achievement gaps increase as classes become smaller. The only interaction effect that indicates smaller gaps with decreasing class size concerns IQ in grades 2, 4 and 6.

The results presented seem to support the conclusion that class size and achievement are differently related across grades, with the earliest grades being the most likely circumstance to detect a negative relationship (cf. Bosker, 1998).

In a re-analysis of the same dataset, Dobbelsteen, Levin and Oosterbeek (1999) use another analytical strategy and come up with different results. First of all they only used grade 2, 4 and 6 data. Then they used an instrumental variable approach to account for endogenous variation in class size due to Dutch staffing rules regulations. These regulations led to a slight see-saw pattern in class size (if schools would use all teachers for classroom instruction) as a function of total enrollment instead of a smooth function. At certain intervals higher enrollment therefore leads to a slight drop in the pupil-to-teacher ratio. The instrumental variable approach then uses a new class size variable, namely the class size as predicted. The prediction is based on regressing actual class size on the average formal class size of a school allowed for following the staffing rules and all other available variables. As a consequence the new class size variable is uncorrelated with all the other variables in the model as a result of which one can be sure that the effect of the new class size variable on achievement is unique. The results indicate the absence of a relationship between class size and pupil achievement in grade 2 (both for maths and language) and positive relationships in grades 4 and 6 (with the exception of language in grade 4). The problem with both studies using the same dataset is, as was said before, that achievement is the cumulative effect of a number of years of schooling and -due to the lack of a pre-test- not the effect of being in one class for one school year. The second problem pertaining to both studies is the implicit assumption that class size is fixed, whereas in actual fact the size of a class may vary during the year, during the week or even during the day depending on the subject matter taught. It is not unthinkable that large multigraded classes in particular are split into smaller instruction groups for basic subjects, but from the data source to be used it is simply not known. A specific problem with the study of Dobbelsteen et al. is that they refrain from using pupil's IQ as a covariate in the design, which results in an unwarranted undercorrection of achievement before assessing the effect of the newly created class size variable.

5.4.4   A renewed statistical meta-analysis

A recently reported meta-analysis on class size and pupil achievement is more strict than the one of Glass and Smith (1979) and statistically more refined than the best evidence synthesis of Slavin (1989) (Goldstein & Yang, forthcoming). The researchers found nine studies that met the following criteria: they used a matched design or randomization, the outcomes were achievement scores, the studies covered at least one school year period and had pre-test and post-test scores, the smaller classes were no smaller than 15 and the larger classes no larger than 40.

Contrary to what was noted before, this meta-analysis does not reveal grade specific class size effects. The estimated effect size across all studies involved (including STAR) is 0.19. Next to this main effect of small versus large classes, the additional statistically significant linear effect of class size amounts to –0.02, indicating pupil achievement increases as classes become smaller. The effect size found in the experimental randomized control studies is the same as found in the observational studies using a matched design.

5.5   The missing link between class size and achievement

Although many studies have been conducted on class size effects, relatively little is known about the underlying causal mechanisms. There are certainly more hypotheses than there is empirical evidence. Smith and Glass (1980) managed to find 59 studies with somewhat less than 400 results on the relation between class size, attitudes and instruction. The results demonstrate positive effects of smaller classes when compared to larger classes for student attitude (effect size 0.81), individualization (effect size 0.50), student participation (effect size 0.61), quality of instruction (effect size 0.44) and teacher attitude (effect size 2.26). Not much is known, however, on the quality of the studies used in this meta-analysis, nor on the specifics of the designs used. In trying to find plausible explanations (i.e. sensible hypotheses) for the class size effects one might refer to the knowledge base on instructional effectiveness (Creemers, 1994; Scheerens & Bosker, 1997) that goes back to the well-known Carroll model. In this model time and quality of instruction are seen as the predominant facilitators of pupil learning.

The time related factors may affect achievement as follows. Firstly, it is argued that with fewer pupils the teacher has less discipline and classroom management problems, thus leaving more time for instructional activities. As a result the teacher of a small class can do more of everything (CSR, 1999) whilst reducing whole class instruction time. This would possibly lead to the curriculum being delivered with more variety, breadth and depth (Blatchford & Mortimore, 1994), although the actual content covered might remain the same. Because a classroom climate in small classes is more conducive to learning, pupils' engaged learning time might increase and they become more involved in the learning process.

It also is likely, as Blatchford and Mortimore (1994) argue, that quality of instruction also increases when class size decreases, in the sense of, for instance, providing advance organizers, regular assessment of pupil progress, and positive feedback. It should be clear, however, that, contrary to the time factor, the mentioned aspects of quality of instruction are not directly related to class size. Another crucial element that may mediate class size effects is high standards and the accompanying expectation that pupils can achieve these standards. This may be an alternative explanation of the effects of class size in the experimental STAR study (Finn & Achilles, 1990; Word, 1990). Since teachers had to prove the point that a reduction in class size would boost pupil achievement they may have imposed higher standards on their pupils. In actual fact these teachers may have improved on the other instructional characteristics also for this reason (and this then would be the Hawthorne effect).

We can summarize the elements indicating high quality of instruction by using the concept of appropriateness of instruction, i.e. gearing instruction to individual pupil needs (Stringfield & Slavin, 1992). Hill (1998) uses the term 'focused instruction' in this respect, meaning that instruction should be focused to match prior achievement levels of individual pupils. Focused instruction starts with an adequate assessment of initial achievement levels of all pupils to be instructed, for which a proper reliable and valid test should be available. Next to this, intermediate and ultimate learning objectives need to be formulated and on the basis of both a carefully planned instructional strategy chosen and implemented for the group as well as for pupils that need a more individualized route. Then evaluative information on pupil progress should be collected, once again using, amongst others, standardized tests, which should be interpreted at both pupil and group level. Moreover didactical activities and materials used should be regularly evaluated, and when pupils fail teachers call for expert help.

Following from and related to the aforementioned time and quality factors, teacher and pupil interaction as well as pupil-pupil relations may be another intermediating mechanism between class size and pupil achievement. Pate-Bain, Achilles, Boyd-Zaharias & McKenna (1992, 254) report on the basis of STAR:

> "A common benefit cited by teachers in small and regular plus
> aide classes was that they were better able to individualize
> instruction. These teachers reported increased monitoring of
> student behaviour and learning, opportunities for more immediate
> and more individualized reteaching, more enrichment, more
> frequent interactions with each child, a better match between each
> child's ability and the instructional opportunities provided, a more
> detailed knowledge of each child's needs as a learner, and more
> time to meet individual learners' needs using a variety of
> instructional approaches."

A meta-analysis of small class instruction conducted by Lou, Abrami, Spence, Poulsen, Chambers and D'Apollonia (1996) showed the benefits of teaching small groups within classes. Regardless of the type of grouping, heterogeneous or homogeneous, pupils in these classes achieved better than those who were subject to whole-class teaching (+.17). Blatchford and Martin (1998) suggest that one factor will be within-class grouping strategies, for example, the size and number of groups in a class. Results from a large scale longitudinal study of class size effects in the first stage of schooling in England (5-7 years), show that class size and within class group size are related. In larger classes teachers were more likely to be forced to have large groups of 7-10 pupils, larger than they themselves would like, and they felt this had negative consequences in terms of pupil involvement and concentration. Class size may therefore work as a general contextual factor that affects learning experiences indirectly through effects on 'micro', or within class contexts (see Blatchford, Baines & Kutnick, 1999).

In a review of studies about enhancing science and mathematics in early childhood education, Friedrich (1994) showed that "a hands-on" approach to learning in which the child is an active participant, favours the development of young children. The younger children are, the more dependent they are on face to face interaction with adults. Therefore children-to-staff ratios in day care centres is about 7 to 1. Learning from the environment in the very early years has to be mediated by close supervision of the instructor. These arguments indicate that indeed class size effects may be most relevant in the early stages of schooling where pupils are more dependent on their teachers, whereas in the latter stages independent learning becomes increasingly frequent.

Pupil-to-pupil relations are reported to be more negative in larger classes, including aggression, annoyance and teasing (Smith, McMillan, Kennedy & Ratcliffe, 1989). Grouping seems important here since in a small class smaller groups can be formed, thus providing pupils with opportunities for cooperative and peer-tutoring type learning activities, and thus leaving the teacher more time for each group to assist (CSR, 1999, 13-15).

Dobbelsteen, Levin and Oosterbeek (1999) hypothesize quite the opposite mechanism: pupils learn more if they are surrounded by classmates with a similar aptitude level. The chance of having such matched classmates increases as class size increases. They find empirical support for this hypothesis, but unfortunately the measure they have taken is not valid: for each pupil they count the number of pupils within a range of minus and plus one-fifth of a standard deviation on an IQ-test. But since they use an existing database for their research in which only pupils of a certain grade-level are included they miss information on IQ-levels of classmates in a different grade that may be in the same class, the multigraded class. Thus this research is not much help when seeking an answer to the question of whether groups should be homogeneous or heterogeneous.

5.6   Discussion and implications for future research

Resourcing is seen as the major cause of large classes in Dutch primary schools. The pupil-to-teacher ratio formally allows for somewhat smaller classes (3 pupils per class less), but this would be hard to realize since part of the formation has to be used for managerial leadership activities, remedial teaching, and physical education. Also, schools that are in the position to formulate and implement staffing policies with respect to class size in specific grades generally refrain from doing so. Theoretical considerations, however, clearly point to the importance of class size for young children, since they are more dependent on individual interaction with the teacher than older pupils in making good progress. This is especially true for pupils at risk. Slavin (1989) contends that class size only really matters if classes become as small as one pupil only. For this reason he advocates the Reading Recovery approach, i.e. individual instruction for half an hour a day, for as long as it takes (on average two to three months) for pupils lagging behind in their reading performance to get them back on track. If classes contain many disadvantaged pupils, the Reading Recovery programme should be part of a total approach, called Success for All (Madden, Slavin, Karweit, Dolan &

Wasik, 1993; Slavin, 1996), in which pre-school learning activities, a specifically designed reading curriculum, cooperative learning, parental involvement, regular assessments, and team development and team support are included as key elements. Recently an evaluation study appeared on the effects of two experiments in early education in the Netherlands (Leseman, Veen, Triesscheijn & Otter, 1999). One experiment is derived from Slavins' Succes for All and the other is an alternative version of Weikart's High/Scope Project. The latter stresses a small teacher-to-pupil ratio. In both cases the pupils in the experimental condition groups outperform the pupils in the control groups.

Finn and Achilles (1990) empirically demonstrate that low socio-economic pupils may especially benefit from small classes. This is not what the Dutch results show. In retrospect the intermediating factors may have been time and elements of quality of instruction. But appropriateness of instruction (gearing instruction to prior achievement) may have been lacking in the Dutch case, although it was feasible to achieve this in the smaller classes. One of the reasons may have been the lack of clear standards and an existing value system adhered to by teachers that positive discrimination of low achieving pupils is detrimental to high achieving pupils in that it may impede them to make even further progress. This may be hypothesized to be the reason for the lack of effects of adaptive instruction and multigrade classes (Veenman, 1995 and 1996): schools and teachers may be somewhat reluctant to prioritize. One reason may be that their system of beliefs and understandings does not allow them to do so until the beneficial effects of putting extra effort into low achievers has been empirically demonstrated.

The Ministry of Education, Culture & Science (1997) has developed a policy for extra investments in pre-kindergarten, kindergarten, and grade one and two of primary education, thereby providing schools with the opportunity to achieve a class size reduction of 8 pupils in these early years of schooling. The policy is in place but it is accepted that class size reduction will not automatically generate better results. Thus a framework of standards stating the learning objectives to be achieved at the end of grade two, and supporting policies for recruiting and rehiring retired teachers have been formulated.

Because of the freedom of schools in educational issues the government cannot, unlike the Californian class size reduction initiative, prescribe what schools should do with the extra formation. The only restriction imposed on schools is that part of the formation is earmarked for the early years of schooling, so as to achieve a general 20 to 1 pupil-to-teacher ratio at this stage and a 28 to 1 ratio for grades 3 and up, aside from the extra formation assigned within the national policy framework to enhance opportunities for disadvantaged pupils.

The knowledge base on smaller classes is heavily debated. The only common point in the debate between Achilles, Nye, Zaharias and Fulton (1993) and Slavin (1990) is that both approaches require a substantial decrease in the pupil-to-teacher ratio, be it for a class size reduction or for having a teacher available for one-to-one tutoring.

The Dutch case may provide an opportunity to settle the debate, since the implementation of national policy may vary substantially across schools, with natural experiments evolving over time. Evaluation research set up as monitoring, instead of a more STAR-like experimental design, can then be conducted using a quasi-experimental design. The interesting almost pure approaches to be studied, each of which implies a strategic choice to be made by the schools themselves, may be any of the following. The most obvious way schools can implement the policy is to reduce class sizes in the early stage to around 20. Another way would be a Success-for-All kind of approach, in which one teacher is assigned one-to-one tutoring for pupils at risk. A third way would be to construct what might be called a "reverse pyramid", thus striving for smallest classes for the youngest pupils and then generally increasing class size as they become more independent learners. A fourth approach that may be particular relevant in the first years of the policy when the pupil-to-teacher ratio reduction is gradually implemented, consists of regrouping heterogeneous, maybe even multigrade classes of a regular size (say 24 to 28 pupils) on a consistent basis into two smaller, more homogeneous instructional groups for teaching the basic subjects (cf. Tomlinson, 1989; Odden, 1990).

In evaluating these naturally occurring experiments, special focus should be on the intermediate links, particularly adaptivity of instruction. Moreover, of course, a more economically inspired evaluation of the cost effectiveness of this operation should be undertaken, if only for accountability purposes and to stimulate schools to grasp the opportunity provided.

5.7   References

Achilles, C.M., Nye, B.A., Zaharias, J.B., & Fulton, B.D. (1993). Creating successful schools for all children: a proven step. *Journal of School Leadership, 3,* 606-621.

Blatchford, P., Baines, E., & Kutnick, P. (1999). *The effect of class size on within class grouping practices.* Paper to British Educational Research Association Annual Meeting, Sussex University.

Blatchford, P., Goldstein, H., & Mortimore, P. (1998). Research on class size effects: a critique of methods and a way forward. *International Journal of Educational Research,* 29, 691-710.

Blatchford, P., & Martin, C. (1998). The effects of class size on classroom processes: 'It's a bit like a treadmill - working hard and getting nowhere fast!' *British Journal of Educational Studies,* 46(2), 118-137.

Blatchford, P., & Mortimore, P. (1994). The issue of class size for young children in schools: what can we learn from research? *Oxford Review of Education,* 20(1), 411-428.

Bosker, R.J. (1998). The class size question in primary schools: policy issues, theory, and empirical findings from the Netherlands. *International Journal of Educational Research,* 29, 763-778.

Bosker, R.J., & Hox, J.J. (1996). Klassengrootte en het functioneren van leerlingen en leerkrachten in het basisonderwijs. Een onderzoek op basis van de PRIMA-cohort data. In Commissie Kwalitatieve Aspecten van de Groepsgrootte in het Basisonderwijs, *Klassenverkleining* (pp. 107-118). The Hague: SDU.

Burstall, C. (1992). Playing the numbers game in class. *Education Guardian,* 7th April.

CKAG, Commissie Kwalitatieve Aspecten van Groepsgrootte (1996). *Klassenverkleining.* The Hague: SDU.

Creemers, B.P.M. (1994). *The effective classroom.* London: Cassell.

CSR (1999). *Class size reduction in California 1996-98. Early findings signal promise and concerns.* Palo Alto: CSR.

Dobbelsteen, S., Levin, J., & Oosterbeek, H. (1999). *The causal effect of class size on scholastic achievement. Distinguishing the pure class size effect from the effect of changes in class composition.* Amsterdam: Mimeo.

Finn, J.D., & Achilles, C.M. (1990). Answers and questions about class size: A statewide experiment. *American Educational Research Journal,* 27(3), 557-577.

Friedrich, K.R. (1994). *Building a foundation: developing quality early childhood programs to enhance the science and mathematics education of all children.* Paper presented at the annual meeting of the AERA, New Orleans.

Glass, G.V., & Smith, M.L. (1979). Meta-analysis of research on class size and achievement. *Educational Evaluation and Policy Analysis,* 1(1), 2-16.

Glass, G.V., Cahen, L.S., Smith, M.L., & Filby, N.N. (1982). *School class size.* London: Sage Publications.

Goldstein, H., & Blatchford, P. (1998). Class size and educational achievement: a review of methodology with particular reference to study design. *British Educational Research Journal,* 3(24), 255-268.

Goldstein, H., & Yang, M. (forthcoming). Meta analysis using multilevel models with an application to the study of class size effects. *Journal of the Royal Statistical Society* (Series C).

Hanushek, E.A. (1986). The economics of schooling: Production and efficiency in public schools. *Journal of Economic Literature,* 24, 1141-1177.

Hanushek, E.A. (1994). Money might matter somewhere: A response to Hedges, Laine, and
·   Greenwald. *Educational Researcher,* 23(4), 5-8.

Hedges, L.V., Laine, R.D., & Greenwald, R. (1994a). Does money matter? A meta-analyses of studies of the effects of differential school inputs on student outcomes. *Educational Researcher,* 23(3), 5-14.

Hedges, L.V., Laine, R.D., & Greenwald, R. (1994b). Money does matter somewhere: a reply to Hanushek. *Educational Researcher,* 23(4), 9-10.

Hill, P. (1998). Shaking the foundations: empirically driven school reform. *School Effectiveness and School Improvement,* 9(4), 419-436.

Inspectorate of Education (1995). *Groepsgrootte in het basisonderwijs.* The Hague: SDU.

Inspectorate of Education (1996). *Schoolkenmerken en groepsgrootte in het basis-onderwijs.* Utrecht: Inspectorato of Education.

Kral, M. (1997). *Instructie en leren in combinatieklassen.* Nijmegen: ITS.

Leseman, P., Veen, A., Triesscheijn, B., & Otter, M. (1999). *Evaluatie van Kaleidoscoop en Piramide. Verslag van de tussentijdse resultaten.* Amsterdam: SCO-Kohnstamm Insituut.

Lou, Y., Abrami,, Ph.C., Spence, J.C., Poulsen, C., Chambers, B., & D'Apollonia, S. (1996). Within-class grouping: a meta-analysis. *Review of Educational Research,* 66(4), 423-459.

Madden, N.A., Slavin, R.E., Karweit, N.L., Dolan, L., & Wasik, B.A. (1993). Succes for all: Longitudinal effects of a restructuring program for inner city elementary schools. *American Educational Research Journal,* 30(2), 123-148.

Ministry of Education, Culture & Science (1997). *Groepsgrootte en kwaliteit: investeren in de onderbouw van de basisschool.* The Hague: SDU.

Nye, B.A., Achilles, C.A., Zaharias, J.B., Fulton, B.D., & Wallenhorst, M.P. (1993). Tennessee's bold experiment: using research to inform policy and practice. *Tennessee Education,* 22(3), 10-17.

Odden, A. (1990). Class size and student achievement: research-based policy alternatives. *Educational Evaluation and Policy Analysis,* 12(2), 213-227.

OECD (1995). *Education at a Glance.* Paris: OECD.

Pate-Bain, H., Achilles, C.M., Boyd-Zaharias, J. &, McKenna, B. (1992). Class size makes a difference. *Phi Delta Kappan,* 74(3), 253-6.

Polder, K.J., & Gijtenbeek, J. (1995). *Inkomsten en besteding van basisscholen. Survey naar de werkin van Londo- en FBS-bekostiging op katholieke basisscholen.* Amsterdam: SCO-Kohnstamm Institituut.

Raudenbush, S.W., & Willms, J.D. (1996). The estimation of school effects. *Journal of Educational and Behavioral Statistics,* 20(4), 307-335.

RISE (1994). *Class size regulation. A dossier of international comparisons.* London: The Research and Information on State Education Trust.

Robinson, G.E. (1990). Synthesis of research on the effects of class size. *Educational Leadership,* April, 80-90.

Ross, K.N., & Postlethwaite, T.N. (1994). Differences among countries in school resources and achievement. In W.B. Elley (Ed.), *The IEA study of reading literacy: Achievement and instruction in thirty-two school systems.* Oxford: Elsevier Science Ltd.

Scheerens, J., & Bosker, R.J. (1997). *The foundations of educational effectiveness.* Oxford: Elsevier Science.

Slavin, R.E. (1989). Achievement effects of substantial reductions in class size. In R.E. Slavin (Ed.), *School and classroom organization* (pp. 247-257). Hillsdale, N.J.: Lawrence Erlbaum.

Slavin, R. (1990). Class size and student achievement: is smaller better? *Contemporary Education,* 62(1), 6-12).

Slavin, R.E. (1996). *Education for All.* Lisse: Swets & Zeitlinger.

Smith, M.L., & Glass, G.V. (1980). Meta-analysis of research on class size and its relationship to attitudes and instruction. *American Educational Research Journal,* 17(4), 419-433.

Smith, A.B., McMillan, B.W., Kennedy, S., & Ratcliffe, B. (1989). The effect of improving preschool teacher/child ratios: an 'experiment in nature'. *Early Child Development and Care,* 41, 123-138.

Stringfield, S.C., & Slavin, R.E. (1992). A hierarchical longitudinal model for elementary school effects. In B.P.M. Creemers & G.J. Reezigt (Eds.), *Evaluation of Effectiveness.* Enschede/Groningen: ICO.

Tomlinson, T.M. (1989). Class size and public policy: politics and panaceas. *Educational Policy,* 3(3), 261-273.

Tomlinson, T. (1990). Class size and public policy: the plot thickens. *Contemporary Education,* 62(1), 17-23.

Veenman, S. (1995). Cognitive and noncognitive effects of multigrade and multi-age classes: A best-evidence synthesis. *Review of Educational Research,* 65(4), 319-382.

Veenman, S. (1996). Effects of multigrade and multi-age classes reconsidered. *Review of Educational Research,* 66(3), 323-340.

Wenglinsky, H. (1997). *When money matters.* Princeton: ETS.

Word, E. (1990). *Student/Teacher Achievement Ratio (STAR). Tennessee's K-3 Class Size Study.* Washington: ERIC Report ED320 692.

6. QUALITY AND OPPORTUNITIES IN SECONDARY EDUCATION: IMPLEMENTATION AND EFFECTS OF THE COMMON CORE CURRICULUM

Greetje P.C. van der Werf[1], Hennie P. Brandsma[2], Lidwien M.C.M. Cremers-van Wees[2] & Miranda J. Lubbers[1]
[1]*Gion, University of Groningen, the Netherlands*
[2]*Faculty of Educational Science & Technology, University of Twente, the Netherlands*

In August 1993 every secondary education school in the Netherlands began implementing the Common Core Curriculum [Basisvorming]. By modernization and harmonization of the curriculum and stating core objectives to be achieved for (almost) all pupils, it was anticipated that three objectives could be reached: increased levels of excellence, providing pupils with skills and knowledge for future technological and socio-cultural developments, and postponing the selection of pupils into one of the main four curricular tracks in secondary education until the age of 15. This chapter describes the evaluation conducted using a.o. a series of repetitive large scale pupil cohorts to see whether the objectives were attained. The results indicate that the objectives of the innovation have hardly been reached yet, since schools are still organized and working as if the implementation had not yet started.

6.1 Introduction

Until 1993 the Dutch educational system for pupils aged 12 to 16 was organized in four different educational tracks. Immediately after leaving primary school pupils were placed in a specific track. Track assignment took place according to performance level assessed in the final grade of primary school. These tracks reflected different levels of secondary education. The lowest level was Junior Vocational Education (VBO), the second and third level were Lower and Higher General Secondary Education (MAVO and HAVO) and the highest level was Pre-University Education (VWO). The length of the courses also varied: VBO and MAVO 4 years; HAVO 5 years; and VWO 6 years.

In August 1993 every secondary school began implementing the Common Core Curriculum [CCC]. This offers a common learning content to all pupils in the first stage of secondary education and usually covers three grades. In some school types the duration may cover two or four years.

The implementation of the CCC is based on social-political aims which are:

1. Improvement of the general quality of education;
2. Strengthening and enlarging common knowledge and skills, adapted to technological and social-cultural developments;
3. Postponing the moment at which pupils have to make decisions about their further educational career.

The curriculum covers general and subject specific core goals, which form the basis for the learning content of the subjects. Every pupil takes lessons in at least 15 mainly traditional subjects from the old secondary school curriculum. The new subjects are technology, computer science and 'household skills'. Besides the 15 subjects, on which 25 50 minutes lessons on average are spent per week, schools have seven free lessons that they may spent on subjects of their own choice.

The implementation of the CCC did not imply a structural change since the CCC is only offered in the first stage of secondary education, while the original tracks are maintained.

Schools have to link up the CCC with the educational tracks they offer later. They can choose three curriculum variations: 1) Three years CCC followed by transition to grade 10 (secondary 4) of MAVO, HAVO or VWO; 2) Two years CCC and then VBO; or 3) Two years CCC and a one year combined CCC and VBO track.

Standardized tests developed by the National Institute for Test Development (CITO) determine whether pupils have succeeded in mastering the objectives of the CCC. However these tests are not final examinations since schools are free to decide when they apply the tests and to decide whether pupils have taken the tests successfully in order to finalize the CCC.

It is clear that the Dutch CCC is not entirely comparable with the common one in England. In England all pupils follow a common curriculum until the age of 14 when they then select different combinations of subjects. All pupils must follow courses in English, mathematics and science and then take a central General Certificate of Secondary Education (GCSE) exam in each subject. Pupils are also able to choose a wide or restrictive range of other subjects or vocational options. After the age of 16 all pupils are entitled to enter full-time further education and their GCSE results are decisive in determining what courses they take (Wolf & Stedman, 1999). In comparison with the Dutch CCC the English one seems more differentiated according to content (number of subjects), while the Dutch is more differentiated according to performance level. The English curriculum is also more prescriptive with respect to the final standards to be achieved, whereas the Dutch CCC only has core objectives without prescription of standards.

In implementing the CCC schools have to make choices on how to organize the first stage of secondary education regarding the grouping of pupils with different achievement levels into homogeneous or heterogeneous classes, the length of the CCC, lesson schedules and embedding the CCC into the educational tracks. Schools have much freedom in these decisions which may result in large differences between schools in the way the CCC is implemented. These differences may have important consequences for pupil achievement and educational careers.

This chapter is about the degree to which the CCC has been implemented in schools and the effects of the CCC on pupils' achievement and educational careers.

The questions that will be addressed are:

1. What changes in school and instruction characteristics have been implemented in secondary schools since 1993?
2. To what degree has the quality of secondary education improved since 1993?
3. To what degree have educational opportunities been improved since 1993?

6.2   Theoretical background

The research questions comprise three central concepts that need further elaboration. To answer research question 1 *school and instructions characteristics* should be elaborated upon since it may be expected that they will change in schools as a result of the new CCC. To answer the research questions 2 and 3 the concepts of *quality of education and educational opportunities* should be defined.

6.2.1   Characteristics of schools and instruction

In choosing the relevant school and instructional characteristics it is necessary to look in detail more at the 'policy perspective' of the CCC. This can give an impression of the school organizational and instructional arrangements that are supposed to be in place in order to reach the desired social political goals of the CCC. The introduction section has already given us a broad idea of the political aims of the innovation. By and large it is a curricular innovation. Firstly its content is aimed at *'modernization'* and has been adapted to meet changing societal demands and the demands of a changing pupil population. In subjects there is a shift from mere content learning (knowledge) towards application of knowledge, general skills (skills that are not related to specific subject domains) and cohesion between subjects. Secondly specific subjects are integrated into broader curricular areas, e.g. integrating mathematics, physics and biology into 'science', or integrating subjects like history, geography and politics into 'social studies'. Thirdly new subject areas have been introduced, like information technology, basic technical skills (simple repairs, use of electric appliances) and household skills (food, cooking, childcare, health, cleaning etc.).

Secondly the innovation is aimed at *'harmonization of the curriculum'*. This means that the same curriculum content is offered to all pupils irrespective of their former school career, abilities, gender and social and ethnic background. Although all pupils are offered the same 15 prescribed subject areas there are no well defined prescriptions with regard to the level of attainment each student has to achieve within each subject. Only core goals for each subject and for six general skills are defined and described by law. The core goals are statements about the content of the knowledge and skills pupils need to possess, or in any case that have to be offered to pupils. These core goals are at the heart of the innovation and can be interpreted as curricular guidelines or as a curricular grid. There are, however, no proficiency levels connected to these core goals; the core goals are stated as aspirations (e.g. "The pupils have knowledge on consumer rights and obligations"). Thus proficiency levels can be adjusted or translated to the specific population of pupils within the specific context of the school. This also means that there are no formally and centrally stated attainment standards (like external examinations), and tests developed to determine whether the pupils have finished the CCC cannot be considered as formal because no standards or norms are given. It is more or less up to the school to decide whether a pupil has acquired the necessary knowledge and skills. It is also at the discretion of the school (or even the teacher) to decide at what point in time pupils have finished the CCC. In practice this can be after one to four years.

Despite the fact that schools are somewhat free to decide about the curriculum content for pupils there are some legal prescriptions, sometimes as 'advice' and sometimes 'formal', concerning the timetable for the whole curriculum and for every subject separately. During the first two years some 2,500 50 minute lessons have to be offered. Some 75% (1,000 hours yearly) should be spent on 15 CCC subjects, the remaining 25% can be used for other subjects like Latin, vocational orientation, counselling or even extending the hours for CCC subjects. Schools may vary considerably however in the amount of hours for specific subjects and the period or grade in which subjects are offered. Some rules however are more formal, for instance number of hours that have to be spent on certain well-described specific subjects, like physical education and the moment when pupils are to be given an advice for their next curricular track at the end of grade two.

The CCC also sets explicit goals, i.e. postponing the time at which pupils have to make decisions about their further educational career. It is an objective that such choices are made as late as possible. Although no explicit prescriptions are given by law, schools have several means to achieve this. Firstly at school and organization level. Over the last 10 years Dutch policy has stimulated the merging of 'small' schools that offer one or two educational tracks, with other schools, into larger and more broader units offering all or most of the tracks. Secondly within the first phase of secondary school the aim is to group together pupils with varying abilities into more heterogeneous classes. These two educational approaches have as a consequence that schools can create more options for pupils to choose from. Thirdly by improving counselling provisions for pupils with respect to their individual coaching throughout their school career, i.e. intellectually, socially, emotionally and regarding the choices they have to make. Finally by integrating the necessary skills to make optimal choices and knowledge about educational and professional options into the CCC as so-called general and subject specific core goals.

6.2.2   Quality of education and educational opportunities

The concept *quality of education* has three dimensions: *effectiveness*, *personal profit* and *efficiency*. Firstly the quality of education is the result of what pupils learn at school in terms of measurable knowledge and skills (De Groot, 1983). This implies goal realization or what we call educational *effectiveness*. If the CCC is aimed at improving education, this means that pupils should now learn more than before and thus have more knowledge and skills at the end of the curriculum. Some people will argue that the CCC is aimed at different knowledge and skills than the old curriculum since the focus is less on knowledge and more on the application of knowledge and learning of skills (Procesmanagement Basisvorming, 1993). With this opinion however the aim of the CCC is not to improve the quality of education but only is a change to the content of education, which makes a comparison with the former curriculum impossible. To compare the quality of education of the new curriculum with the former in terms of acquired knowledge and skills we suppose that the new curriculum has the minimal aim that pupils learn more and thus achieve better than before. This does not imply that other aims are not important enough to be evaluated.

A second aspect to quality of education is the *profit* pupils have from education, i.e. the level of education they reach indicated by the track they follow in secondary school, the value of the diploma they gain and the progress they make in further education.

The third aspect to quality of education is *efficiency,* indicated by the time a pupil needs to complete a certain educational track or to reach a certain level of education. Those who repeat grades or who transfer from one track to another loose time and are thus less efficient than those who progress continuously through a track.

Both the second and third aspect of quality of education are based on the idea that delay of choice of education and profession should result in better choices and in more effective and efficient careers throughout secondary school and beyond.

It will be clear that these three aspects are strongly interrelated. The aim of the CCC is to improve all three aspects of quality and the question is also for which pupils the quality of education should be improved. The answer can be found in the second aim of the CCC - strengthening the common cultural basis. This means that in the first three grades the curriculum should be modernized and the same curriculum content offered to all pupils (harmonization). However one may also expect that all pupils profit as much as possible from that curriculum. In other words, the CCC aims to offer *equal opportunities* to all pupils. It is known however from research into educational opportunity that student achievement and school careers are largely influenced by the capacities or the motivation of pupils themselves. Not all pupils are able or willing to learn to the same degree. Therefore equal opportunity should be conceived as 'as many pupils as possible should learn and profit from education as much and as efficiently as there capacities allow for'. This means that pupil achievement and school careers should only be related to their capacity or willingness to learn and not to SES, gender or ethnicity. The CCC has improved educational if the relationship between achievement and school careers and SES, gender and ethnicity has become weaker since 1993 in comparison with before.

6.3   Design of the evaluation

The research questions will be answered with data collected in the 'Longitudinal Cohort Studies in Secondary Education' (VOCL). These studies were designed especially for evaluating the CCC (Peschar, 1988). The first cohort study started in 1989, the second in 1993, when the CCC was first implemented. The data of the first cohort study may be considered as pretest data, with which the data of the second cohort study can be compared to establish the effects of the CCC. Below we describe the sample, variables and instruments, procedures of data collection and method of analysis.

6.3.1   Sample

The sample population for the first cohort study consisted of 1,800 secondary schools with about 185,000 pupils in the first grade of five tracks: Individualized Junior Vocational Education (IVBO), Junior Vocational Education (VBO), Lower General Education (MAVO), Higher General Education (HAVO) and Pre-University Education (VWO). The aimed sample size was 400 schools, stratified according to the tracks offered by the schools. The sample realized consisted of 381 schools. First grade classes were sampled at random. The total number of classes was 868; the total number of pupils was 19,524.

As a consequence of policy to create larger secondary schools in 1993 the sample population of schools was decreased to about 800. It was the aim of the second cohort study to sample as many schools as possible that were also in the 1989 sample. This was not very successful. Only 121 schools were willing to cooperate with the second cohort study. Of the remaining 680 280 new schools had to be sampled to conduct the new cohort study again in about 400 schools. The new sample realized was only 212, which produced a total sample for the second cohort study of 333 schools. Although the number of schools in the second cohort study is lower than in the first, the number of classes and first grade pupils is comparable since secondary schools in 1993 are larger than in 1989. The number of classes in the second study is 880, the number of pupils is 20,331. The section on the results illustrates whether both samples are comparable with respect to pupils background characteristics and the school tracks followed.

6.3.2   Procedure of data collection

The first cohort study started in the 1989/1990 school year by collecting data on enrolling pupils. Entrance tests were taken and data were collected about pupils' background characteristics and their school tracks. Tests were administered by the schools' teachers, while information about pupil characteristics was partly provided by the school administration and partly by parents who filled in a questionnaire. Information on school and instruction characteristics was collected by interviews with school principals and by grade 7 teachers completing questionnaires. In the 1991/1992 school year, when pupils were now in grade 9 (secondary 3) tests were administered again as well as interviews with the school principals and questionnaires for grade 9 teachers. Information about the school careers of pupils (track and grade, further education after secondary school) was collected yearly. Until now data are available until the 1997/1998 school year (the ninth year of secondary schooling of the cohort pupils).

In the 1993/1994 school year the pupils in grade 11 (secondary 5) of the two highest tracks (HAVO and VWO) filled in a questionnaire about their choice of examination subjects, plans for further education, study skills and achievement motivation. Pupils who left secondary diploma without a diploma and those who had completed the three lowest tracks (IVBO, VBO or MAVO) also filled in a questionnaire about their examination subjects, examination results, transfer to further education or labour market and future plans.

The second cohort study started in the 1993/1994 school year. The procedure was almost the same as the one for the first cohort study although there are two differences. Firstly grade 7 tests were administered by test assistants and grade 9 tests were administered either by test assistants or by teachers of the schools who were paid for this. Secondly in grade 9 there was one test more than in the first cohort study. From the second cohort data are available until the 1997/1998 school year (the fifth year of secondary schooling of the cohort pupils).

6.3.3   Variables and instruments

In this section only the variables and instruments are described that are relevant for the research questions. Comparisons are made between the two cohorts with respect to 1) school and instruction characteristics; 2) pupil achievement in grade 3; 3) educational careers of pupils until the fifth year of secondary schooling; and 4) relationships between achievement and educational position and background characteristics. The four groups of variables are described below.

School and instruction characteristics

As stated before two core elements of the innovation are modernization and harmonization of the curriculum, whereby modernization relates to the content of the curriculum and harmonization to its organizational and structural aspects.

Subject specific core goals were measured at the level of subject teacher and subject department. For this study two subjects, mathematics and Dutch language, were selected. For both subjects information was gathered concerning chosen method (textbook), i.e. purchase of a new CCC method, specific method used and the allocated teaching time for the subjects selected.

With respect to 'application of knowledge' and 'skills' two scales were developed for each subject in order to measure the perceived realization of the general skills goals (α reliabilities vary with subject and time from .69 to .76) and subject specific core goals (α reliabilities vary with subject and time from .57 to .76). Next to this a scale was developed in order to measure teacher attitude towards the subject specific core goals (α ranges from .64 to .79). A scale was also developed in order to measure the degree to which specific learning skills (also called meta-cognitive skills) should be part of the curriculum (α Dutch .86; Math .79) and are taught to pupils (α Dutch .93; Math .92). These scales were administered to subject teachers in 1996 (grade 9) only.

In order to measure the concept of cohesion between subjects information was gathered at teacher level (1994) or head of the subject department (1996). Cohesion was measured both within the department with respect to the level of cooperation between subject teachers (α varies from .63 to .74), as well as with respect to the importance of CCC topics (e.g. integration and attunement between subjects (α varies from .70 to .80).

Within the broad concept of harmonization several indicators can be distinguished, i.e. adaptive instruction and postponement of career choices. Adaptive instruction was measured at the subject teacher level through several variables like the (differentiation in) setting of minimum goals for all pupils, the use of a differentiation model within classrooms and the allocated time for subjects. At school level information was collected about adaptive arrangements for two specific groups of pupils, i.e. those with a non-Dutch background and special needs pupils.

Postponement of career choices was measured by collecting information on the 'broadness' of the educational tracks offered within schools and about the way pupils with various abilities were grouped into homogenous or more or less heterogeneous classes; the duration of the heterogeneous grouping; the possibilities pupils have to switch between educational streams; and the points in time when pupils have to decide on the desired school type and their selection of subjects. Also information was gathered on counselling provisions for pupils with respect to individual coaching throughout their school career, i.e. intellectually, socially, emotionally and with respect to the choices pupils they must make like the orientation on further education and the professional career.

For more information about the school and instruction characteristics and the instruments measuring them we refer to Cremers-Van Wees, Akkermans and Brandsma (1999).

Achievement of pupils

Grade 7 pupil achievement was measured by tests for mathematics, Dutch language skills and information processing developed by the National Institute for Test Development (CITO). Each test consisted of 20 multiple choice items with four alternatives of which only one alternative was correct. The content of the tests was the same in both cohort studies. The reliabilities were .76, .84 and .78 respectively. The reliability of the total test was .91.

Grade 9 pupil achievement in the first cohort study was measured by a test for text comprehension and mathematics. Both tests were also developed by CITO. The test for text comprehension consisted of 40 multiple choice items with four answer alternatives of which only one answer was correct. The reliability of the test was .80. The mathematics test consisted of two versions, version A for MAVO, HAVO and VWO and version B for IVBO and VBO. Version A had 12 multiple choice items with four answer alternatives and 20 open questions; Version B had two multiple choice items and 30 open questions. The score values of the correct answers were different, depending on the difficulty of the item. The maximum score was 140 for the A-version and 80 for the B-version. The reliabilities were .80 and .87 respectively.

In the second cohort study grade 9 achievement was measured again by a test for text comprehension and for mathematics. CITO had changed the content of the tests: in the text comprehension test 13 items of the old test were replaced by new items. The reliability was now .79. In the A-version of the mathematics test 15 items were replaced by 16 new ones; in the B-version two items were replaced by three new ones. The maximum scores in the new tests were 101 and 77 respectively for the A-version and B-version; the reliabilities were .81 and .87 respectively.

In order to compare both cohorts regarding the achievements in grade 9 both versions of the text comprehension test and the four versions of the mathematics test were equated using the one-Parameter Logistic Model (Verhelst, Glas & Verstralen, 1995). This was possible because the different versions of the mathematics and text comprehension test contained several overlapping items. The reliability of the equated test for comprehensive reading was .73 for the 1989 version and .75 for the 1993 version. The reliabilities of the equated mathematics tests varied between .84 and .88.

All test scores were transformed into T-scores with a mean of 50 and a standard deviation of 10.

Educational position

The educational position of pupils reached in the fifth year of schooling was expressed in both cohorts as a combined score of the grade and track pupils were in. This is what we call the 'grade ladder' (Bosker, Van der Velden & Hofman, 1985). The score on this ladder indicates the distance in years until the top level of the educational system. The maximum score is 12, which can be reached if pupils have completed the highest track (VWO) without repeating grades. It takes 6 years to reach this score. Because in the 1993 cohort pupils were in their fifth year the maximum score which can be reached is 10 if pupils are in grade 11 of VWO and have not repeated grades. Pupils in grade 11 of HAVO had a score of 9. Pupils who left full-time education with an IVBO, VBO or MAVO diploma received the value of their last position plus one point. Pupils who left education without a diploma keep their last position. For more details we refer to Van der Werf, Kuyper and Lubbers (1999).

Background characteristics

The first background characteristic is secondary education level recommended to a pupil at the end of primary school. This recommendation is based on prior achievement of the pupil in primary school as well as on the final primary education test score that most primary schools elect to offer. The recommendation may be considered as an indicator of the initial level of achievement at entering secondary school. As with the educational position in the fifth year this recommendation can also be transferred into a score on the grade ladder. This is the starting position (position 0) with a score range between 1 (IVBO recommendation) and 5 (VWO recommendation). Combined recommendations have an in-between score, for example recommendation VBO/MAVO is 2.5.

The second background characteristic is the track (class type) in which pupils are placed in the first grade, which can also be expressed as a score on the grade ladder. This is position 1, which has a score range between 2 (IVBO) and 6 (VWO). Heterogeneous class types have an in-between value, for example a MAVO/HAVO class has a 4,5 score.

The third background characteristic is the socio-economic status of the family, indicated by the highest level of education completed by both parents. The SES score ranges between 2 (only primary education completed) and 6 (university completed).

The fourth background characteristic is the ethnic origin of pupils, indicated by a combination of nationality/country of birth of a pupil and nationality/country of birth of parents and grandparents. The following categories are identified: 1) Dutch; 2) Turkish; 3) Moroccan; 4) Aruban, Surinam or Antillean; 5) Other.

The fifth background characteristic is the intelligence of the pupil, measured in grade 1 with two non-verbal subtests of the Prüfsystem für Schul- und Bildungsberatung PSB (Horn, 1969). The first subtest (PSB-3) measures 'reasoning skills', the second (PSB-8) 'abstraction abilities' and both subtests consist of 40 items.

6.3.4 Data analysis

Descriptive analyzes were conducted by computing frequencies, average scores and standard deviations of the four categories of variables. Differences between the cohorts were tested with respect to school and instruction characteristics as far as the same information was available for the several points in time, achievements in grade 1 and 3 and the educational position in the fifth year of schooling. The relationship between background characteristics and achievements and educational position was analyzed separately in each cohort and the results were compared between the cohorts. Multiple regression analyzes were conducted to predict the achievements and educational position from pupil background characteristics and additionally from the classtype (homogeneous, heterogeneous or mediate heterogeneous) the pupils were in in grade 7, Finally to test the differences between the cohorts, the cohort effect was added to the model.

6.4   Results

6.4.1   Implementation of CCC: modernization of the curriculum

In the first VOCL cohort study, started in 1989, it was not yet known what the core goals of the CCC would be. So in that cohort it was not possible to operationalize and measure the specific curricular changes that would take place at the onset of the innovation in 1993. For this reason we cannot report about differences between cohorts as far as 'modernization' is concerned. It is possible however to make some comparisons in the development of CCC between 1993 and 1996, three years later. We start by generally indicating the level of implementation in 1996 of the main elements of the CCC as reported by school management.

In general schools succeeded in implementing the CCC to a satisfactory degree (2.8 out of a maximum score of 4). Some elements, however, specifically those linked to 'cohesion' between subject matter and between teachers, the realization of general skills goals, and the link-up with the later stages in education have been implemented to a much lower degree. Some elements not so closely connected with CCC as such, like arrangements for pupil counselling, reveal the highest degree of implementation.

For modernizing the curriculum educational publishers developed new textbooks for CCC subjects, based on guidelines issued by the government and advisory committees. As a measure of the level of implementation of the CCC the purchase of new textbooks serves as a good indicator. The number of subjects for which new textbooks were purchased increased considerably between 1994 and 1996. High ranking subjects in 1996 were Dutch language (84% new textbooks), maths (83%), economics (76%), physics (77%) and new subjects like 'household skills' (84%) and 'basic technical skills' (75%). However for another new subject 'information technology' only 55% of sample schools purchased a new textbook. Low ranking subjects were mainly the creative subjects like drawing (50%) and crafts (36%).

Regarding the use of the new textbooks teachers generally used the prescribed order in which the topics were presented (for Dutch 88% and form maths almost 100%). However teachers do not use all the topics described in the textbooks. In general, some 11% (maths) and 16% (Dutch language) of the offered content in the textbooks is not used by teachers. This is replaced with material from other methods and/or self developed materials.

The next three indicators of a modernization of the curriculum are the teachers' attention to *realizing general skills*, to achieve the *intended subject specific goals* and their agreement with the premises of CCC. The emphasis on realizing general skills within both subjects was rather low, hardly differed between subjects and had not increased during the three years of the CCC. The level of realization was higher than that of the general skills in respect of subject specific core goals, but had not improved much during the three years of implementation. The level of agreement with the subject specific CCC premises for both subjects was only moderate and had not increased since the start of the CCC.

In order to measure the concept of cohesion between subjects information was gathered at teacher level (1994) or the head of the subject department (1996). Cohesion was measured within the mathematics and Dutch language department with regard to the level of cooperation between subject teachers. The level of cooperation can be labelled as very low (average score of 1.9 on a scale from 1 to 4). In general cooperation is not on a regular basis and has not improved over the years. Also the level of integration into broader subjects and the level of attunement with other subjects is rather low. However the latter has improved during the time of the innovation, especially for mathematics.

6.4.2   Implementation of CCC: harmonization of the curriculum

Harmonizing the curriculum has to do with its organizational and structural aspects both at school and classroom level. Harmonization means that pupils are offered the 'same' curricular content and that career choices can be postponed. As stated before this can be achieved through several measures. Firstly by offering a broader range of tracks under the same educational roof. This implies that pupils with highly different ability levels can enter school without hardly any entry selection. Secondly by grouping pupils with different abilities into one classroom, thereby keeping different educational career possibilities open to pupils. Thirdly these grouping procedures will give rise to within-class differentiation and forms of adaptive instruction. Finally there is a stronger need for a highly sophisticated 'care system' like counselling provision for pupils in schools.

Firstly our data showed that a major shift in the educational landscape had taken place within six years. Largely through the use of financial incentives the Dutch government had succeeded in their aim to create larger and especially broader schools. From a landscape at the start of the decade that mainly consisted of a large number of small schools offering only one or two curricular tracks it has evolved into fewer schools that are much larger and offer more curricular tracks. Whereas in the old situation selection and track determination of pupils took place at entry to secondary school on the basis of recommendation and even entrance exams, it is now possible for schools to place pupils into tracks at a later stage in their educational career and this then is based on their attainments in the first phase of secondary school.

However, because of the fact that schools have a lot of freedom in the way they organize the curricular tracks it still remains to be seen whether schools also use the possibilities open to them to make their system less selective at entrance level. The data show that more heterogeneous instead of homogenous classes are created in the first two grades on the one hand, but on the other the broad heterogeneous classes consisting of three or four tracks are replaced by those with only two tracks. Also the number of years pupils are in heterogeneous classes has been reduced, which implies that the actual placing of pupils into a track has become earlier (in general at the end of the second grade) than before the implementation of the CCC.

One of the objectives of the innovation was that schools make it possible for pupils to switch between curricular tracks as early as possible without losing time. Sometimes pupils are placed in a certain secondary school type that proves to be too academically high or low. Compared to the pre CCC period possibilities for pupils moving up or down a curricular track in either their own or another school, without losing time, has increased considerably. In the pre CCC system, where most schools only had one track, pupils had to resit a year or had to change over to another school.

Another measure to harmonize the curriculum is adaptive instruction at classroom level: differentiation in the setting of minimum goals for all pupils and the use of within-classroom differentiation. However whole classroom instruction is still dominant in teaching mathematics and especially Dutch language. Some form of small group teaching is used to a considerable level in grade 1 but is decreasing as the pupils move on to grades 2 and 3. Individual teaching hardly is practiced. Compared to the situation before the implementation of the CCC, Dutch language teachers have made a slight shift from a mixed use of models to using a specific type of group teaching. Maths teachers however have shifted considerably from whole class teaching to group teaching and the mixed use of several models.

Looking at the aspect of setting minimum goals for all pupils the data show that this was paramount for most teachers, especially maths teachers (90%) before the implementation of the CCC and has decreased considerably after

1993 (65%). Since the CCC teachers differentiate much more through setting goals individually.

Finally we have information on instruction in schools with pupils from a non-Dutch origin or that have individualized provisions for special needs pupils. Almost all of these schools have created special arrangements like extra counselling, use of adaptive tests and remedial teaching. However more than 70% of schools with individualized departments for special needs pupils had not purchased any of the new CCC textbooks developed specifically for the purpose.

6.4.3   Effects of CCC: effectiveness, personal profit and efficiency

Before comparing the achievements and educational position of the pupils in both cohorts we needed to check whether the cohorts are comparable with respect to their background characteristics. It turned out that the average scores on SES and both intelligence subtests are higher in 1993 than in 1989. The differences are significant and the effect sizes are .30 and .40 respectively. Also the percentage of non-Dutch pupils is higher in the 1993 cohort, with a difference of one percent. The cohorts do not differ with respect to the recommendations given by primary school teachers regarding the curricular track the pupil is able to succeed in. So in establishing the effects of the CCC we had to take into account that there were differences in pupils' intake characteristics.

Table 1 presents the average scores and standard deviations of both cohorts on the achievement tests in grades 7 and 9 and on the indicator of the educational position in grade 11. The test scores are T-scores with an overall mean (across both cohorts) of 50 and a standard deviation of 10. The differences between the cohorts were tested with t-tests. The results of the testing are also in the table as well as the effect sizes.

Table 1. Comparison between the cohorts on achievement in grades 1 and 3 and on educational position in grade 5

	VOCL 1989			VOCL 1993			t-test	
	Mean	Sd.	N	mean	Sd.	N	t	eff. size
Grade 1								
Dutch language	49.5	10.1	18,526	50.5	9.9	19,131	9.10	.10
mathematics	49.6	10.0	18,456	50.4	9.9	19,144	8.53	.08
information	49.6	9.9	18,335	50.4	10.1	19,117	7.26	.08
total test	49.5	10.0	18,159	50.4	10.0	19,097	8.51	.09
Grade 3								
text compreh.	50.0	9.6	10,496	50.0	9.6	8,903	-.21	.00
mathematics	49.7	10.2	10,831	50.4	9.7	8,100	4.53	.07
Cohort year 5								
educ. Pos.	7.5	1.5	18,926	7.5	1.5	19,692	4.23	.05

T-values greater than 3.10 are significant with $p < .001$

With the exception of text comprehension in grade 3 all differences are significant in the advantage of the 1993 cohort. However all effect sizes are less than .25, the value that may be considered as a relevant effect size. So in general we can conclude that educational results have not changed since the implementation of the CCC. We also analyzed whether this conclusion holds for all curricular tracks.

The results of the comparison between the cohorts for each track separately show that achievement in text comprehension in the 1993 cohort is lower in IVBO, VBO and VWO. The differences are significant for IVBO and VWO. The effect sizes vary between .03 for MAVO to -.12 for VWO. For mathematics the achievements have improved significantly in VBO and MAVO and decreased significantly in VWO. The effect sizes vary between .01 for IVBO to -.16 for VWO. With respect to the educational position in the fifth year, there is a small improvement in IVBO, VBO and MAVO and a small decrease in HAVO and VWO. The improvement is significant in VBO and MAVO as is the decrease in VWO. The effect sizes vary between .01 in HAVO to -.05 in VWO.

The conclusion thus far is that there is not a relevant improvement of the educational results for the different tracks. In some tracks there is a small improvement, while in others, especially in the higher ones, there is deterioration. The most important result is the small but consistent deterioration for VWO pupils and the small but consistent improvement for

MAVO pupils, without taking into account the differences in intake characteristics.

6.4.4   Effects of CCC: equal opportunities

Table 2 presents the relations between gender, SES and ethnicity on the one hand and achievements in grade 9 and the educational position in year 11 on the other. For gender and ethnicity the average scores are in the table as well as the t-values and F-values of the testing of differences between the categories of pupils. Correlations are presented for SES.

Table 2. Relationships with background characteristics, per cohort (ASA is short for Aruban, Surinam and Antillean pupils)

	text compr		maths		edu. pos.	
	>89	>93	>89	>93	>89	>93
boys	49.5	48.5	50.3	51.0	7.29	7.39
girls	50.2	51.5	49.1	49.7	7.63	7.70
t-value	-5.48	-13.91	6.27	5.88	-16.18	-14.47
effect size	-.07	.31	.12	.13	-.23	-.21
Dutch	50.3	50.2	50.2	50.8	7.56	7.59
ASA	46.7	47.5	45.4	44.3	6.91	6.95
Moroccan	44.7	43.7	41.4	42.2	6.61	6.61
Turkish	44.2	42.1	42.4	41.2	6.58	6.62
others	50.4	50.9	50.5	50.7	7.49	7.59
F-value	33.03	35.40	61.64	66.21	84.18	110.22
eff. size ASA	-.37	-.28	-.47	-.67	-.44	-.44
eff .size Moroc.	-.58	-.68	-86	-.89	-.65	-.67
eff. size Turkish	-.63	-.84	-.77	-.99	-.67	-.66
eff. size others	.01	.07	.03	.01	.05	.00
correlation SES	.30	.33	.36	.37	.42	.40

All t-values, F-values and correlations are significant at p<.001

The difference in text comprehension achievement between boys and girls has become larger while the difference in mathematics achievement and the educational position in grade 11 have remained about equal. In both cohorts girls score higher in text comprehension and on educational position in grade 11 but lower in mathematics.

The effect sizes for the ethnic groups show a remarkable picture. Firstly the disadvantages of Turkish and Moroccan pupils in comparison with

Dutch ones have increased for text comprehension scores, while the disadvantage of ASA pupils has decreased. Mathematics scores have decreased for Turkish, Moroccan and ASA pupils, while those of others have increased when compared with Dutch pupils. The disadvantage in educational position in grade 11 has improved for Moroccan pupils, has remained the same for ASA pupils and has decreased for Turkish pupils. The advantage of the other pupils when compared to Dutch ones has disappeared. In both cohorts Turkish and Moroccan pupils have an equal disadvantage compared to Dutch pupils, ASA pupils have less disadvantage than Turkish or Moroccan and other pupils have an almost equal position as Dutch pupils.

Finally the table shows that SES correlates highest with educational position in grade 11 and least with the text comprehension score. Comparison between the cohorts shows that the correlations with test scores are slightly higher in the 1993 cohort, while the correlation with educational position is slightly lower.

In general we may conclude that equality of educational opportunities has not improved since implementing the CCC. The differences between boys and girls, different ethnic groups and different categories of socio-economic status are almost equal in both cohorts.

6.4.5   Testing the effects of CCC, taking background characteristics into account

It appeared from the former sections that the educational results of pupils have hardly improved since the CCC was implemented and that it did not affect the equality of educational opportunity for specific categories of pupils. But we also discovered that both cohorts of pupils differ substantially in intake characteristics (background characteristics and initial abilities) at the start of secondary education. Further we know that pupils in both cohorts were in different classes as far as grouping is concerned. The final section examines whether there is a cohort effect after taking into account differences in background characteristics, initial abilities of pupils and the composition of the grade 7 class they were in. We analyzed the data using multilevel analysis in order to take into account the hierarchical structure of the data (pupils nested within schools). The criterion variables were the achievement scores for mathematics and text comprehension in grade 9 and the educational position in grade 11. The predictors at student level were: recommendation, intelligence, entrance test score in grade 7, educational track in grade 9 (only in the models with mathematics and text comprehension as criterion variables), SES, gender, ethnic origin, achievement motivation and well-being, classroom composition in grade 7 and cohort. The numbers of pupils in the analyzes were 13,797 for mathematics, 14,258 for text comprehension and 26,370 for educational position. The results are summarized in table 3. For more detailed information we refer to Van der Werf, Lubbers and Kuyper (1999).

Table 3. Establishing the effects of the CCC, taking into account the differences in intake between the cohorts (regression parameters with standard errors in brackets)

	Text comprehension	Mathematics	Educational position
intercept	49.75 (.19)	50.70 (.18)	7.46 (.02)
recommendation	1.00 (.14)	1.24 (.11)	.54 (.01)
intelligence	.18 (.07)	.98 (.06)	.03 (.01)
entry information	2.27 (.09)	1.01 (.08)	.16 (.01)
entry mathematics	.32 (.10)	3.13 (.08)	.16 (.01)
entry language	1.46 (.09)	.40 (.08)	.13 (.01)
track grade 9	2.80 (.12)	2.73 (.10)	n.a.
gender (girls)	1.16 (.13)	-1.44 (.11)	.20 (.01)
ethnicity (ethn. min.)	-1.00 (.32)	-1.50 (.26)	.07 (.02)
SES	.16 (.07)	.15 (.05)	.10 (.01)
achievement motivation	.25 (.07)	.36 (.06)	.15 (.01)
school well-being	.15 (.07)	-.03 (.06)	.02 (.01)
class type grade 7 (homogeneous)			
-mediate heterogeneous	-1.26 (.25)	-.37 (.22)	.13 (.02)
-heterogeneous	-1.29 (.32)	-.50 (.29)	.15 (.02)
cohort 1993	-.59 (.18)	-.13 (.16)	.05 (.01)
school level variance	5.04	6.58	.03
student level variance	47.17	29.52	.60
perc. school level	10%	18%	5%
perc. variance reduction	49%	70%	36%

If the ratio regression parameter/standard error is greater than 3.10 the effect is significant at p < .001

The data in table 3 show that pupil background characteristics and initial abilities have a significant effect on all three criterion variables, with the exception of SES on text comprehension. The higher the scores on SES, recommendation, intelligence and the entry tests, the higher the achievement level in grade 9 and the educational position in grade 11. The effects of gender and ethnicity are different for the criterion variables: girls score higher on text comprehension and educational position, while boys score higher on mathematics. Ethnic minority pupils score lower on achievements in text comprehension and mathematics, but higher on educational position. This last result can be explained by the fact that most ethic minority pupils have a very low level of recommendation so that their score on the grade ladder can hardly decrease during five years of secondary schooling.

Achievement motivation has a significant positive effect on all three criterion variables. The effects of class type are significant for text comprehension and educational position, but the directions of the effects are different: heterogeneous classes have a negative effect on achievement but a positive effect on the educational position that is reached in grade 11 of schooling.

Finally the cohort effect is also only significant for text comprehension and educational position. The pupils in the 1993 cohort scored lower on text comprehension but reached a higher educational position compared to the 1989 cohort.

6.5   Conclusions

The conclusions from the data presented are quite clear. Firstly we found that the CCC had not been properly implemented by schools until 1996, neither at school level nor classroom level. Secondly the quality of education in terms of effectiveness, personal profit and efficiency has hardly improved. On the one hand the effectiveness - the degree of goal realization in terms of learned knowledge and skills - has decreased slightly, on the other hand the educational positions indicated by scores on the grade ladder have improved. The effects are stronger for the higher educational tracks. In HAVO and VWO (the two highest) 1993 test scores are lower than those of the 1989 cohort, while the educational positions (as indicated by level of the track and pupil grade) are higher. This is a remarkable phenomenon. The educational positions have improved while the achievements have decreased. This implies that in secondary education achievement plays a less important role since the implementation of the CCC in decisions about progress to higher grades or transitions to higher tracks.

Although the differences are small the results may point to a cumbersome trend. If this becomes the case, in the long term the quality of education will decrease. Teaching knowledge and skills as the most important aim of schooling will become less important than striving to improve the profit and efficiency of education. On the other hand it also might be the case that pupils' achievements on the tests in this study do not fully reflect their actual achievement. The test scores do not have consequences for their further educational careers (there is no high stakes testing involved). It is possible that pupils may not have done their utmost to complete the tests. Additionally it is possible that in decisions by teachers (and pupils themselves) about educational careers, other criteria than test scores also play a role, like motivation and efforts, or that teachers themselves apply tests that are more suitable to evaluate the aims of the CCC (Roelofs, Vermeulen & Houtveen, 1998; Roelofs & Houtveen, 1999).

The third conclusion from the results is that equality of educational opportunities has not yet improved since the CCC was implemented. The differences in pupil achievement and educational position, related to gender, SES and ethnicity in the 1993 cohort are almost equal to those in the 1989 cohort.

We must conclude that the CCC has not yet resulted in improved educational quality, at least not in terms of the definitions used in this article. About any other effects nothing as yet can be said on the basis of our results. However there is no real reason for pessimism. The 1993 cohort was the first cohort of pupils who were confronted with the CCC. Their teachers had to teach new methods for the first time, which had other subject-independent aims and modernized didactic strategies. For these pupils the curriculum was more extensive compared to earlier cohorts. Given this, it is probably a favourable sign that the quality of education has not decreased dramatically, as sometimes occurs when implementing innovations.

6.6   References

Bosker, R.J., Velden, R.K.W. van der, & Hofman, W.H.A. (1985). *Een generatie geselecteerd. Deel I: De loopbanen.* Groningen: RION.

Cremers-Van Wees, L.M.C.M., Akkermans, L.M.W., & Brandsma, H.P. (1999). *Ontwikkelingen in de Bavo in de periode 1990-1998. Modernisering en harmonisering in de basisvorming.* Enschede: OCTO.

Groot, A.D. de (1983). Is de kwaliteit van het onderwijs te beoordelen? In B. Creemers, W. Hoeben & K. Koops (Eds.). *De kwaliteit van het onderwijs* (pp.54-73). Groningen: Wolters-Noordhoff.

Horn, W. (1969). *Prüfsystem für Schul- und Bildungsberatung PSB.* Göttingen: Verlag für Psychologie.

Peschar, J. (1988). *Evaluatie van de basisvorming. Kader voor het uitvoeringsplan.* Den Haag: SVO.

Procesmanagement Basisvorming (1993). *Inrichtingsbesluit VWO-HAVO-MAVO-VBO. Besluit kerndoelen en adviesurentabel basisvorming 1993-1998.* Almere: Procesmanagement Basisvorming.

Roelofs, E.C., Vermeulen, C.J., & Houtveen, A.A.M. (1998). *Basisvorming op weg. Onderzoek naar de mening van docenten over de realisatie van de Basisvorming.* Utrecht: ISOR.

Roelofs, E.C., & Houtveen, A.A.M. (1999). Didactiek van authentiek leren in de Basisvorming: stand van zaken bij docenten Nederlands en wiskunde. *Pedagogische Studiën,* 76(4), 237-258.

Verhelst, N.D., Glas, C.A.W., & Verstralen, H.H.F.M. (1995). *One-Parameter Logistic Model (OPLM).* Arnhem: CITO.

Werf, M.P.C. van der, Kuyper, H., & Lubbers, M.J. (1999). Achtergrond- en gezinskenmerken van leerlingen en opbrengsten van het voortgezet onderwijs. Groningen: GION.

Werf, M.P.C. van der, Lubbers, M.J., & Kuyper, H. (1999). *De onderwijsresultaten van VOCL-89 en VOCL-93 leerlingen.* Groningen: GION.

Wolf, A. & Stedman, H. (1999). Basic Competence in Mathematics: Swedish and English 16 year old. *Comparative Education,* 34 (3), 241-261.

7.   EVALUATING THE IMPACT OF A RAISING SCHOOL STANDARDS INITIATIVE

Brenda Taggart & Pam Sammons
International School Effectiveness & Improvement Centre, Institute of Education, University of London, United Kingdom.

Concern about the quality of schooling in disadvantaged urban areas has been especially marked throughout the United Kingdom during the 1990s. This led to the instigation of a major school improvement project in Northern Ireland, known as the Raising School Standards Initiative, that was intended to help schools address significant disadvantage and under-achievement amongst their pupils. The project, based on the knowledge base of the school effectiveness tradition, was designed to target a small number of secondary schools and their main contributory primary schools. The project sought to improve the quality of school management, the pupils' standards of literacy and numeracy, the levels of qualifications, links with local industry, parental involvement in schools, attendance and punctuality, and to deal with problems of discipline in class. The improvement strategy selected can be seen as an attempt to integrate a 'top down' external approach (distal) with a 'bottom up' (proximal) strategy developed within individual schools. This chapter describes selected aspects of the full evaluation: the launch and selection of schools and the process of 'action planning'. It also looks at the impact of the project on management, teaching and learning and educational standards. It concludes with findings which will have implications for other initiatives which seek to raise school standards in the urban context.

7.1   Introduction

Concern about the quality of schooling in disadvantaged urban areas has been especially marked throughout the UK during the 1990s. This led, in part, to the then Minister for Education in Northern Ireland, announcing in May 1994 a major school improvement initiative under the Making Belfast Work (MBW) programme. The Raising School Standards (RSS) initiative was intended to help schools address significant disadvantage and under-achievement amongst their pupils. The project was designed to target a small number of secondary schools and their main contributory primary schools. Additional funding of £3m, over the three year period was allocated. A major difference between this initiative and other school improvement projects was the substantial financial investment agreed over a three year period and the strong emphasis placed specifically on pupil outcomes.

During the last fifteen years there has been a growth in public and policy concern about educational standards, particularly in literacy and numeracy, and widespread recognition of the importance of raising standards to meet the increasingly complex economic and social needs of society in the 21st century. This, in turn, has led to the demand for greater accountability of schools and teachers from policy makers, inspectors and parents. Adding to the debate has been increasing evidence from school effectiveness research (Rutter, Maughan & Ouston, 1979; Reynolds, 1992; Mortimore, Sammons, Stoll, Lewish & Ecob, 1988; Sammons, Thomas, Mortimore, Owen & Pennell, 1994) and more recently school improvement (Hopkins, Ainscow, West, 1994; Myers, 1995; Stoll & Fink, 1996; Barber & Dann, 1996; Sammons, Thomas & Mortimore, 1997) about what makes an effective school. This research evidence has highlighted the existence of 11 key characteristics of effective schools (Sammons, Hilman, & Mortimore, 1995).

The school effectiveness research base provides evidence of the need to develop value added approaches for the evaluation of school performance. Such approaches are becoming increasingly widespread and a number of Local Education Authorities have introduced innovative schemes (for a review see Barber and Dann, 1996). In the Northern Ireland context the Department of Education Northern Ireland has funded research to develop a comprehensive value added framework for the evaluation of school performance as part of the expanded Raising School Standards Initiative (Thomas & Sammons, 1996).

In evaluating the success of the original MBW RSS initiative it is important to remember the context of civil unrest, the highly selective nature of secondary education in Northern Ireland as well as the high levels of unemployment and socio-economic disadvantage evident amongst many schools in Belfast. Pupil choice at the secondary phase in particular is complicated by selection by aptitude (11+), geographical boundaries and religious background. It is known that there is a relationship between the concentration of socio-economically disadvantaged pupils (those eligible for free school meals and those with low attainment at entry) and general levels of pupil achievement. Contextual effects on secondary school pupils' achievement have been identified by a number of school effectiveness researchers (Goldstein, Rasbash, Yang, Woodhouse, Pan,

Nuttall & Thomas, 1993; Willms, 1986; Sammons, Thomas, Mortimore, Owen & Pennell, 1994; Sammons, Thomas & Mortimore, 1997). Inevitably, a selective educational system is likely to exaggerate such contextual effects amongst the least popular and most disadvantaged secondary schools.

7.1.1   The aim of the project

The project focused on four secondary schools (two maintained Catholic and two controlled Protestant) identified as having high levels of under achievement and their ten main contributory primary schools. The primary aim of the project was to provide additional support and resources to schools with the overall objective of accelerating an improvement in the performance and employability of school leavers by:

1. improving where appropriate the *quality of management*, teaching and learning within the school;
2. improving the *standards of literacy and numeracy* and overall standards at both primary and secondary level;
3. improving the *level of qualifications* which they achieve at school and access to further education;
4. improving *links with local industry;*
5. increasing *parental involvement*;
6. dealing with problems of *discipline* in class;
7. improving *attendance and punctuality.*

It should be noted that of these seven foci, three contain measurable pupil outcomes (2, 3 and 7) whereas two focus on school and classroom processes which influence the quality of the educational experience (1 and 6). By contrast, 4 and 5 concern aspects of links with the broader community.

7.2   The external evaluation of the project

In May 1995 the Belfast Education and Library Board (BELB) commissioned the International School Effectiveness and Improvement Centre (ISEIC) at the Institute of Education, University of London to undertake an external evaluation of the initiative. As well as an investigation of the impact of the overall project it was thought desirable to examine the experience of implementing the project in individual schools in order to identify the factors which facilitate improvement and barriers to success. The evaluation was also intended to examine the general implications of the project for school improvement projects elsewhere and to identify examples of good practice for dissemination to other schools.

Individual schools involved in the RSS initiative were required to submit action plans for approval by the Central Management Committee (CMC) demonstrating how they proposed to meet the stated aims and objectives of the initiative. This has become a common feature of school improvement initiatives on both sides of the Atlantic (Stringfield, Ross & Smith, 1996). Schools were also required to engage in self-evaluation and to collect relevant information to enable BELB to review the impact of the initiative, including the identification of a range of targets and baseline measures. A key feature of the initiative was to be focus on the use of measures of pupil achievement to establish the extent to which improvements in standards occur.

A number of commentators have pointed to the value of a case study approach to increase understanding of the processes which foster school effectiveness and positive change and provide the "rich description" of processes needed by practitioners concerned with school improvement. The National Commission on Education's (1996) *Success Against the Odds* study of 11 schools in disadvantaged areas provides a source of evidence relevant to policy makers and practitioners concerned with school improvement. Other school effectiveness research, which combined detailed qualitative case studies of both more and less effective secondary schools and departments with quantitative value added analyses of academic effectiveness at GCSE, of relevance to the evaluation of the project is provided by Sammons, Thomas and Mortimore (1997) and Smith (1996).

The results of research on the impact of School Development Planning (SDP) (MacGilchrist, Mortimore, Savage & Beresford, 1995) also has implications for the evaluation of the project. This drew particular attention to the need to examine the extent to which activities included in schools' written plans actually affect classroom practice and the extent of staff ownership of, and involvement in, preparing the plan.

The MBW RSS evaluation adopted a case study approach in considering the four secondary and ten feeder primaries involved in the BELB project. The case studies recognised both the overall aims of the initiative and the differing aims of individual schools expressed in their individual Action Plans. A variety of sources of data and evidence were considered:

- document analysis: school and authority (BELB and Department of Education) level e.g. school development plans, RSS Action Plans, school policy documents, Inspection reports;
- schools' statistics: pupil outcome data, attendance, expulsions and suspensions as well spending patterns of the additional resources;
- interviews to explore the views of key personnel: BELB advisors, principals, co-ordinators and Chairs of Governors;
- questionnaires to explore perceptions of the school: pupils/parents (Primary Year 5 and 7, Secondary Year 9 and 11) and all teachers.

This chapter cannot cover all aspects of the evaluation covered in the main evaluation report (Sammons, Taggart & Thomas, 1998) but will focus on the launch and selection of schools and 'action planning'. It will also consider the impact the initiative had on some of its stated aims: the quality of management; teaching and learning and educational standards. The evaluation was commissioned to explore the impact of an *educational initiative* and the factors which influenced its implementation and success. It does not attempt to evaluate the success of individual schools.

7.2.1   Launching the initiative

How any project is launched is important in terms of setting the tone for what is to come. The Minister's press release referred to schools "who are presently achieving no or only very poor qualifications" but did not publicly name those schools. One of the newspapers however, published names of the four secondary schools and called them "schools identified as having the highest levels of under-achievement." This high profile public naming was not well received by school staff who were mindful of their institution's reputation in the community. Clearly, the same issues have been debated elsewhere in the UK concerning the relative merits of the popularly coined 'naming and shaming' policy concerning failing schools. Public naming is seen by some to be a necessary stimulus for improvement for schools with serious weaknesses, but others believe it can exacerbate schools' difficulties, lowering staff morale, making recruitment harder and exacerbating problems due to falling rolls (Mortimore & Whitty, 1997).

The reaction of secondary principals to being included in the initiative was on the whole more negative than positive. Primary school principals saw the criteria for selection (low achievement) being unique to secondary schools with feeder primaries chosen to support the four secondary schools. The most common reaction to inclusion in the initiative in the primary sector was excitement about the additional funding. This was not however all that primary principals considered. In three schools there were concerns about work load issues. The majority of principals disliked the title of the initiative because it suggested that their standards were too low.

For BELB the choice of the secondaries was an acknowledgement that these schools were "faced with problems" but, given the publicity, being included on the initiative brought the public stigma of "failing". All of the four secondaries knew they scored poorly in terms of examination performance but staff would not necessarily have described the school or pupils as failures. It should be noted there was also a feeling amongst colleagues in non-selected schools with high levels of disadvantage that failure was being rewarded and that more able principals were being penalised for "being effective managers who run successful schools." It is important to recognise that the RSS schools had the advantage of considerable additional resources and external support for school improvement as a result of the project. Nevertheless, the demands for accountability and the requirements for successful improvement strategies are not easily reconciled as experience elsewhere in the UK also demonstrates.

7.3   Action planning: developing action plans

One of the key features of the MBW RSS was that selected schools had to submit for approval an "action plan" focusing on a whole school approach to meeting the objectives of the initiative. In many respects the plan was intended to be the school's blueprint for improvement. As the initiative was to extend over three years, it was considered important that schools build in improvements to their structure and working arrangements so they could maintain and further improve standards within the normal funding arrangements after the conclusion of the project. Schools also had to seek approval from their Board of Governors who were asked to give undertakings to assist in the monitoring and evaluation of the programme. The action plans were designed to broadly detail the problems which schools wished to tackle and the methods they would use to do so. All action plans had to be agreed upon and any additional funding was to be determined on their judgements of the merits of each individual proposal.

The action plans were intended to be specific to the needs of individual schools. Nonetheless, the programme was expected to include some or all of the following elements:
- developing effective management at all levels within the school;
- the development of literacy/numeracy across the school;
- raising expectations amongst pupils, parents and teachers;
- increasing educational achievements;
- involving parents in the support of schools provision;
- improving attendance and punctuality;
- increasing and improving links between the school and employers;
- developing appropriate certifiable vocational courses;
- developing and implementing effective procedures to monitor and evaluate the curricular and organisational feature of the school;
- preparing and planning programmes.

The very short time in which schools were asked to formulate and present plans, resulted in action plans being submitted which would be problematic when it came to implementation. The most commonly reported problem in the first action plans was their tendency to be over-ambitious. It was believed, with hindsight, that schools planned to cover too much in too short a time scale. Where some schools identified strategies for improvements in all of the nine key areas, advisors had serious doubts about the extent to which the schools could deliver all the improvements they were aiming for simultaneously.

The analysis of schools' action plans showed considerable variation and little consistency in how an action plan could be approached in the first year. The evaluation mechanisms in particular showed wide variations and targets were often non-specific. It is clear that at the start of the MBW RSS no consistent approach was adopted for action planning. This had important consequences for the later evaluation of the impact of RSS (for details see Sammons, Taggart & Thomas, 1998).

7.3.1   Implementing action plans

A number of factors helped coordinators implement their action plans. The most significant factors were:
- having the co-operation of staff;

- linking the school's staff development programme to the plan;
- the monitoring and evaluation of target setting;
- being given the opportunity to keep staff informed of developments through regular meetings;
- work at the very beginning of the project which had an immediate impact on the school e.g. the redecoration and re-equipping of rooms for library and reading club, the introduction of new books and resources etc.;
- providing in-service courses for staff.

Two groups of factors mitigated against co-ordinators implementing their action plans. The first were concerned with staffing and personnel issues and the second with the central organisation of the initiative. Staffing issues included:
- staff with entrenched attitudes;
- poor departmental leadership;
- not having the right people in post at the right time;
- the co-ordinator feeling isolated.

Central organizations issues included:
- the time scale for developments being too rushed at the outset;
- the time scale between the submission of the action plan and the arrival of funding being too long;
- complications in the system for ordering resources;
- not enough support for staff development.

It was recognised that the quality of the first action plans were often poor, given the short time scale and lack of expertise and experience in writing plans which existed in school. The poor quality of the initial action plan coupled with the emphasis on resources and the budget cycle, sent out mixed messages to schools. Schools were advised not to focus on financial matters but then felt pressured to spend large amounts of money very quickly without time for adequate reflection and planning in order to fit in with the demands of the financial year. This meant that the initiative was perceived, in the early stages (possibly the first six to nine months) as being "resources driven." In response to these difficulties the project's Education Advisors began to look at other school improvement initiatives, other school improvement networks and to recognise that new strategies needed to be put in place if the initiative was to be refocused on its underlying aims. This led to a conference with a keynote speaker who focused on questions of urban disadvantage and school effectiveness and improvement. There was a particular stress on:

- the conditions which foster academic achievement;
- reward based control systems with reference to areas of consistency, cohesion and constancy; and
- the role of the head teacher.

In relation to school development in Raising School Standards the emphasis was on:
- the means of achieving outcomes;
- organizational change and the change culture;
- focusing on teaching and learning; and
- the development cycle.

After this keynote conference delegates were asked to get involved in workshop sessions which explore practical steps towards improvement. They also had the opportunity to analyse a practical example of an action plan teasing out from this example the key factors which could assist their own school improvement. The conference was reported to have helped principals, co-ordinators and advisors identify the important small steps which would help lead towards improvement.

Using action planning as an "effective management tool" was also seen to have enabled advisors to work with principals and co-ordinators "on monitoring and evaluation and how you tie in finances and resources to your objectives." Whereas schools were thought to be very weak at this before the initiative, subsequent training and guidance was felt to have done much to help them to improve this area of their work significantly. The approach to action planning taken after the first year appeared to help principals and co-ordinators narrow the focus of their action plans and make their improvement programme much more realistic and manageable. Advisors encouraged schools to focus on one or two of their key objectives so that change could go beyond the cosmetic.

7.3.2   Schools' internal evaluation of the impact and baseline measures

The evaluation mechanisms used to determine the success or otherwise of the initiative were inextricably linked to the schools' action plans. The schools' internal capacity to evaluate the initiative improved markedly after the first year as schools became more adept at producing annual action plans which showed a greater focus on the aims of RSS. Although schools were given suggestions as to the type of monitoring and evaluating procedures they could engage for the initiative, this was not made a requirement at the start of the project. Advisors reported that some baseline measures were in place for evaluation purposes but this was inconsistent across the fourteen schools and practice in this area showed a great deal of variation. The mechanisms for evaluation identified ranged from some quantifiable data such as monitoring statistics, to more subjective perceptions of "how things were going". The establishment of baseline measures can assist in the monitoring, evaluation and management of any new development. They can be used as the basis for the development of 'success criteria' and enable issues of impact to be examined critically and objectively for example, baseline measures have been used to provide value-added feedback to primary schools (e.g. Sammons & Smees, 1998; Yang & Goldstein, 1996) and at secondary level (Thomas & Mortimore, 1996). There use has been demonstrated by the Improving School Effectiveness project in Scotland (Robertson & Sammons, 1997) as part of a research initiative and development explicitly designed to link school effectiveness and improvement approaches. Although baseline measures were advocated at the start of MBW RSS (in 1994), schools did not appear to have received clear guidance on which to use and there was little consistency in approach across the schools as a consequence.

Clearly some areas of the initiative are much easier to evaluate than others. In the core curriculum subjects of English language and mathematics pupil progress can, and was, in some schools explored by analysing gains in pupils' standardised test scores although not all schools adopted this strategy. An overall lack of data on baseline measures appears to have seriously weakened most schools' ability to take meaningful measures. As noted by OFSTED (1994/5), "the absence of success criteria in some initiatives makes it difficult for participants to know and understand the impact of their work and means that they depend on subjective judgement or anecdotal evidence, neither of which are likely to be accurate about the past or a good guide to future planning" (36). The first year of the MBW initiative clearly reveals this as a problem in many schools.

7.4   The impact of MBW: Raising School Standards

The primary purpose of the RSS initiative was to tackle under-achievement and by considering 'pupil outcomes,' to assist teachers to raise standards and improve the quality of pupils' educational experience. When considering 'impact' the external evaluation addressed not only 'pupil outcomes' but also changes in other areas identified in the original proposal as important to the project (management, the quality of teaching and learning and educational standards in literacy and numeracy).

7.4.1   The extent of the impact

For some areas of the initiative it has been possible to demonstrate clearly, on standardised measures, the impact of the initiative in the short term. These tend to be curriculum areas that have established assessment practices such as reading/maths tests. For other areas the evidence is more subjective reflecting participants' perceptions and in some instances may not be calculable for several years to come. Given the length of the initiative and the scope of the external evaluation, the evaluation could only speculate on any long terms effect RSS might have.

7.4.2   The impact on management

The importance of leadership and management which can help to enhance a shared vision for improvement has been highlighted in much of the literature on school effectiveness and school improvement both in Britain and internationally (Gray, 1990; Stoll & Fink, 1996; Teddlie & Stringfield, 1993; Hallinger, 1996; Sammons, Thomas & Mortimore 1997). The starting point for exploring the impact which RSS had on management was the analysis of the teachers' questionnaire which sought views on the extent to which teachers (in all fourteen schools), thought their school had improved over the period of the initiative for a range of management indicators. This was compared with the extent to which teachers thought RSS had influenced these improvements. The three areas were the initiative was perceived to have had the most impact were school development planning, vision development, staff development and communication.

Developing a vision of what the school is trying to achieve
The vast majority of teachers thought their school's vision had improved, by far the highest rating for any item. Over a third thought RSS had had a significant effect on this change. Teachers wrote that RSS had helped develop vision by making staff more aware of the direction the school is moving because

the aims of the school had been made clear. Teachers had been set clear goals and had a firmer notion of what to achieve.

School development planning

Nearly three quarters of teachers thought school development planning had improved during the period of RSS with 40 per cent crediting RSS as strongly instrumental in this. Teachers reported that the emphasis on planning (action plans) had given direction for overall school development which had also contributed to the development of schemes of work.

Improvements in the staff development programme

Improvements in this area were also seen as significant. In written comments the schools' staff development programme was perceived to have been the area most affected by RSS. Whilst RSS enabled teachers to update their skills on in-service courses outside of school, teachers thought the opportunities for intra-school staff development of greater importance. In conclusion RSS was said to have enabled teachers to work together in the classroom and learn from each other in a non-judgemental situation which enabled staff members to share experiences and support each other. This perception concurs with the observations made on the importance of staff development programmes for school improvement by Barber and Dann (1996, 22) who concluded that: "a successful urban school requires a learning staff". In all, for seven schools improvement in the staff development programme was reported by more than two thirds of teachers. An important consideration in staff development was that the local authority advisors where prepared to work in classrooms and model good practice for teachers involved in the project. The importance of this 'coaching' method is explored in Showers (1982). In a comparison of school improvement projects on both sides of the Atlantic, Joyce, Calhoun and Hopkins (1999) identifies good staff development as a key factor in successful school improvement initiatives.

Improved communication

Overall, improvements in communication between the Senior Management Team (SMT) and the staff was reported by over two thirds of teachers. However this was not always seen to have been as a direct result of RSS. The difference between those teachers who thought RSS had no effect on this and those who thought it had a significant effect was small. The general benefits reported in this area were improved communications, staff being kept informed and made to feel part of a school team. By contrast, RSS was not perceived to have led to improvements in the area of communication in schools where the project was seen as a primarily senior management initiative, little shared with the rest of the staff.

The two areas of management in which RSS would appear to have had a relatively lower impact were staff morale and staff involvement in financial decisions.

Staff morale

Just over half the teachers in the survey thought staff morale had improved over the period of RSS. In some cases this was accounted for by factors outside of the scope of RSS. Where RSS was thought to have had no influence on morale, teachers reported difficulties in coping with the pace and nature of change brought about by initiative type developments. Where RSS was thought to improve teacher morale this appeared to be as a direct result of additional resourcing. The morale of staff working in disadvantaged urban areas is an extremely important issue which need to be taken into consideration when discussing school improvement. For example, Maden and Hillman (1996, 335) state that "schools serving disadvantaged and frequently troubled areas, an abundance of energy and commitment is needed just to tread water." Schools in such areas often find it hard to recruit and attract staff and the stigma of being associated with a 'failing school', in raw league table terms may exacerbate recruitment difficulties.

Staff having a 'say' in financial decisions

The questionnaire asked teachers nine questions about management issues in their school. Teachers reported the least improvement in this area and over half felt RSS had not affected their involvement in financial decisions. By contrast less than one in ten of teachers believed RSS to have had a significant effect on this area. Whilst principals and SMT may have been increasingly willing to consult with teachers on other matters there still appears to be a reluctance in most schools to include teachers in financial decision making. This lack of involvement in financial decisions was a theme mentioned in Stringfield, Ross and Smith (1996) when reporting on experiences of American teachers engaged in school improvement initiatives. They argue that "school staff lacked the ability to effectively use power granted in these areas because they had not been trained to do so" (310).

7.4.3   The impact on teaching and learning

The MBW RSS set out to tackle under-achievement and raise school standards. Any attempt to improve pupil outcomes needs to focus on the quality of teaching and learning (Creemers, 1994; Slavin, 1996). The teacher questionnaire contained a number of items which attempt to address the impact on classroom practice. The area were the initiative appears to have the most impact are curriculum development, teacher collaboration, and the quality of teaching.

Curriculum development
Curriculum development was seen to have improved by nearly 90 per cent of teachers and over half felt RSS had played a significant part in this. Teachers reported that RSS enabled curriculum development to have a greater time allocation which resulted in greater opportunity for curriculum development and the ability to target certain areas of the curriculum. Developments were reported at both institutional level because RSS facilitated curriculum panels to function and allowed us to maximise the curriculum/subject expertise present on the staff and at an individual level where teachers have been free to follow up discussions and develop their ideas on curriculum delivery. Curriculum development in this context for many teachers was regarded as synonymous with staff development. Where improvements in teaching and learning occurred, particularly in the areas of language and maths, teachers reported that the following had brought about change:
- in-service training opportunities;
- updating policies and the introduction of new programmes; and
- practical in-service training which included demonstration lessons by Advisors.

The majority of teachers in all schools thought there had been improvements in curriculum development in their school over the last three years.

Teacher collaboration and resourcing lessons
Over 80 per cent of teachers reported being drawn together in schools to work on various aspects of RSS. The result of this increased collaboration appears to have been more collegiate planning and, in some cases, the development of new schemes of work. A common comment from teachers was that there were better schemes of work and better forward planning which led to greater improvements in development of the curriculum. This emphasis on

planning has felt to have led to great improvements in the quality of teaching and learning within many of the schools. As well as reporting greater collegiality in planning the content of lessons, RSS appears to have encouraged more thought to be given to resourcing activities. Where this happened teachers reported that the additional resources offered to the schools as a result of RSS made an important difference to the quality of teaching and learning in their classrooms.

The quality of teaching generally and teachers' focus on learning

Teachers were asked about both the quality of teaching and about teachers' focus on learning. Teachers reported that there had been improvements in both areas. Over a third indicated a significant effect of RSS on the quality and on the focus of teaching and learning. The comments teachers made split them into three distinct sub-categories. The largest group were teachers who thought the initiative had enabled them to consider the *learning* taking place in their own classrooms: "emphasis now on learning rather than teaching" and "teachers are encouraged to focus on pupils' learning and completion of tasks." The second, slightly smaller group were teachers who considered both *teaching and learning*, "RSS has allowed teachers to focus on their teaching and the children's learning and make significant changes." These teachers indicated an added depth to their work as a result of RSS, "the staff have come together to look at all aspects of teaching and learning more thoroughly." The third group, equal in size to the second group, placed the emphasis on *teaching* which was being done more thoughtfully: "teachers are putting more thought now into what they are teaching and standing back more and thinking about the best way to put over a topic" and "teachers more aware of what they deliver."

Where changes in teaching and learning were reported teachers often put this down to the development of their own expertise arising from extra time to examine and develop their classroom practice. Views about improvements in the quality of teaching over the last three years were generally positive.

The areas in which the initiative appeared to have had the least impact were feedback, and consistency.

The feedback given to pupils about their work

The importance of appropriate teacher feedback on work has been identified in reviews of school effectiveness research (Sammons, Hillman & Mortimore,

1995). Research by Tunstall and Gipps (1996) has likewise highlighted this aspect. Although feedback was not targeted specifically by RSS it is an important aspect of pedagogy. Fifty-nine percent of teachers reported improvements in teacher feedback to pupils about their work, although relatively few attributed RSS as having a significant effect. It is possible that teachers did not regard this area as important in determining the quality of teaching and learning and /or that the focus of RSS development work did not give a priority to this area.

Consistency in regular setting and marking homework

Just under half of teachers thought that this area had improved in the last three years and only a small minority thought RSS had had a significant impact. There is a strong tradition in Northern Ireland schools (both primary and secondary) of homework being set on a regular basis. Whilst there has been little directly reported differences in the teachers attitudes to homework, there is evidence to suggest that parental attitudes have improved, with parents being more involved in 'learning at home schemes', especially in reading. The action plans do not suggest that schools saw homework as a focus of RSS and the teachers' responses support this conclusion.

7.4.4   The impact on educational standards

The MBW RSS initiative was specifically instituted to improve levels of pupil performance in reading and numeracy in schools identified as under-achieving. Changes in pupil performance and access to Higher Education and Further Education was evaluated from questionnaire, interview and schools' performance data.

The four secondary schools' examination results were analysed to establish whether any trends could be discerned over the four year period 1993/4 - 1996/7. Secondary schools tended to focus their efforts on entry cohorts (aged 11-12 years old) giving priority to literacy and numeracy. It is therefore too early to trace any impact on these pupils' performance at GCSE. Nevertheless, it is disappointing that in terms of published examination results, there was limited evidence of any improvement. None of the secondary schools showed any noticeable increase in the percentage of pupils gaining 5 GCSE passes (Grade A-C). In terms of the measure 1 - 4 GCSE (Grade A - C) there was also no evidence of improvement. Using a broader measure (% 5 GCSE passes A-G) there was slight evidence of improvement for two schools for the percentage gaining five A - G passes. In terms of no passes at GCSE or other examinations there was also some evidence of improvement. There was also evidence of improvement in the percentage of pupils obtaining one or more passes in non-GCSE examinations for three out of the four secondary schools schools.

The majority of teachers (over three quarters) in 12 schools believed reading and educational standards had improved over the last three years. The focus on reading is common to many school improvement project particularly in the USA (Joyce, Calhoun & Hopkins, 1999, 94) where it is reported that "eight million students now enrolled in Grades 6 to 12 do not have the level of literacy to profit fully from current secondary education programs." For numeracy a similar trend was evident although in two secondaries and one primary less than two thirds thought standards had improved. An analysis of schools' action plans indicated that, during the first year of the initiative, all schools focused on reading with numeracy receiving more attention in the second or third year. With respect to target setting for pupils, teachers' views again varied at the school level. Although the majority reported improvement the range was from 11 to 100 per cent. Only in three schools, however, did over half the teachers attribute a significant effect to RSS (one secondary and two primaries).

Teachers generally had very positive views about the extent of improvement over the last three years. Nonetheless, only a minority attributed a significant effect to RSS. The interview data, however, indicated unanimous agreement between principals, co-ordinators, and BELB Advisors that RSS had improved standards in reading and general numeracy across all schools. Several reasons were given for the improvements in reading which included the introduction of:
- additional reading time on the timetable;
- Reading Recovery programmes;
- new approaches to reading such as 'paired/peer reading' and 'Reading Clubs';
- the purchase of new published commercial schemes;
- new library facilities and reading/library clubs;
- a special focus on one curriculum area by all staff leading to consistency;
- new equipment and book provision (which was reported to have motivated children who were "displaying enthusiasm for and enjoyment of reading" unseen before RSS).

Numeracy was seen to have benefited mainly because of the additional resources provided by RSS. This was said to have affected the work of teachers by extending their teaching repertoire, most notably in the areas of practical work. The extra equipment acquired enabled classes to benefit from practical activities. Test scores were also cited in support of the assertions of improvement in reading and numeracy. Whilst improvements were noted in connection with both of these core curriculum areas the emphasis in the first year of RSS for many schools was literacy with the focus on numeracy coming later, consequently test score evidence for numeracy was less widely available.

The evidence from school effectiveness research that reading performance is a crucial component of later academic performance (Sammons, Hillman & Mortimore, 1995) also indicates that socio-economic disadvantage has a greater influence on attainment and progress in this area than in mathematics (Mortimore, Sammons, Stoll, Lewish & Ecob, 1988; Brandsma & Knuver, 1989; Sammons, 1993). Given its importance for access to the curriculum, the focus on reading during the project's first year can be seen as an appropriate top priority for schools.

Where improvements were reported in the area of outcomes teachers said RSS had helped their school give greater consideration to measured standards because of better tracking systems for monitoring progress. Many principals and co-ordinators indicated that RSS had made them more aware of pupil outcomes and performance scores and the importance of monitoring these.

The MBW RSS schools varied in the approaches they used to monitor the impact of their initiatives on pupils' educational outcomes. Schools varied in their specific objectives, the pupils or year group targeted and the kinds of evidence collected. Because of this it is not possible to make systematic comparisons across schools of, for example, rates of pupil progress over the period of the initiative. By contrast, the expanded RSS has used a value added framework, with common baseline and post-test measures to enable such analyses to occur.

Whilst teachers thought there had been general improvements in many areas they appeared reluctant to ascribe this as a significant effect of RSS because the programme has not really been in long enough to calculate improvements to standards through academic results. Principals were able to cite improvements in specific areas but were cautious in making claims for sustained improvements. Given the emphasis paid to the intake year (grade 6) in secondary schools' action plans it is clear that a three year evaluation cannot pick up any longer term effects. Follow up at age 16 would be needed to examine improvements in public examination and further education participation.

Teachers, principals and co-ordinators identified areas outside of those addressed by the questionnaire which they said had contributed to improvements in educational standards. These were:

- *special needs:* having additional teaching help in the form of a special needs or remedial teacher, as a result of RSS was specifically reported as factor in raising standards in several schools especially in the area of remedial mathematics;
- *staff development:* teachers considered that standards had been raised by teachers updating their skills through in-service, "practical in-service training which included demonstrations by Advisors has helped in the teaching of reading and practical mathematics" and "money made available to release staff for up-to-date training in new materials and new approaches" contributed to raising standards;
- *consistency:* where policies and targets were being applied consistently across a school, teachers reported improvements in standards. Teachers also appreciated having "clearer goals so that each teacher should know what to do." The setting up of curriculum panels was thought to have aided this process;
- *smaller classes:* a small group of teachers (11 from 6 schools) commented that standards had risen specifically because RSS enabled them have smaller teaching groups.

7.5   Conclusions and implications for other standards initiatives

In evaluating the overall achievements of the MBW RSS initiative, it is crucial to recognise the nature of the particular socio-economic and political context in which the 14 project schools are set. If the challenges for education in the inner city are many, then the particular problems which face Belfast's schools can only multiply these challenges. The initiative sought to tackle under-achievement in schools whose communities have had a long history of socio-economic disadvantage and in a highly selective system with a history of civil unrest. This initiative recognised that improvements do not necessarily come cheap. Nonetheless, the true benefits of the MBW RSS may not as yet be fully apparent. It must be recognised that in school improvement there are "no quick fixes" (Gray & Wilcox, 1995; Stoll & Myers, 1997; Joyce, Calhoun & Hopkins, 1999) and that the seed sown today may take some time to come to harvest. Given the rushed and problematic start to the project in 1994 much of the first year was taken up with planning and in some schools it was not until the second year that developments really took off. Moreover, the focus on younger age groups in the secondary schools means that any long term impact on public examination results and higher education/further education participation will not be picked up until 1999 onwards.

7.5.1   Management

The initiative was conceived with clear and ambitious aims and addressed a real need to focus on the difficulties faced by under-performing secondary schools in particular. Given the nature of educational funding it was right that the opportunity to use significant central funding for the development of schools was taken. However, the lack of a realistic planning period to consider the nature of school improvement and the question of the most appropriate methods for tackling under-achievement meant that the start of the project was problematic. In an Authority with a history of innovative developmental projects an audit of past strengths and weaknesses associated with both management and development would have greatly assisted the MBW RSS in the initial phases.

The significant workload issues associated with managing the initiative were overcome and by the middle of year two, as the initiative progressed, the management became firmer. Personnel changes which occurred during the period of the work were dealt with effectively. There were many benefits for non-school based personnel from working on the RSS initiative. Involvement in the initiative has resulted in a greater understanding of the issues associated with school development and improvement which should be of great benefit for future projects. Much of the learning which has occurred on this initiative is already assisting in planning and developing the on-going expanded RSS which began in 1995.

7.5.2   Launching an initiative and selection of schools

The public naming of schools by newspapers as "under-achievers" soured the launch of the initiative in the secondary schools because schools appeared unprepared for the publicity this attracted. There is a real need to ensure that the approaches made to schools to become involved in such a wide ranging initiative are uniform. Many of the problems associated with the launch were overcome, but this delayed commitment to the project in some schools. The relative merits of so called 'naming and shaming' approach to school improvement remains of course controversial elsewhere in the UK (Mortimore & Whitty, 1997). The experience of this policy in the USA prompted Joyce, Calhoun and Hopkins (1999, 223) to underline the fact that "schools need help rather than admonition." The selection of schools in both phases was controversial. Despite clear criteria there was misunderstanding and suspicion from both schools which were included as well as those excluded. These problems were also overcome but made for a difficult period at the beginning of the initiative and meant that progress in the first year was limited in many ways.

7.5.3   Action planning

The schools involved in MBW RSS were not familiar in the initial stages of the initiative with the process of action planning. Schools struggled with trying to produce an action plan without, in many cases, sufficient training and support to tackle this complex operation. Where insufficient expertise was coupled with a time-table, perceived as unrealistic, and what appeared to be arbitrary decisions made about funding, many principals in particularly, became jaded with the action planning process. Within the first year it was recognised that action planning was a difficult issue for schools and this was addressed directly. From this point onward the initiative gained more credibility both in and outside schools and greater progress was evident subsequently. Schools and BELB staff made great gains in planning, targeting and implementing action plans during the second year and the enhanced capacity to plan and manage change in schools was perceived by many involved to be an enduring legacy of the initiative.

7.5.4   Monitoring and evaluation

Whilst the procedures put in place for monitoring the initiative were adequate these could have been much improved if those involved with making the system work had been involved in the planning phase. In this way a more realistic time-table could have been set and the duplication of information avoided. Although monitoring was consistent outside schools, opportunities for evaluating the progress made in schools was often hampered by a lack of comparable baseline measures. Where such measures were in place they tended to be standardised tests. The approach schools took to evaluation improved markedly as the initiative progressed, this appeared to be related to the ability to set clearer and more realistic targets in action plans. Because schools focused on different groups of pupils and did not adopt a common approach to baseline assessment of pupils and later follow up testing, it has not been possible to make direct comparisons of rates of progress across all schools.

In some schools evidence of considerable short term gains in pupils' reading ages was submitted. If sustained in future years these gains should have a very beneficial impact on these pupils' subsequent progress at school and therefore on their long term educational outcomes. The adverse impact of poor literacy skills on young people's future ability to function in various aspects of adult life has been well documented. Although the action plans in most schools emphasised reading, numeracy received much less attention in the first year. However, by the second and third year many schools had started baseline screening in mathematics and there was some evidence of attempts to transfer the success and achievements in focusing on reading into this core curriculum area.

7.5.5   Time scale

Bollen (1989) argued that school improvement is a process and not an event, and that time is a major factor that cannot be manipulated without a strong influence on the quality of the process. He noted that innovation is often set on a three year scheme which can be too short for institutional change to be embedded or for the impact of change to be fully assessed. This would bear out the findings from a number of studies in the USA (Stringfield, Ross & Smith, 1996) where with short time frames, "it is premature to expect significant changes in student outcomes" (290). A five year programme may be more appropriate and it is likely that a follow up of pupil achievement, attendance and behaviour over the next two years by BELB would provide valuable evidence of any longer term gains in the 14 schools involved in the MBW RSS experience.

7.5.6   The impact on the aims of the initiative

The evaluation data used to examine the initiative's impact were collected during the second and third year of the initiative (October 1996 - July 1997). Development continued in schools after the data collection period and schools were encouraged to engage in planning for continued improvements after the end of the initiative (exit planning). Joyce, Calhoun and Hopkins, (1999) identify four conditions which have been seen to be present in successful school improvement projects: a reasonable level of agreement by the staff and parents: an adequate amount of staff development to develop the necessary knowledge and skill; a related organisation of the faculty (staff) so that it can work together to achieve implementation; and, a focus on the learning environment. The MBW RSS had all of these conditions to a greater or lesser extent. There is clear evidence that the majority of schools involved in this initiative made improvements related to the main aims of the initiative. Nonetheless, there was variation between schools and within schools in the extent to which the 'school improvement' message had become embedded in practice. In schools that used the initiative to foster a whole school approach to developments, significant improvements were made, often transforming areas of practice. In schools where the principals and co-ordinator were less successful in involving all of the staff, little other than the benefits of three years of additional resources may be the legacy of the project. Although schools were able to produce information on attendance, suspensions, exclusions and other statistical measures, there was only limited evidence in their paperwork to suggest that this information was interrogated or analysed to set targets and aid the development of consistency in policy and practice. The encouragement of principals and their staff to consider *critically* how the MBW RSS experience relates to their own institution and staff and their approach to school development may enable others to learn from the initiative's legacy.

Impact - management

One of the major success of MBW RSS was that it broadened the focus of many other initiatives that had gone before to include a 'whole school approach' to development. It provided a vehicle for staff to articulate a 'vision' for the school and to identify the steps that need to be taken if the 'vision' is to be turned into a reality. It appeared that many senior management teams were able to focus specifically on teaching and learning shifting the emphasis in some schools away from a management dominated by administration. There was evidence to suggest that the improvements in staff development programmes, linked to better long, medium and short term planning will foster further developments in the future. Clearly the stability of staff who received additional help and the extent to which they are able to share this with other colleagues will also have an impact on the extent of long term cultural change in individual schools.

Impact - teaching and learning

The MBW RSS enabled schools to develop more systematic and relevant staff development programmes which have fed into curriculum improvements. It provided time for key personnel to consider both subject knowledge and approaches to pedagogy. Linked to these developments has been a greater emphasis on collegiate planning which has had practical classroom application. The quality of lesson material has been improved and the awareness of the importance of a more appropriate curriculum, particularly at secondary level. It was clear that improvements in this area have been made in most schools. Nonetheless, it must be stressed that some (particularly the secondary schools which were operating from very low baselines) still have considerable scope for further improvements. The focus RSS gave to teaching and its links with learning, coupled with an emphasis on measuring pupil outcomes could be extremely important to future developments in many of these schools.

The MBW project has provided a considerable attempt to develop the improvement capacity of schools. There is evidence (Bollen, 1989; Hopkins, Ainscow & West, 1994), that school improvement is related as much to the quality of the policy (raising standards) as the improvement capacity of schools. The school improvement literature suggests that, given greater school autonomy in many systems in recent years, the concept of the thinking (self-reflecting) school has to be promoted. The evaluation suggests that the MBW RSS initiative did indeed stimulate reflection for staff, both individuals, and at an institutional level. It sharpened the measurement, monitoring, target setting and evaluating capacity of schools through the action planning process. In several schools significant curriculum development appears to have occurred which should have benefits over the longer term.

Impact - educational standards

Without standard baselines measures it is difficult to be precise about improvements made across the board on this initiative. There is evidence to suggest that for individual children in some schools there have been considerable gains from being involved in RSS, especially for poor readers. The evidence for gains in mathematics however, is weaker. How much these short term gains can be sustained is difficult to predict, but it appears that, particularly at secondary school level, pupils are now better able to access the national curriculum as a result of their experiences. It is too early to make assertions about the impact of RSS on public examination results and access to higher and further education. Improvements in primary pupil outcomes should mean higher baselines for grade 6 on entry into secondary schools. Given knowledge of the links between reading performance at age 7 and public examination grades improvements in primary pupils' reading ages are likely to have a positive impact on their later examination results and employment prospects (Sammons, 1995). In the long term the improvement of primary pupils' skills would do much to reduce the significant challenges faced by certain secondary schools where (as illustrated by some of the schools) over 60 per cent of children may be two years or more below their chronological age in reading.

The considerable difficulties faced by so called 'under-achieving' schools especially at the secondary level have been highlighted by inspectors and the media during the 1990s. The research evidence suggests that turning round such schools is extremely difficult (Gray & Wilcox, 1995). The culture of such schools may be fragmented and focus on teaching and learning weak (Reynolds, 1996). The MBW RSS initiative provided a major opportunity for schools to re-evaluate their approaches and a strong impetus for curriculum development. In most schools the capacity for planning was much improved during the three years and clear strategies for regular monitoring of reading was made in most schools, although the impact on numeracy to date appears weaker. There was some evidence of greater staff cohesion and clearer goals setting, although problems in senior management remain in some schools. The positive impact of a change of principal was a noticeable feature in some schools and attributed with a greater impact in effecting improvements than the RSS initiative by teachers in these schools. The adverse impact of amalgamation on a school's ability to focus on the RSS initiative is also a relevant factor.

There is no doubt that the four secondary schools at the heart of the MBW RSS initiative continue to face considerable challenges in low levels of literacy and numeracy of their intake. It is likely that this applies to several other secondaries serving socio-economically disadvantaged communities in Belfast. Ways of effectively targeting resources at the pupil level (without rewarding failing schools) to provide specific programmes to promote rapid gains to enable these pupils to access the national curriculum may be needed if standards are to be raised in the long term. There may even be a case for temporary disapplication of the full national curriculum requirements in such schools to ensure a focus on basic skills for those with measured performance two or more years behind their chronological age. Intensive holiday clubs prior to secondary transfer may also be appropriate for pupils below a certain level although it is clear that raising achievement in the basic skills at the primary level is crucial. A number of RSS primaries had some success in these areas and ways of maintaining this emphasis and spreading good practice should be explored.

The MBW RSS initiative provides an important example of a school improvement initiative which had very clear and laudable aims focusing on promoting pupil outcomes and which combined considerable financial support with external advice and guidance in seeking to develop participating schools' capacity to improve. It thus attempted to integrate both a 'top down', external approach to improvement with the encouragement of 'bottom up' strategies developed within individual schools. The majority of those involved valued the opportunities the initiative provided and believed that much was learnt from the MBW RSS experience. As with any initiative, there were areas of success and aspects where less progress was made than anticipated. Schools developed their capacity to plan, monitor and evaluate school improvement, and the evidence suggests that the quality of teaching and learning was improved in many cases. Nonetheless, significant challenges remained in several schools, especially at the secondary level. Some positive effects on pupils' reading were identified, and attempts to transfer this to mathematics were being made. Behaviour, discipline and attendance remained areas of concern especially for the secondaries, although modest improvements in attendance were found in most schools. On the whole, secondary schools faced greater challenges and experienced more difficulties in implementing their improvement strategies than their feeder primaries. Similar results were reported by Stringfield, Ross and Smith (1996) in their analysis of school restructuring in the US context.

As yet the long term benefits of the MBW RSS are hard to judge, given the three year time scale. There is evidence that the experience of the project's first year provided a helpful input into the planning process for the expanded RSS province wide (Thomas & Sammons, 1996). A further follow up of pupil cohorts which were targeted in schools' action plans at Key Stages and in terms of public examinations and post-school destinations would be valuable to explore this issue in subsequent years.

In the U.K. current work is attempting to develop ways of contexualizing school performance and setting results in context to facilitate its policy of target setting and national strategies to raise standards. Moreover, the recently announced policy relating to Education Action Zones bears strong similarities to the strategy adopted in the MBW RSS initiative by focusing on low attaining secondary schools serving highly disadvantaged intakes and selected feeder primaries. The evaluation this chapter is based on (Sammons, Taggart & Thomas, 1998) may therefore have implications which extend beyond the particular context of the 14 Belfast schools involved.

7.6   References

Barber, M., & Dann, R. (Eds.). (1996). *Raising educational standards in the inner city. Practical initiatives in action.* London: Cassell.

Brandsma, H.P., & Knuver, J.W.M. (1989). Effects of school classroom characteristics on pupil progress in language and arithmetic. *International Journal of Educational Research, special issue Developments in School Effectiveness Research*, 13(7), 777 -788.

Bollen, R. (1989). *School improvement: A dutch case in international perspective.* Leuven/Amersfoort:Acco.

Creemers, B.P.M. (1994). *The effective classroom.* London: Cassell.

DfEE (1998). *Numeracy matters: The preliminary report of the numeracy task force* (published for consultation). London: DfEE.

Goldstein, H., Rasbash, J., Yang, M., Woodhouse, G., Pan, H., Nuttall, D., & Thomas, S. (1993). A multilevel analysis of school examination results. *Oxford Review of Education*, 19(4), 425 – 433.

Gray, J. (1990). The quality of schooling: Frameworks for judgement. *British Journal of Educational Studies*, 38(3), 204 – 223.

Gray, J., & Wilcox, B. (Eds.). (1995). *Good school bad school: Evaluating performance and encouraging improvement.* Buckingham: OUP.

Hallinger, P. (1996). *The principal's role in school effectiveness: an assessment of substantive findings, 1980 - 1995.* Paper presented at the Annual Meeting of the Research Association, New York.

Hopkins, D., Ainscow, M., & West, M. (1994). *School improvement in an era of change.* London: Cassell.

Joyce. B., Calhoun, E., & Hopkins, D. (1999). *The new structure of school improvement. inquiring schools and achieving students.* Buckingham: Open University Press.

MacGilchrist, B., Mortimore, P., Savage, J., & Beresford, C. (1995). *Planning matters. The impact of development planning in primary schools.* London: Paul Chapman.

Maden, M., & Hillman, J.(1996). Lessons in success. In National Commission on Education, *Success against the odds: Effective schools in disadvantaged areas* (pp. 312-363). London: Routledge.

Mortimore, P., Sammons, P., Stoll, L., Lewish, D., & Ecob, R. (1988). *School matters: The junior years.* Somerset: Open Books (Reprinted in 1994 by Paul Chapman, London).

Mortimore, P., & Whitty, G. (1997). *Can school improvement overcome the effects of disadvantage?* University of London: Institute of Education.

Myers, K. (Ed.). (1995). *School improvement in practice: Accounts from the school made a difference project.* London: Falmer Press.

National Commission on Education (1996). *Success against the odds: Effective schools in disadvantaged areas.* London: Routledge.

Office for Standards in Education (OFSTED). (1994/5). *Inspection Quality.* London: HMSO.

Reynolds, D. (1992). School effectiveness and school improvement in the 1990s. In D. Reynolds & P. Cuttance (Eds.), *School Effectiveness.* London: Cassell.

Reynolds, D. (1996). Turning around ineffective schools: some evidence and some speculations. In J. Gray, D. Reynolds, C. Fitz-Gibbon & D. Jesson (Eds.), *Merging traditions* (pp. 150-164). London: Cassell.

Robertson, P., & Sammons, P. (1997). *Improving school effectiveness: A project in progress.* Paper presented at the Tenth International Congress for School Effectiveness and Improvement, Memphis, TN.

Rutter, M., Maughan, B., & Ouston, J. (1979). *Fifteen thousand hours: Secondary schools and their effects on children.* London: Open Books.

Sammons, P. (1993). *Measuring and resourcing educational needs: Variations in LEA's LMS policies in inner London.* Clare Market Paper No. 6. London: Centre for Educational Research, LSE.

Sammons, P. (1995). Gender, ethnic and socio-economic differences in attainment and progress: a longitudinal analysis of student achievement over 9 years. *British Educational Research Journal, 21*(4), 465-485.

Sammons, P., Thomas, S., Mortimore, P., Owen, C., & Pennell, H. (1994). *Assessing school effectiveness: Developing measures to put school performance in context.* London: OFSTED.

Sammons, P., Hillman, J., & Mortimore, P. (1995). *Key characteristics of effective schools: A review of school effectiveness research.* London: OFSTED and Institute of Education.

Sammons, P., Thomas, S., & Mortimore, P. (1997). *Forging links: Effective schools and effective departments.* London: Paul Chapman.

Sammons, P., & Smees, R. (1998). Measuring pupil progress at key stage one: Using baseline assessment to investigate value added. *School Leadership and Management* 18(3), 389-407.

Sammons, P., Taggart, B., & Thomas, S. (1998). *Making belfast work: Raising school standards. An evaluation.* Report prepared for the Belfast Education and Library Board. University of London: ISEIC Institute of Education.

Showers, B. (1982). *Transfer of training: The contribution of coaching.* Eugene, OR: Centre for Educational Policy and Management.

Slavin, R.T. (1996). *Education For All.* Lisse: Swets & Zeitlinger.

Smith, G. (1996). Urban education: Current position and future possibilities. In M. Barber & R. Dann (Eds.), *Raising educational standards in the inner city. Practical initiatives in action.* London: Cassell.

Stoll, L., & Fink, D. (1996). *Changing our schools: Linking school effectiveness and school improvement.* Buckingham: Open University Press.

Stoll, L., & Myers, K. (1997). *No quick fixes perspectives on school in difficulty.* London: Falmer Press.

Stringfield, S., Ross, S., & Smith, L. (Eds.) (1996). *Bold plans for school restructuring. The new American schools design.* Mahwah, NJ: Erlbaum.

Teddlie, C., & Stringfield, S. (1993). *Schools made a difference: Lessons learned from a 10-year study of school effects.* New York: Teachers College Press.

Thomas, S., & Sammons, P. (1996). *Raising school standards initiative: The development of baseline and value added measures for DENI.* London: ISEIC Institute of Education.

Thomas, S., & Mortimore, P. (1996). Comparison of Value Added Models for Secondary School Effectiveness. *Research Papers in Education*, 11(1), 5 - 33.

Tunstall, P., & Gipps, C. (1995, september). *How does your teacher help you to make your work better? Childrens understanding of formative assessements.* Paper submitted to BERA Conference. Bath, England.

Willms, J.D. (1986). Social class segregation and its relationship to pupils' examination results in Scotland. *American Sociological Review*, 51, 224-241.

Yang, M., & Goldstein, H. (1996). Multilevel Models for longitudinal data. In U. Engel & J. Reinecke (Eds.), *Analysis of Change, Advanced Techiniques in Panel data Analysis* (pp. 191-220). Berlin: Walter de Gruyter.

8. SYSTEMIC, WHOLE-SCHOOL REFORM OF THE MIDDLE YEARS OF SCHOOLING

Peter W. Hill & V. Jean Russell
Centre for Applied Educational Research, The University of Melbourne, Australia

A large scale longitudinal study into the cognitive and affective development of pupils in Australian schools between kindergarten and grade 11, shows stagnation both in math and language in the middle years of schooling. Moreover, attitudes towards schools are rapidly declining during this stage. Building on the educational effectiveness knowledge base guiding principles for a reform of the middle years are outlined, and it is advocated that a whole school design instead of an incremental approach is needed to bring about the desired changes.

8.1 The need for reform

Some of the more persistent problems in education are those associated with provision for pupils in early adolescence. Pressures to resolve these problems are mounting in many countries as evidence accumulates regarding the prevalence of symptoms such as underachievement, disaffection, alienation and disengagement from productive learning among pupils, especially boys.

Within the Australian context, there has been a veritable groundswell of interest in taking a fresh look at the 'so-called' middle years of schooling (typically grades 5-9), particularly in the light of research findings regarding endemic problems associated with this period of schooling. Foremost among these findings have been those of the Victorian Quality Schools Project (Hill, Holmes-Smith & Rowe, 1993; Hill & Rowe, 1996, 1998; Hill, Rowe, Holmes-Smith & Russell, 1996; Rowe, Hill & Holmes-Smith, 1994, 1995).

The Victorian Quality Schools Project was a longitudinal study of school and teacher effectiveness, comprising a three-year quantitative study and a one-year qualitative follow-up study (1992-1995). The initial sample of 90 schools from the three educational sectors in Victoria (government, independent and Catholic) provided data on some 931 teachers and 13,909 pupils in grades K, 2, 4, 7 and 9. Repeated measures were obtained on the five year-level cohorts over a three-year period of students' progress in literacy and mathematics, their home background characteristics, behaviour, attitudes and opinions. Information was also obtained on aspects of classroom organization, teacher participation in professional development, parent opinion, teacher attitudes and perceptions of their work environment, and on aspects of leadership within the 90 schools.

The mapping of pupil learning progress across the compulsory years of schooling revealed that there was virtually no growth during the middle years in reading, writing, speaking and listening. As is evident from figure 1, reading progress plateaus in grades 5 to 8 for most pupils, while for the lowest 25 per cent there is an actual decline in achievement, particularly in the first year of secondary school (grade 7). It is also evident that underachievement persists longer and is greater among boys than girls.

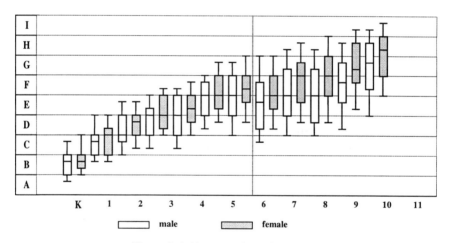

Figure 1. Achievement in reading, K-11

The developmental pattern of pupil attitudes to school throughout the compulsory years, placed alongside their pattern of learning progress, provides supporting evidence. A marked decline in students' enjoyment of schooling in the middle years can be seen in the results shown in figure 2, with some slight improvement beginning to emerge only towards the end of the compulsory schooling years (K-10).

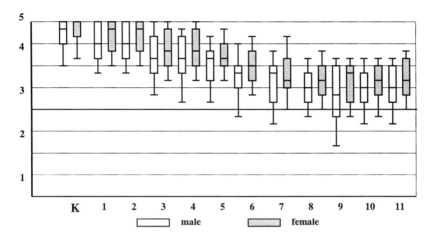

Figure 2. Attitude to school, K-11

Boys are consistently and significantly more negative than girls in their attitudes to school and signs of a tentative improvement in their attitude are not found until about twelve months later than for girls.

Such findings are consistent with what is known of the education of young adolescents. As the literature indicates, the decline in pupil enjoyment of school during the middle years and the associated lessening of their engagement in learning affect not only students' learning progress but many other aspects of the educational experience of young people (Anderman, 1994; Hargreaves, Earl & Ryan, 1996; Galton & Willcocks, 1983; Power & Cotterell, 1981).

Early school leaving or 'dropping out' is one of the most serious and extreme consequences. Others, which can be indicators of impending or likely early leaving, include truancy; habitual lateness; dislike of teachers; anger and resentment towards school; disruptive behaviour in class; delinquent behaviour; suspension and expulsion; passivity and withdrawal; failure to complete work or do homework; low self-esteem; social isolation; peer conflict or gang behaviour; substance abuse; unsafe sexual practices; and self-injury (Batten & Russell, 1995; Brooks, Milne, Paterson, Johansson & Hart, 1997; Withers & Russell, 1998). Such characteristics are familiar to those working with pupils at risk.

The word 'alienation' encapsulates the overall experience of pupils who demonstrate their disengagement either actively (as above) or passively through responses such as switching off and simply failing to learn. Within the Australian context, the concept of alienation was used as a focus for a national project on reform in the middle years of schooling, initiated in 1994: *The Pupil Alienation During the Middle Years of Schooling Project*, which was funded as a Project of National Significance. The report of the project, entitled *From alienation to engagement* (Australian Curriculum Studies Association, 1996), provided an outline of common understandings of, and major theoretical perspectives on, the concept of alienation. Recurring words which convey the meaning of the experience of alienation are 'estrangement', 'detachment', 'fragmentation', 'isolation', 'powerlessness', 'meaninglessness', 'normlessness' and 'disconnectedness'.

8.2   Characteristics and needs of young adolescents

The main characteristics and needs of early adolescence have been summarized by Hargreaves and Earl (1990: 26) as requiring adolescents to:
- adjust to profound physical, intellectual, social and emotional changes;
- develop a positive self concept;
- experience and grow towards independence;
- develop a sense of identity and of personal and social values;
- experience social acceptance, affiliation, and affection among peers of the same and opposite sex; increase their awareness of, ability to cope with, and capacity to respond constructively to the social and political world around them;
- establish relationships with particular adults within which these processes of growth can take place.

While endorsing these characteristics and needs, Eyers, Cormack and Barratt (1992) also direct attention to other characteristics, namely the need for adolescents to think in ways that become progressively more abstract, critical and reflective; to gain experience in decision-making and in accepting responsibility for these decisions; and to develop self-confidence through achieving success in significant events.

Although adolescence is a physical, emotional and cognitive reality, it is, in part, shaped by the social context in which young people live. Hargreaves, Earl and Ryan (1996) draw attention to the 'triple transitions' which adolescents currently experience by viewing the profound transition of adolescent development within the context of two other major transitions: the rapidity and unpredictability of change in the social, economic and political life of society; and the widespread educational reform and restructuring which is producing rapid and continuing movement away from traditional forms of schooling. Other writers point to the effects on adolescent development of societal influences such as the media, high levels of unemployment, ready availability of drugs, advances of technology (Barratt, 1998) and even the way in which life style changes are reducing the age of onset of puberty, thus confronting primary schools increasingly with the challenge of educating young adolescents (Eyers, Cormack & Barratt, 1992).

While it is possible to discern common characteristics and needs of young adolescents, it is also true that there is a wide variation to be found within any group of adolescents.

> *'While some seem bold, argumentative and assertive, others are withdrawn and even submissive. They pass through developmental stages at different times, and in uneven ways. Some have difficulties, others do not. In one moment, teachers may feel they are dealing and reasoning with a virtual adult in mental capacity and insight; at the next, with a child needing care, reassurance and direct instructional 'scaffolding'. This heterogeneity provides one of the joys of working with a group of young adolescents, and one of its deepest challenges to a teacher' (Eyers, Cormack & Barratt, 1992, 8).*

8.3   Responsive forms of schooling

There has been a concerted attempt in many countries, particularly in the last decade, to develop forms of schooling which are responsive to the characteristics and needs of young adolescents and which sustain their involvement, engagement and participation in learning. The imperative for such reform is summarized well in the report of the Junior Secondary Review of South Australia (Eyers, Cormack & Barratt, 1992, 48):

> *'Along with the pleasure and satisfaction to be gained from knowing these young people better in order to promote their growth, and the work which this entails, is the hard-edged realization that in today's schools we ignore this involvement at our mutual peril. Alienation among young adolescents is commonplace in western society. Handing on alienated young*

> *people from schooling into an economic community which has few employment prospects for them is a recipe for disaster. Schools do not have all the cards to play in this scenario, but the chance they have is one which the whole society needs to value and use.'*

The relationship between the developmental characteristics and needs of young adolescents within today's ever-changing social context and the educational provision made for them within the schooling system is of critical importance to the reform of the middle years of schooling.

For schools to achieve and sustain the engagement of young adolescents in learning, it is essential that they provide the approaches, opportunities and experiences that enable young people to accomplish the developmental tasks they face, within their own social context, as a result of their expanding physical, social, emotional and cognitive capacities (Barratt, 1998; Braggett, 1997; Cumming, 1998b; Eyers, Cormack & Barratt, 1992; Hargreaves, Earl & Ryan, 1996). On this basis is built the gathering advocacy for reform of the middle years of schooling, generally defined as the phase of schooling that bridges the conventional primary/secondary (elementary/high) divide and usually said to encompass grades 5 to 8 (approximately ages 10 to 13).

The challenge of establishing new forms of schooling attuned to adolescents' needs and characteristics is increased by the very fact that this phase of schooling overlaps the traditional boundaries of both primary and secondary schools. Pupils who are already experiencing the demanding transitions of adolescence itself are thus required to deal simultaneously with the discontinuities and anxieties of moving from a primary school culture and adapting to a different secondary school culture. Hargreaves, Earl and Ryan (1996) note that the primary school culture is conventionally based on the principles of care and control whereas the traditional secondary school culture is characterized by an academic orientation, pupil polarization and fragmented individualism. Although structural solutions aimed at bridging these two cultures have at times been sought (and are common in the USA) through the establishment of separate middle schools or middle years sections of K-12 schools, structural solutions are not seen as either a necessary or a sufficient response (Eyers, Cormack & Barratt, 1992).

Guiding principles for the development of appropriate schooling in the middle years have been proposed by many, including the Australian

Curriculum Studies Association (1996), the Australian National Middle Schooling Project (Barratt, 1998; Cumming, 1998a), Beane (1991; 1993); Braggett (1997), Cormack, Johnson, Peters & Williams (1998); Cumming (1993), the Junior Secondary Review of South Australia (Eyers, Cormack, Barratt, 1992), Hargreaves, Earl and Ryan (1996), the Schools Council report on schooling for young adolescents (Schools Council, 1993), and Scott (1997). Commonly identified principles are:

- educational provision based on the characteristics and needs of young adolescents;
- a holistic, integrated approach to change, involving all aspects of schooling including curriculum, teaching and learning strategies, assessment, school organization and school culture;
- establishment within schools of a sound philosophical base and a shared set of theoretical constructs and beliefs about middle years reform;
- partnerships with pupils in the development of the curriculum, the ways learning is organized and monitored and in other aspects of the life of the school community;
- a close relationship between pupils and teachers, so that teachers know and understand each pupil and pupils feel supported and connected to the school;
- collaborative work by teachers in the planning and teaching of groups of young adolescents;
- flexible use of time, space and other resources, replacing the rigidities imposed by existing structures such as traditional timetables and room allocation which run counter to the learning needs of young adolescents;
- use of an outcomes-based approach, with ongoing recording of progress and achievement in relation to explicit expectations of pupils;
- continuity between the three phases of schooling: the early, middle and later years, while giving recognition to the different needs of each phase;
- involvement of parents and the community in productive partnerships in relation to the education of young adolescents;
- fair and adequate share of resources, especially in terms of staff, facilities, technology, equipment and materials;
- implementation of new approaches through strategies based on theories and understandings of change.

Many different strategies and practices, based on such principles, have been put forward as the means of achieving middle school reform. The proposals vary from descriptions of single, specific strategies, such as classroom collaboration and negotiation (Campbell, 1997; Illman, 1997) and the team/small-group approach (Roberts, 1997) to comprehensive and global ones, such as the full-service school (Dryfoos, 1994; Wehlage & Stone, 1996; Withers & Russell, 1998).

The take-up of these proposals typically has been piecemeal, localized and short-lived, with most time and energy being directed towards implementing single, specific strategies, typically through 'add-on' projects. Most attempts have been undocumented, with no evaluation of their impact and with little evidence that they succeeded in bringing about institutionalized change. While there is a growing interest in more comprehensive approaches to reform, there are few well-documented models that adopt a whole-school approach to the middle years (Cumming, 1998c; Pogrow, 1993). In addition, little is known regarding their efficacy. As Slavin (1997, 25) notes, "for 20 years, various versions of "middle school models" have been advocated, implemented and debated, but rarely evaluated".

In following sections of this chapter, we make a number of suggestions regarding the development of a systemic, whole-school approach to reform in the middle years of schooling. These suggestions are couched in terms of:
1. a set of 'strategic intentions' to guide reform efforts; and
2. a set of general design elements that could be used by schools and school systems as the basis for developing a number of specific models for the reform of the middle years of schooling.

8.4   Strategic intentions

8.4.1   Introduction

While the literature presents a consistent and coherent view as to the general direction to be taken in reforming the middle years, it does not indicate that there is one best way that all schools or school systems should follow. This suggests that reform needs to be guided by a set of 'strategic intentions'. Caldwell and Spinks (1998) define a strategic intention as a statement that suggests a pattern for taking action but which does not specify what shall be done, how, when, and by whom, as these are matters for determination at the local level. Below is a set of 20 strategic intentions that follow from the preceding analysis and the associated literature. They provide signposts for action at the school and system levels.

8.4.2   Securing the curriculum essentials

Any serious reform of the middle years involves a more learner-focused approach to teaching and one less driven by the imperative to cover curriculum content. This does not mean abandoning curriculum content nor under-valuing specialist subject knowledge. Rather, it means being explicit about the aims of education in the middle years, ensuring that there is a clear specification of core knowledge that all pupils are expected to acquire, making time for in-depth learning and having a curriculum that emphasizes thinking and autonomous learning. It is thus suggested that school systems and curriculum agencies need to provide advice regarding curriculum essentials in the middle years to facilitate middle years reform. As strategic intentions, we suggest the following:

1. Attention will be given to articulating aims of education specific to the middle years of schooling that better reflect:
    * developmental characteristics of young adolescents; and
    * changing educational needs of pupils in the light of broader changes in society and the economy;
    * and to ensuring that these aims become part of the shared beliefs and understandings of all staff.

2. Action will be taken to:
    * curb uncontrolled expansion in the breadth of the curriculum for pupils in the middle years;
    * identify a manageable core of knowledge appropriate to this stage of schooling; and
    * allow greater opportunity for sustained personal endeavour, in-depth learning and the pursuit of excellence.

8.4.3   Managing the transitions

Reform of the middle years inevitably involves managing transitions from one stage of schooling to another to ensuring continuity of care and of educational provision. It often involves bridging the gaps between different models of provision, namely that of the primary school, based around the concept of a class of pupils who spend most of the school day with a single teacher, and that of the secondary school in which pupils go to different teachers for different subjects.

3. While reform will affect both primary and secondary schools, the greatest changes will occur in secondary schools as they seek to place greater emphasis on a learner-centered as opposed to curriculum-centered approaches to education.
4. There will be increased attention to coordinating the transition of pupils from the early years to the middle years, from the middle years to the later years, and from primary to secondary schools.
5. There will be regular interchanges of primary- and secondary-trained teachers between secondary schools and feeder primary schools and a growth in the number of K-12 schools (schools for 5 to 17 year olds).

8.4.4   Creating a new model of provision

While the traditional model of primary schooling works appears to be appropriate for pupils in the early years, and the traditional secondary model is appropriate for pupils in the senior years, neither model would appear to be optimal for the middle years. For some time, researchers and commentators have pointed to the need for a different model of provision for the middle years that provides a middle ground between teaching across the curriculum and subject specialization.

6. There will be a convergence in structures and approaches to teaching and learning between the final year of primary schooling and the first year of secondary schooling.
7. The core curriculum for most pupils in the middle years will be taught by small teams of teachers that share responsibility for the care and education of around 70-80 pupils, who they will teach for at least two consecutive years.
8. Teachers will be organized into teams to facilitate planning and co-ordination of teaching programs and ongoing improvement of teaching and learning within the classroom.
9. Changes will be made in the internal organization of schools to ensure larger, uninterrupted blocks of time for learning and close relations between pupils and teams of teachers.

10. Schools will set up high-status, intensive programs or 'academies' to cater for the needs of identified groups of pupils and to offer pupils the opportunity to achieve at a high level in a particular area of the curriculum (e.g., music or sport) or to learn in different ways (vocationally-oriented as opposed to academic learning).

8.4.5   Transforming teaching and learning

One of the most frequent comments of young adolescents when talking about school is that they regard it as 'boring'. This comment reflects a deep need for learning that is exciting, engaging at a personal level, that is challenging and connected to issues or problems that young people regard as meaningful and important. It implies a constructivist view of learning, deep rather than surface learning approaches, and a curriculum that requires pupils to be active and to think creatively and solve problems. Given the importance to young adolescents of peer influences, it also implies the use of co-operative learning strategies that tap into the positive potential of peer group influences. Sophisticated approaches to the use of the new information technologies will play a critical role in the transformation of teaching and learning in the middle years.

At the same time, schools will need to become more effective at providing assistance to pupils who experience difficulties coping with the normal demands of academic work. These include considerable numbers of pupils who have inadequate levels of literacy and numeracy. It is no longer satisfactory that many secondary schools and secondary school teachers lack any real capacity to teach pupils how to read and write. Reading and writing are examples of foundational learning that need to be promoted and developed continuously at all levels of education. Society cannot afford to have significant numbers of people who slip through the early years 'net' unable to cope with the literacy demands of schooling and the modern world.

11. There will be substantial and sustained investment in transforming teaching and learning with the aim of producing autonomous learners who perceive schooling to be worthwhile, challenging and enjoyable.
12. There will be a massive increase in the use of new information technologies to provide continuous access to new and powerful ways of learning and sources of knowledge.

13. All pupils will be expected to achieve to high standards in core areas of the curriculum, and pupils who fall behind their peers will be closely monitored and provided with special assistance and extra time and support to enable them to achieve these standards.

8.4.6   Creating outward-looking learning communities

The middle years are characterized by increasingly infrequent contact between the school and the home. To some extent this is a natural part of pupils growing up and becoming more independent. There is an ongoing need, however, for parents to be informed of what is going on, to be supportive of their child's learning and to be a partner in the learning process. Schools are one (although in most cases the most important) of the sources of support for young people but the effectiveness of other agencies and service providers can be enhanced greatly when all providers of services for youth work together. Early adolescence is also a time when young people increasingly need to interact with the wider community in a structured way and to make use of the rich opportunities for productive learning in society at large. This is a further reason why the reform of educational provision in the middle years must result in more outward-looking learning communities.

14. There will be a renewed emphasis on creating close links between the home and the school and on reaching out to all families to secure their support for and involvement in their children's learning.
15. Schools will establish close links with outside organizations and individuals who can support the work of the school and provide role models for pupils, as well as becoming the key component of integrated systems of service provision for young people.
16. There will be increasing use of off-campus learning and the use of learning resources in the wider community.
17. Schooling in the middle years will become less bureaucratic and more concerned with developing and sustaining committed communities of learners.

8.4.7   Tooling up for reform

Reform of the middle years may require significant changes to current patterns of pre- and in-service training and systems of support for schools. It certainly requires attention to the development of highly trained professionals whose particular focus and expertise is the education of young adolescents in the middle years. It is essential that middle year's educators enjoy recognition and job satisfaction comparable to those of teachers in the early years of the primary school or the senior years of the secondary school.

Above all else, resources need to be devoted to developing, implementing and evaluating fully articulated and comprehensive models of provision that can then be adopted more generally across school systems. The reform of the middle years is too complex for schools to be expected to undertake this design task unaided. Moreover, it is desirable that there is a degree of consistency of approach from one school to the next, within the one system.

18. Pre- and in-service education and training, and support structures for schools will increasingly be organized to reflect the distinctive nature of schooling in the early, middle and later years and the need for continuity and smooth transitions between stages.
19. All teachers in the middle years will:
    • have in-depth knowledge of at least two specialist areas;
    • be trained in strategies for integrating specialist knowledge through topic-, issues-, problem- or vocationally-based approaches to learning;
    • be qualified to promote high standards of literacy, numeracy and other core knowledge, including the use of new information technologies.
20. Resources will be directed towards developing, evaluating and implementing comprehensive and integrated design approaches to improving educational provision in the middle years of schooling.

8.5   General design elements of a comprehensive school reform model

How might the above set of 20 strategic intentions be built into a plan for comprehensive reform of the middle years? The traditional approach to improvement in schools has been through the introduction of new *programs* aimed at enhancing one or more aspects of the school's operation while keeping other aspects constant. This represents an incremental approach in that it assumes that the basic structures and processes of schooling should remain constant while attention is focused on those most in need of improvement.

As was foreshadowed in the last of the above 20 strategic intentions, however, the reform of the middle years calls for a response that goes beyond the adding-on of yet another program. What is required is a 'design approach'. This is consistent with recent developments in school reform within the USA, where the focus has shifted to whole-school 'designs' that represent deliberate attempts to transform the entire ecology of formal education. They are predicated on the notion that in order to bring about quantum improvements in learning outcomes, each of the critical elements of schools and of school systems needs to be identified, those aspects that need to change in order for them to operate effectively and in alignment with all the other elements need to be attended to, and each element needs to be redesigned accordingly. Wilson and Daviss (1994, 22) describe the redesign process as follows:

> *'The redesign process is the integration of research, development, dissemination, and refinement by which innovations and the procedures that create them are originated, improved, and made affordable....the redesign process is an institutionalized method of strategic, systemic change that works unceasingly to enact a vision of excellence as well as to redefine excellence itself when changing conditions make it necessary.'*

In the USA, there are now a number of 'designs' that adopt a comprehensive, whole-school approach to improvement of learning outcomes. The best-known of these designs are the nine designs promoted by the New American Schools Development Corporation (see especially Stringfield, Ross, & Smith, 1996). Each design required many hundreds of hours of design work by teams of educators all working to create a coherent and consistent approach to improvement, based wherever possible on 'best practice' and findings from discipline-based research and the research literature on school effectiveness and improvement. These designs were piloted in a small number of schools and subject to external evaluation before being implemented more widely.

More recently, the American Institutes for Research (1999) have undertaken an evaluation of 24 school-wide designs, all of which span at least one of Grades 5-9 and may thus be considered as relevant to the middle years, but none of which is specifically targeted at these years (see table 1). This indicates how important it is that work be done that specifically addresses the issue of a school-wide approach to the middle years.

Table 1. List of 24 school-wide Reform Models Reviewed by the American Institutes for Research and the Grade Levels of Pupils Targeted by each Design.

Accelerated Schools (K-8)	The Foxfire Fund (K-12)
America's Choice (K-12)	High Schools That Work (9-12)
ATLAS Communities (PreK-12)	High/Scope (K-3)
Audrey Cohen College (K-12)	League of Professional Schools (K-12)
Basic Schools Network (K-12)	Modern Red Schoolhouse (K-12)
Coalition of Essential Schools (K-12)	Onward to Excellence (K-12)
Community for Learning (K-12)	Paideia (K-12)
Co-NECT (K-12)	Roots and Wings (PreK-6)
Core Knowledge (K-8)	School Development Program (K-12)
Different Ways of Knowing (K-7)	Success for All (PreK-6)
Direct Instruction (K-6)	Talent Development High School (9-12)
Expeditionary Learning Outward Bound (K-12)	Urban Learning Centers (PreK-12)
Expeditionary Learning Outward Bound (K-12)	Urban Learning Centers (PreK-12)

Within the Australian context, there is no parallel (as yet) to the NASDEC process for generating whole-school designs. However, work has been undertaken within the Centre for Applied Educational Research at The University of Melbourne with the aim of identifying a set of *general* design elements that need to be taken into account in the development of any *specific* designs for improving pupil learning outcomes.

An analogy may be helpful in explaining the notion of a 'general design element'. In creating a new model of car, the automotive design team know that the basic design elements of the car (e.g., the four-stroke engine under the hood, the steering wheel, the floor-mounted accelerator and brake pedal) are likely to remain constant: the scope for change lies in how effectively, efficiently and reliably each element performs. Likewise, in schools, the elements that are critical to ensuring pupils achieve success in core areas of the curriculum are likely to remain relatively unchanged over extended periods of time. On the other hand, in schools that succeed in institutionalizing on-going improvement into their operations, there is constant attention to improving each element and ensuring that when integrated with all others, the school operates smoothly and effectively.

Figure 3 summarizes a set of general design elements that are hypothesized to be fixed elements in all schools, but which need to be constantly subject to re-design in the ongoing quest for more effective models of schooling. These general design elements were identified in the course of research and developmental work undertaken as part of the *Early Literacy Research Project (ELRP)* (Crévola & Hill, 1998a and b; Hill & Crévola, 1997 & 1998). They have subsequently been used to inform the work of 12 schools that have participated over the past year in the Middle Years Research and Development Project (MYRAD). This project has been a joint initiative of the Victorian Department of Education and the Centre for Applied Educational Research at The University of Melbourne. The aim of the project is to develop and test a whole-school design for the middle years (grades 5-9) capable of bringing about significant improvements in the achievement of pupils, in their attitudes to schooling and learning, and in their behaviours. The general design elements summarized in figure 3 have been used within MYRAD as a template or conceptual framework for developing specific programs and whole-school designs targeted at the middle years of schooling. Each of the nine elements is described briefly below. They are highly interconnected and interdependent, however, and thus change in any one of the nine elements can be expected to entail change in the others.

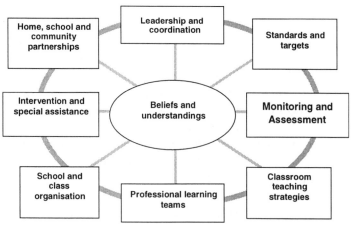

Figure 3. General design for improving learning outcomes

8.5.1   Beliefs and understandings

Central to any whole-school design are the beliefs and understandings that teachers have about their professional efficacy - whether they believe that as teachers they can make a difference to the learning of virtually every pupil in spite of obstacles (general teaching efficacy) and whether they hold this believe in relation to their own individual teaching (personal teaching efficacy) (Ashton & Webb, 1986; Lee, Dedrick & Smith, 1991; Rosenholz, 1989).

Underlying a sense of efficacy is the fundamental belief that virtually every pupil is capable of learning, given the right support and pace of instruction, a belief which means that teachers do not give up on pupils, but try different approaches until success is achieved. As one perceptive grade 5 pupil in the VQSP case study said:

> *'They feel they're not doing their job properly if the kids don't catch on they're trying their best, but if they don't succeed very fast the teacher thinks 'There's got to be something else I can do for them!' '*

When teachers believe that they can affect pupil learning, they accept responsibility, individually and collectively, for pupil progress, rather than assigning responsibility or blame for failure to learn to the pupils or their home backgrounds.

With respect to the middle years, there are particular understandings that teachers need to have regarding the developmental needs of pupils during early adolescence (Hargreaves & Earl, 1990) and more especially their need for a curriculum that emphasises in-depth learning and develops abstract and critical thought, decision-making and taking responsibility for decisions (Eyers, Cormack & Barratt, 1992).

8.5.2   Standards and targets

The setting of specific targets against system-wide standards for the whole school, each grade level and each class group, provides important and explicit goals and expectations for pupils and teachers to meet. Given the principle of knowing and meeting the individual learning needs of each pupil, the objective should be to set individual learning targets for each pupil.

In many school systems *content* standards exist that specify what schools are expected to teach pupils in the middle years. It is much rarer to find systems that have undertaken detailed work to define appropriate *performance* standards for pupils in the middle years, suitably benchmarked against those of other systems. Increasingly, however, systems and curriculum authorities are ensuring that in addition to providing content standards and statements of expected outcomes suitably illustrated by examples of pupil work, they are also developing performance standards specifying particular levels of achievement and associated targets specifying which pupils are expected to meet the nominated standards and when.

8.5.3   Monitoring and assessment

All scientific approaches to improvement depend on systematic observation of the phenomenon in question. Within the school context, it is critical that there is regular, frequent, systematic and detailed monitoring, assessment and recording of pupil learning progress. Clay (1993) makes the distinction between the measurement of outcomes, the measurement of abilities and the observation of learning behaviours in order to inform teaching. All three are important, but the latter (often referred to as diagnostic assessment) needs special emphasis in the middle years in order to accommodate the learning styles and to understand the learning difficulties of individual pupils, as well as to ensure that instruction is focused within the 'zone of proximal development' of pupils (Vygotsky, 1978).

The regular monitoring of the progress of individual pupils in areas other than the academic is valuable in encouraging and enabling the school to perceive pupils as whole persons. The sharing of information between primary and secondary schools about pupil achievement is also critical.

8.5.4   Classroom teaching strategies

Research evidence indicates that the greatest contribution made by schools to students' achievement is at the classroom level (Scheerens & Bosker, 1997). When pupil achievement is adjusted for entry characteristics of pupils and their prior levels of performance, school effects are relatively modest - say between 8-15 percent of the variance in value-added scores as Reynolds c.s. (1994) show. On the other hand, there is often substantial variation in effectiveness between classes within schools - as much as 30-50% (Hill & Rowe, 1996; Scheerens, Vermeulen & Pelgrum, 1989). Furthermore, the variables that best predict whether pupils make progress tend to be those integrally concerned with the quality of teaching and learning (Wang, Haertel, & Walberg, 1993) and what happens within the classroom, such as: high expectations, time on task or engaged learning time, and focused teaching that succeeds in engaging all pupils within their 'zone of proximal development'.[1]

Teachers need to have available a repertoire of strategies to enable them to meet individual needs. Approaches that are attuned to the characteristics and needs of young adolescents include pupil involvement in classroom decision-making about curriculum, including the ways learning is organized, monitored and assessed; learning that connects with and is relevant to students' personal and social concerns, and their out-of-school experience and culture; active learning experiences; engagement in complex, higher order and critical thinking activity; and co-operative as well as independent learning (Australian Curriculum Studies Association, 1996; Beane, 1993; Eyers, Cormack & Barratt, 1992; Forte & Schurr, 1997; Hargreaves, Earl & Ryan, 1996; Marks, Newmann & Gamoran, 1996; Wehlage, Newmann & Secada, 1996).

8.5.5   Professional learning teams

A crucial element in any design aimed at improved teaching and learning in schools is the provision of effective, ongoing and practical professional learning opportunities for teachers. High quality professional development that has a positive impact on classroom practice is essential (Goertz, Floden & O'Day, 1996).

---

[1]   Scheerens & Bosker (1997) conclude on the basis of meta-analyses of findings and best-evidence syntheses that the basic factors are: time on task; closeness of content covered to assessment instrument; a structured approach: specific objectives, frequent assessment and corrective feedback; and types of adaptive instruction that can be managed by teachers. Hill & Crévola (1997) argue, on the basis of the same evidence, that the literature on effectiveness supports just three factors which closely resemble the four factors of Scheerens and Bosker, namely: high expectations of student achievement; engaged learning time, and structured teaching focused on the learning needs of students.

Effective professional learning assumes effective leadership to create the motivation and commitment to change and improve. It also involves intensive, sustained, theoretically-based yet practically-situated learning, with opportunities to observe good practice, to be involved in coaching and mentoring processes and to take time for reflection (Fullan, 1991 & 1993; Hargreaves & Fullan, 1991). Moreover, professional learning is most powerful when it occurs within the context of teachers working as members of a team and in pursuit of specific learning outcomes for pupils.

Teachers are unlikely to develop as practitioners by remaining professionally isolated in their classrooms. The establishment of 'professional learning teams' is a critical strategy in 'de-privatizing' teaching (Wehlage & Stone, 1996, 300) and in creating both a culture and a process for ongoing improvement in the quality of teaching in schools.

In the context of the middle years, the establishment of professional learning teams enables a closer relationship between pupils and their teachers. Teachers working collaboratively in a small, multidisciplinary team with the one group of pupils, sharing responsibility for the planning, teaching, assessment and pastoral care of those pupils, learn much more about each pupil as a person and about their individual learning needs. Teachers also gain professional stimulation, professional growth, confidence and commitment from the team experience (Ashton & Webb, 1986; Barratt, 1998; Brennan & Sachs, 1998; Forte & Schurr, 1997; Lee & Smith, 1993; Rosenholtz, 1989).

8.5.6   School and class organization

The organization of the school can help or hinder learning; time on task can be maximized, for example, through time-tabling in large blocks of time, having few public address announcements, minimizing the number of visitors entering classrooms and the number of times pupils or teachers are withdrawn from class for other purposes. School organization can also provide a positive, secure but challenging environment for pupils when, for example, pupils are respected, supported and treated equitably; pupils are partners in decision-making; discipline is firm and consistent, not authoritarian and repressive; school policies are constructive rather than restrictive and inflexible; peer relationships are positive, and bullying and harassment are negligible (Batten & Russell, 1995; Withers & Russell,

1998). The classroom culture needs also to be positive and secure but challenging.

School substructures, such as the teams/small group structure, mitigate against pupils being overwhelmed by anonymity within a large school, especially when class size is kept to a level that allows pupils to be known individually, to gain a sense of belonging and have their individual learning needs met. The stability of class composition across subject areas and through grades 7 and 8, also means pupils have a sense of continuity during that time. Mixed ability classes and the use of flexible instructional groupings within these classes provide positive learning environments that nevertheless allow teaching to be focused on the learning needs of each pupil (Slavin, 1988a, 1988b & 1990).

8.5.7   Intervention and special assistance

There are critical, negative consequences if pupils who fail to make progress in regular classroom settings are not identified quickly and assisted. The initial identification of and response to such pupils is the responsibility of teaching teams who meet on a regular (weekly) basis to review, on a case by case basis, the progress of their pupils and who develop and implement action plans to assist the most 'at risk' pupils to make progress. This implies that the school will not only establish professional learning teams, but also schedule time when they can meet as a team to monitor pupil progress and formulate action plans.

Some pupils will have needs which call for more specialized and intensive assistance than can be provided by the regular teaching team. Unfortunately, the track record of specialized programs for pupils in the middle years is not good (Pogrow, 1993) and cannot be compared to the kinds of results produced by interventions such as Reading Recovery for grade 1 pupils. This does not mean the abandonment of such programs, but rather more intensive work on the development of effective programs. Wilson and Daviss (1994, 47) claim that:

> *'Reading Recovery is consistently effective because it is based on careful research, teaches educators how to make practical use of its findings and supervises them continuously.'*

These are characteristics that should apply to support programs for pupils in the middle years. In addition, there need to be clear and realistic expectations as to what such programs can be expected to achieve, the programs need to be integrated with other aspects of provision within the school, especially with regular classroom teaching, and they need to be matched to the cognitive needs and styles of young adolescents.

8.5.8   Home/school/community links

The interactive involvement of the family and community with the school has many benefits. Regular, informative reporting to parents/guardians on pupil progress and communication about education and school life to families means parents/guardians have the opportunity to understand and appreciate a major aspect of their young adolescent's life, and also to develop approaches to behaviour management and learning which are consistent with those of the school. Parents/guardians can increase teachers' knowledge and understanding of individual pupils; they can also become resource people contributing to the school's programs.

Cooperative, active and supportive relationships between the community and school are also advantageous. Business, industry and community organizations can provide out-of-school learning experiences for pupils, as well as giving input (ideas and resources) to the school's programs. Provision of services by community agencies for young people and their families, through the school where possible, helps both the school and the community to develop a holistic approach to young adolescents, in contrast to the usual fragmented approach. The collaboration of teachers and professionals from other service areas also extends the knowledge, understanding and effectiveness of all professional groups (Australian Curriculum Studies Association, 1996; Barratt, 1998; Dryfoos, 1994; Wehlage & Stone, 1996; Withers & Russell, 1998).

Close professional links between secondary schools and their feeder primary schools are critical if understanding of cultures and purposes, continuity of curriculum, sharing of knowledge of pupils, and successful transition experiences for pupils are to be achieved. The amount to be learned by both primary and secondary teachers from such collaboration is significant. Visits by primary and secondary teachers to one another's schools are strongly encouraged (Braggett, 1997; Stringer, 1997).

8.5.9   Leadership and coordination

Leadership's consistent, continuing support for initiatives and improvement in the middle years is thought to be critical (Australian Curriculum Studies Association, 1996; Barratt, 1998; Brennan & Sachs, 1998; Cormack, Johnson, Peters & Williams, 1998; Cumming, 1998b). Such support is demonstrated through actions such as leaders' moral support and enthusiasm; communication with the school community; provision of time, staff, funds and other material resources; ensuring staff professional development; giving priority in relation to time-tabling; giving recognition, praise and constructive feedback, and the sharing of leadership with others.

Leaders are important in developing a strong instructional focus within the school by ensuring the establishment of clear instructional goals and the co-ordination of the curriculum; securing adequate resources and targeting these to meet school goals and priorities; protecting class time from interruption; arranging appropriate class size and composition; encouraging collaborative teamwork among staff; improving teacher effectiveness; establishing standards and targets and the frequent and regular assessment and monitoring of pupils against these.

Leaders also play a significant role in the development of strong, positive school cultures through ensuring the following: a clear vision and set of goals; high expectations of staff and pupils; involvement of school community members in decision-making; supportive, fair and open relationships with staff and between staff and pupils; collaborative professional learning and personal support among staff members; high quality teaching; the giving of recognition and feedback; and the establishment of a safe and orderly school environment (Fullan, 1993; Hallinger, Bickman & Davis, 1996; Hallinger, & Heck 1996; Heck, Larsen & Marcoulides, 1990; Louis & Smith, 1992; Stoll & Fink 1996).

Finally, leaders have the key role to play in implementing and institutionalizing a whole-school design approach incorporating the elements summarized in figure 3. Only they have the authority to bring about the degree of transformation required and the capacity to maintain an overview of each of the design elements and ensure that each is operating effectively and in alignment with all other elements. They also need to appoint key staff with significant time release to act as team leaders who coordinate teaching and learning and manage the design on a day-to-day basis.

8.6 Translating strategic intentions into action at the school level

8.6.1 Introduction

The above general design elements provide a framework for developing particular designs for pursuing reform of the middle years of schooling. In moving from a set of strategic intentions and general design elements to action at the school level, we suggest reform is likely to proceed broadly in three overlapping phases, with schools and systems operating simultaneously at different points on a change continuum. The three phases are described below:

Phase 1: The end of the old paradigm

During this phase there is increasing evidence of problems with traditional patterns of provision in the middle years and increasingly calls are heard for something to be done. It becomes evident to more and more participants that significant gains are unlikely to come from simply working harder within current structures and using current approaches, so individual schools and teachers begin experimenting with different approaches and structures. These piecemeal responses tend to be short-lived, however, not so much because they do not work, but because they run counter to the prevailing paradigm and any reduction in the momentum for change and innovation leads to the old paradigm re-asserting itself. Nonetheless, the seeds of the new paradigm are sown: all that remains is for the moment to come when it is possible to put together the pieces into a comprehensive model that is clearly perceived to provide a better way of doing things. That moment comes when there is both conceptual clarity about the new paradigm and the will to cut loose from the old.

This is the phase that many schools and school systems are in at the present moment. There has been a growing groundswell of dissatisfaction with traditional patterns of provision. While the dissatisfaction began many years ago amongst forward-thinking schools and educators, it has now grown to the stage at which the time is ripe for moving on. It is important to recognize, however, that the new is already manifest in the present. Many hundreds of schools are experimenting with structures and processes that help define the new paradigm and are implementing various of the strategic intentions referred to earlier. In this sense, it is true to say that there is nothing new about these proposals. But few if any schools have managed to implement *all* of the changes necessary to create and sustain a comprehensive and effective model of provision.

It is nevertheless important that we learn from the work of the pioneers in the field, from the schools that have found pieces of the jig-saw puzzle that is the future for education in the middle years.

Phase 2: Successful implementation of a new, school-wide middle school model

During this phase, teams of expert educators - whether within school systems, universities or the private sector - initiate projects to develop specific designs for school-wide reform focusing on the middle years. The new designs are field tested in a small number of progressive schools (typically volunteer secondary schools and their feeder primary schools), and there is close monitoring of all facets of their implementation, with external, third-party evaluations to assess their impact. These schools receive additional support to enable them to take the tough decisions and implement fundamental changes. Independent, third-party evaluations of the journeys and experiences of these schools in implementing new designs are critical in refining designs and in generating the momentum for the third phase - the scale-up of successful designs and models of provision.

Phase 3: Large-scale, systemic reform of the middle years

During this third phase, large number of schools and school systems seek to implement design-based reform of the middle years. Schools are given options about which model they will adopt and the time-scale over which they will implement reforms, since it will be apparent that there is no 'one best way' to pursue reform and that some schools are more ready for reform than others.

This phase is associated with changes to pre- and in-service education and training and to structures for supporting schools. This results in a new kind of educational professional who specializes in the education of young adolescents. The third phase is also one in which a renewed emphasis is placed on the instructional leadership and change management roles of principals and others in leadership positions in schools.

8.6.2   Concluding Comments

The above phases assume that the trend towards whole-school reform in the middle years is not a passing fad but a major issue confronted by systems everywhere in order to better meet the needs of young people. It also implies that the problems evident in schools that operate in traditional ways are amenable to solutions and that these solutions can be implemented widely. In other words, they imply an optimistic view of schooling and of the capacity of educators in leadership positions to bring about reform through a deliberate process of design rather than a 'hit-and-miss' process of trial and error. It is a particularly optimistic view given the fact that the directions advocated for the middle years imply a paradigm shift in thinking and practice.

Over recent decades, most change in education has happened as a result of external pressures rather than internal pressures for change. Pressures for the reform of the middle years are somewhat unusual in that they are emanating largely from within the education sector itself, which is one reason to be optimistic that educators will see through this challenge and come up with creative solutions to the middle years.

NOTE

The authors wish to acknowledge to the assistance they have received, both directly and indirectly, from colleagues in writing this chapter, particularly Carmel Crévola, Graeme Jane and Tony Mackay, and from colleagues in the many schools that have pioneered new approaches to the middle years.

8.7   References

American Institutes for Research (1999). *An educator's guide to schoolwide reform.* Arlington, VA: Educational Research Service.

Anderman, E.M.M. (1994). Motivation and schooling in the middle grades. *Review of Educational Research,* 64(2), 287-309.

Ashton, P.T., & Webb, R.B. (1986). *Making a difference: Teachers' sense of efficacy and student achievement.* New York: Longman.

Australian Curriculum Studies Association (1996). *From alienation to engagement: Opportunities for reform in the middle years of schooling.* Canberra: National Advisory Committee for the Student Alienation During the Middle Years of Schooling Project.

Barratt, R.E. (1998). *Shaping middle schooling in Australia: A report of the National Middle Schooling Project.* Canberra: Australian Curriculum Studies Association.

Batten, M., & Russell, J. (1995). *Students at risk: A review of Australian literature 1980-1994*. Melbourne: Australian Council for Educational Research.

Beane, J. (1991). The middle school: The natural home of the integrated curriculum. *Educational Leadership, 49*(2), 9-13.

Beane, J. (1993). *A middle school curriculum: From rhetoric to reality*. Columbus, Ohio: National Middle School Association.

Braggett, E. (1997). *The middle years of schooling: An Australian perspective*. Cheltenham, Victoria: Hawker Brownlow Education.

Brennan, M., & Sachs, J. (1998). Integrated curriculum. In J. Cumming (Ed.), *Extending reform in the middle years of schooling: Challenges and responses* (pp. 18-24). Canberra: Australian Curriculum Studies Association.

Brooks, M., Milne, C., Paterson, K., Johansson, K., & Hart, K. (1997). *Under-age school leaving: A report examining approaches to assisting young people at risk of leaving school before the legal school leaving age. A report to the National Youth Affairs Research Scheme*. Hobart: National Clearinghouse for Youth Studies.

Caldwell, B.J., & Spinks, J.M. (1998). *Beyond the self-managing school*. London: Falmer Press.

Campbell, P. (1997). Making classrooms collaborative. *EQ Australia* (1), 41-42.

Cormack, P., Johnson, B., Peters, J., & Williams, D. (1998). Authentic assessment. In J. Cumming (Ed.), *Extending reform in the middle years of schooling: Challenges and responses* (pp. 25-31). Canberra: Australian Curriculum Studies Association.

Clay, M.M. (1993). *An observation survey of early literacy achievement*. Auckland, New Zealand: Heinemann Education.

Crévola, C.A.M., & Hill, P.W. (1998a). Evaluation of a whole-school approach to prevention and intervention in early literacy. *Journal of Education for Students Placed at Risk, 3*, 133-157.

Crévola, C.A.M, & Hill, P.W. (1998b). *Children's literacy success strategy: An overview*. Melbourne: Catholic Education Office.

Cumming, J. (1993). *Middle schooling for the twenty-first century* (Seminar Series No. 28). Melbourne: Incorporated Association of Registered Teachers of Victoria.

Cumming, J. (Ed.). (1998a). *Extending reform in the middle years of schooling: Challenges and responses*. Canberra: Australian Curriculum Studies Association.

Cumming, J. (1998b). Challenges and responses. In J. Cumming (Ed.), *Extending reform in the middle years of schooling: Challenges and responses* (pp. 5-13). Canberra: Australian Curriculum Studies Association.

Cumming, J. (1998c). Support and evaluation. In J. Cumming (Ed.), *Extending reform in the middle years of schooling: Challenges and responses* (pp. 51-55). Canberra: Australian Curriculum Studies Association.

Dryfoos, J.G. (1994). *Full-service schools: A revolution in health and social services for children, youth and families*. San Francisco: Jossey-Bass.

Eyers, V., Cormack, P., & Barratt, R. (1992). *The education of Young adolescents in South Australian government schools: Report of the Junior Secondary Review* . Adelaide: Education Department of South Australia.

Forte, I., & Schurr, S. (1997). *The middle years of schooling: A handbook for success*. Australia: Hawker Brownlow Education.

Fullan, M. (1991). *The new meaning of educational change*. London: Cassell.

Fullan, M. (1993). *Change forces: Probing the depths of educational reform*. London: The Falmer Press.

Galton, M., & Willcocks, J. (Eds.). (1983). *Moving from the primary classroom*. London: Routledge and Kegan Paul.

Goertz, M.E., Floden, R.E., & O'Day, J. (1996). *Studies of educational reform: systemic reform*. Philadelphia: University of Pennsylvania, Consortium for Policy Research in Education.

Hallinger, P., Bickman, L., & Davis, K. (1996). School context, principal leadership, and student reading achievement. *The Elementary School Journal, 96*(5), 525-549.

Hallinger, P., & Heck, R.H. (1996). The principal's role in school effectiveness: An assessment of methodological progress, 1980-1995. In K. Leithwood, J. Chapman, D. Corson, P. Hallinger, & A Hart, *International handbook of educational leadership and administration* (pp. 723-783). Dordrecht: Kluwer.

Hargreaves, A., & Earl, L. (1990). *Rights of passage: A review of selected research about schooling in the transition years*. Toronto: Ministry of Education, Ontario.

Hargreaves, A., Earl, L., & Ryan, J. (1996). *Schooling for change: Reinventing education for early adolescents*. London: Falmer Press.

Hargreaves, A., & Fullan, M. (1991). *Understanding teacher development*. London: Cassell.

Heck, R.H., Larsen, T.J., & Marcoulides, G.A. (1990). Instructional leadership and school achievement: Validation of a causal model. *Educational Administration Quarterly, 26*(2), 94-125.

Hill, P.W., & Crévola, C.A.M. (1997). The literacy challenge in Australian primary chools. *IARTV Seminar Series*, no. 69, November, 1997.

Hill, P.W., & Crévola, C.A.M. (1998). Characteristics of an effective literacy strategy. *Unicorn, 24*(2), 74-85.

Hill, P.W., Holmes-Smith, P., & Rowe, K.J. (1993). *School and teacher effectiveness in Victoria: Key findings from Phase 1 of the Victorian Quality Schools Project*. Melbourne: Centre for Applied Educational Research, The University of Melbourne (ERIC Clearing House, Document No. ED 367 067).

Hill, P.W., & Rowe, K.J. (1996). Multilevel modelling in school effectiveness research. *School Effectiveness and School Improvement, 7*(1), 1-34.

Hill, P.W., & Rowe, K.J. (1998). Modelling student progress in studies of educational effectiveness. *School Effectiveness and School Improvement, 9*(3), 310-333.

Hill, P.W., Rowe, K.J., Holmes-Smith, P., & Russell, V.J. (1996). *The Victorian Quality Schools Project: A study of school and teacher effectiveness*. Report to the Australian Research Council. Volume 1. Centre for Applied Educational Research, Faculty of Education, The University of Melbourne, Melbourne.

Illman, M. (1997). Year 9 negotiators. *EQ Australia* (1), 43.

Lee, V.E., Dedrick, R.F., & Smith, J.B. (1991). The effect of the social organisation of schools on teacher efficacy and sense of satisfaction. *Sociology of Education, 64*(3), 190-208.

Lee, V. E., & Smith, J. B. (1993). Effects of school restructuring on the achievement and engagement of middle-grade students. *Sociology of Education, 66*(3), 164-187.

Louis, K. S., & Smith, B. (1992). Cultivating teacher engagement: Breaking the iron law of social class. In F. M. Newmann (Ed.), *Student engagement and achievement in American secondary schools* (pp. 119-152). New York: Teachers College Press.

Marks, H. M., Newmann, F. M., & Gamoran, A. (1996). Does authentic pedagogy increase student achievement? In F. Newmann & Associates (Eds.), *Authentic achievement: Restructuring schools for intellectual quality* (pp. 49-73). San Francisco: Jossey-Bass.

Pogrow, S. (1993). Where's the beef? Looking for exemplary materials. *Educational Leadership*, 50(8), 39-45.

Power, C., & Cotterell, J. (1981). *Changes in students in the transition between primary and secondary school*. Report No. 27. Canberra: Education Research and Development Committee.

Reynolds, D., Teddlie, C., Creemers, B.P.M., Cheng, Y.C., Dundas, B., Green, B., Epp, J.R., Hauge, T.E., Schaffer, E.C., & Stringfield, S. (1994). School effectiveness research: A review of the international literature. In Reynolds, D., Creemers, B.P.M., Nesselrodt, P.S., Schaffer, E.C., Stringfield, S., & Teddlie, C. (Eds.), *Advances in school effectiveness research and practice* (pp. 25-51). Oxford: Pergamon.

Roberts, J. (1997). To the 3Rs, add the 3Ds. *EQ Australia* (1), 23-25.

Rosenholtz, S.J. (1989). *Teachers' workplace: The social organisation of schools*. New York: Teachers College Press.

Rowe, K.J., Hill, P.W., & Holmes-Smith, P. (1994, January). *The Victorian Quality Schools Project: A report on the first stage of a longitudinal study of school and teacher effectiveness*. Symposium paper presented at the 7th International Congress for School Effectiveness and Improvement, The World Congress Centre, Melbourne.

Rowe, K.J., Hill, P.W., & Holmes-Smith, P. (1995). Methodological issues in educational performance and school effectiveness research: A discussion with worked examples. *Australian Journal of Education*, 39, 217-248.

Scheerens, J., & Bosker, R.J. (1997). *The foundations of educational effectiveness*. Oxford: Pergamon.

Scheerens, J., Vermeulen, C.J.A.J., & Pelgrum, W.J. (1989). Generalizability of instructional and school effectiveness indicators across nations. *International Journal of Educational Research, 13*, 789-800.

Scott, L. (1997). Six principles for the middle years. *EQ Australia* (1), 12-13.

Slavin, R.E. (1988a). Cooperative learning and student achievement. *Educational Leadership,* 46(2), 31-33.

Slavin, R.E. (1988b). Synthesis of research on grouping in elementary and secondary schools. *Educational Leadership,* 46(1), 67-77.

Slavin, R.E. (1990). Achievement effects of ability grouping in secondary schools: A best-evidence synthesis. *Review of Educational Research,* 60(3), 471-499.

Slavin, R.E. (1997). Design competitions: A proposal for a new federal role in educational research and development. *Educational Researcher,* 26(1), 22-28.

Stoll, L., & Fink, D. (1996). *Changing our schools: Linking school effectiveness and school improvement*. Buckingham: Open University Press.

Stringer, W. (1997). Better connections. *EQ Australia* (1), 21-23.

Stringfield, S., Ross, S., & Smith, L. (Eds.). (1996). *Bold plans for school restructuring: the New American Schools designs*. Mahwah, New Jersey: Lawrence Erlbaum.

Vygotsky, L. (1978). *Mind in society: the development of higher psychological processes.* Cambridge, MA: Harvard University Press.

Wang, M.C., Haertel, G.D., & Walberg, H.J. (1993). Towards a knowledge base for school learning. *Review of Educational Research*, 63(3), 249-294.

Wehlage, G.G., Newmann, F.M., & Secada, W.G. (1996). Standards for authentic achievement and pedagogy. In F. Newmann & Associates (Eds.), *Authentic achievement: Restructuring schools for intellectual quality* (pp. 21-48). San Francisco: Jossey-Bass.

Wehlage, G.G., & Stone, C.R. (1996). School-based student and family services: Community and bureaucracy. *Journal of Education for Students Placed at Risk,* 1(4), 299-317.

Wilson, K.G., & Daviss, B. (1994). *Redesigning education.* New York: Henry Holt and Company.

Withers, G.P., & Russell, V.J. (1998). *Educating for resilience: Prevention and intervention strategies for young people at risk.* Report prepared for the Catholic Education Office, Archdiocese of Melbourne, MacKillop Family Services, and the Department of Human Services of the Government of Victoria, Melbourne.

9. REVIEW AND PROSPECTS OF EDUCATIONAL EFFECTIVENESS RESEARCH IN THE NETHERLANDS

Jaap Scheerens[1] & Bert P. M. Creemers[2]
[1]*Faculty of Educational Science & Technology, University of Twente, the Netherlands*
[2]*Gion, University of Groningen, the Netherlands*

A review is presented of recent Dutch research into educational effectiveness and a link is made with evaluations of school improvement projects. The synthesis of the findings of the Dutch educational effectiveness studies show that there is only limited support for effectiveness enhancing conditions that are known from international research literature. The critical review of school improvement projects brings some encouraging findings to the light as well, favouring integral approaches to restructuring schools that penetrate the classroom. New routes are envisioned that bring the educational effectiveness paradigm more in line with the prevailing, constructivistic concept of (independent) learning and (indirect) instruction and with a more economically inspired research tradition.

9.1 Introduction

In the United States and the United Kingdom school effectiveness research received a great deal of attention after publications by Brookover, Beady, Flood, Schweitzer and Wisenbaker (1979) and Rutter, Maughan, Mortimore and Ouston (1979). Although educational research was quite well established in the Netherlands, research into educational effectiveness did not get off the ground until the eighties. Yet in the Netherlands, in a more general sense, educational research before that was related to educational effectiveness, i.e. research on teacher effectiveness, school organization, longitudinal research from a sociological point of view, research into effects of pupil and school characteristics on the individual school career of pupils and the evaluation of educational improvement programmes (Creemers & Knuver, 1989; Creemers & Lugthart, 1989; Scheerens, 1992).

School effectiveness research started with the replication of studies carried out in the United States with the intention of confirming these results or at least finding empirical evidence for the so-called 'five-factor model'. These studies however did not confirm the results of earlier ones in the Anglo-Saxon world. Educational leadership by the principal turned out not to be as effective a measurement as it was in the United States and by the vice-principal in the United Kingdom. There was empirical evidence for some other characteristics of effective schools but not in all studies. In fact, the picture appeared to be quite diverse (Scheerens, 1992; Scheerens & Creemers, 1989). At least in some studies the structuring of instruction, evaluation, time on task, opportunity to learn and a classroom climate conducive to learning turned out to be effective.

Based partly on the results of these replication studies, educational effectiveness research, including school effectiveness and instructional effectiveness, was analyzed. Starting from a methodological and technical critique on past research and a further refinement of the concepts used in the effectiveness research, theories or conceptual frameworks on educational effectiveness were developed (Creemers, 1994; Scheerens, 1992; Scheerens & Creemers, 1989).

From 1990 on, studies took advantage of statistical and technical developments and the further theoretical foundation of educational effectiveness. In the recent past, several PhD studies have been published on issues related to educational effectiveness. Together with other major publications on educational effectiveness, the results of these studies are described in this chapter, which provides an overview of the developments of school effectiveness research and the evaluation of school improvement projects in the Netherlands. Two new directions are also sketched: research on the effectiveness of 'new learning' arrangements and integration of school effectiveness modeling and research and micro-economic theory.

9.2   Research reviews

9.2.1   Overview of research by Scheerens and Creemers

Scheerens and Creemers (1996) present an overview of school effectiveness studies in primary and secondary education (table 1).

In the columns the total number of positive and negative significant correlations of these conditions with educational attainment are shown for 29 studies of primary schools and 13 studies of secondary schools. The main organizational and instructional effectiveness enhancing conditions, as known from international literature, are shown in the rows.

The total number of effectiveness studies in primary education (29) and secondary education (13) indicate that primary education is the main educational sector for effectiveness studies in the Netherlands. In both types of school those with a majority of lower SES-pupils and ethnic minorities are the target group in about 25 per cent of the studies.

Table 1. Number of Dutch studies in which certain school and instructional conditions correlated significantly with outcome variables, after control for pupils' background characteristics (cited from Scheerens and Creemers, 1996).

	Primary level		Secondary level	
	positive association	negative association	positive association	negative association
structured teaching/feedback	5		1	
teacher experience	3	1		1
instructional leadership		2	1	
orderly climate	2		3	1
pupil evaluation	5		0	
differentiation		2	0	
whole class teaching	3		0	
achievement orientation	4		4	
team stability/cooperation		3		3
time/homework	4		4	
other variables	16		8	
average between school variance	9		13.5	
number of studies	29		13	

Note. Not all variables mentioned in the rows were measured in each and every study.

The row that shows the percentage of variance that is between schools indicates the importance of the factor 'school' in Dutch education. The average percentage in primary schools is 9, and in secondary schools 13.5. It should be noted that this is an average not only over studies, but also over output measures. Generally, schools vary more in mathematics than in language/reading. In most cases the between-school variances have been computed after adjustment for covariates at the pupil level so they indicate the 'net-influence' of schooling while controlling for differences in pupil intake. Since at the time these studies were conducted most primary schools had one class for each school year, school and classroom level usually coincide. A final note with respect to the measures of between-school variances shown in table 1 is that only in some cases intraclass correlations have been computed, which will generally be higher than the between-school variances (since the intraclass correlations are computed as the ratio of the between-school variance and the sum of the between-school and between-pupil variance).

When considering the factors that 'work' in Dutch education, the conclusion from table 1 must be that the effective schools model is not confirmed by the data. The two conditions thought to have a significant positive association with the effectiveness criteria in primary education (structured teaching and evaluation practices) are found in no more than 5 out of 29 studies. Moreover, other factors predominate both in primary and secondary education as being associated with effectiveness. It is also striking that if an effect of instructional leadership and differentiation is found, it is negative. The set of other characteristics is very heterogeneous. The most frequently found one being 'denomination', often (but not always) with an advantage for government dependent private schools with a Roman Catholic or Protestant orientation over public schools. The large number of independent variables in most studies, and the fact that only several of these are statistically significant (sometimes dangerously close to the 5 per cent that could have been expected on the basis of mere chance), add to the feeling of uneasiness that the figures in table 1 convey concerning the fruitfulness of research driven by the school effectiveness model. Some consolation can be drawn from the fact that the most positive results come from the most sophisticated study in this area (i.e., Knuver & Brandsma, 1993).

9.2.2   Research review by Scheerens and Bosker

Scheerens and Bosker (1997) present the results of a four-year study summarizing the results of the on-going research programme on school effectiveness of the Department of Educational Organization at the University of Twente. This programme includes conceptual studies, development of models and theories, so called 'foundational' studies into various consistency issues (e.g. stability over time) in educational effectiveness, review studies, meta-analyses and international comparative studies.

In spelling out the conceptual map of schooling the authors consider a broad range of possible *effects*, a set of points of impact or actions to attain particular effects, referred to as the *modes* of schooling (goals, organizational structure and procedures (including management), culture, environment and the technology of the primary process) and *functions or underlying mechanisms* that explain why actions impinged on certain modes lead to effectiveness. The rest of the book summarizes results in terms of impact of the most frequently assessed modes on the predominant effectiveness criterion (productivity) and provides hints on the underlying principles.

According to Scheerens and Bosker alternative ways of modeling cross-level relationships (e.g. between school organizational and instructional conditions) is the most promising direction for improvement and specifications of school effectiveness models. They give examples of multilevel analyses and applications of system dynamics as useful methodological approaches to achieve this.

With respect to overall consistency in school effectiveness, their conclusion is that schools appear to be stable in effectiveness as long as the time interval is tight and if effectiveness is assessed at the formal end of a period of schooling. There is less stability in a longer time interval and when effects are measured at the beginning or in the middle of a certain level of schooling.

Considerable inconsistency in effectiveness measures when different subjects are assessed suggests that, particularly at secondary level, *teacher* effects appear to dominate over *school* effects. Regarding differential school effects, i.e. differential for different groups of pupils, the conclusion is that schools matter most for disadvantaged and/or initially low-achieving pupils.

An in-depth analysis of instruments used in school effectiveness and school self-evaluation studies leads to the conclusion that the operational definitions of the most common concepts are divergent. The following factors are considered: achievement orientation and high expectations, educational leadership, consensus and cohesion among staff, curriculum quality/opportunity to learn, school climate, evaluative potential, parental involvement, classroom climate, effective learning time, structured instruction, independent learning, differentiation, reinforcement and feedback.

In reviewing three major reviews (Levine & Lezotte (1990), Sammons, Hillman & Mortimore (1995) and Cotton (1995)) Scheerens and Bosker conclude that there is a great deal of consensus on factors at school and classroom level that are considered to enhance effectiveness. This optimistic conclusion comes under fire when the results of empirical meta-analyses are brought into the picture. From their own statistical meta-analysis the authors conclude that the impact of school organizational conditions like achievement orientation, leadership, monitoring/evaluation, cooperation among staff and parental involvement appear to be rather modest. Results of re-analyses of an international assessment study (the IEA Reading Literacy study) show even weaker effects.

The authors explore theory-embedded principles and a more theory-driven redirection of educational effectiveness research. According to their views, a synoptic rational planning, proactive approach on the one hand and an evaluation feedback-oriented retroactive approach on the other are the most promising effectiveness-enhancing mechanisms. In their own research programme this has led to an increased emphasis on studying evaluation feedback mechanisms, for example within the context of school self-evaluation. Recent dissertation studies as those by Van der Velden (1996), Heyl (1996), Lam (1996), De Vos (1998) and Doolaard (1999) emphasize the importance of improved instrumentation and advanced techniques of data analysis.

9.2.3   Small scale improvement efforts

The influence of effective school research enhancing the importance of pupil outcomes in policy and practice is relatively small in the Netherlands, although educational policy and schools sometimes explicitly refer to the effective school movement (for example in the Educational Priority Programme for disadvantaged pupils). The educational support system developed several programmes and training courses for schools, but only a few of them are based on the knowledge base of effective schools.

The Friesland project of School Improvement, initially developed at the Local Educational Support Centre, Leeuwarden, is explicitly based on school effectiveness research. The project aims to improve initial reading in grade 1 of primary school, and integrates the development of new reading materials and the improvement of instruction at classroom level by the training of teachers. As in other school improvement projects, most attention is given to teacher behaviour at classroom level incorporating the components of the direct instruction model. Important features of this school improvement project are: emphasis on direct teaching, time on task, opportunity to learn, structuring of the content, a specific set of objectives, evaluation and corrective instruction. The evaluation results were positive (Houtveen & Osinga, 1995).

Another project developed in combination by the Protestant School Support Centre (CPS) and the Catholic University of Brabant focuses on the effectiveness of initial reading (Van de Ven, 1994). This programme is inspired by the ideas of Slavin (Slavin, Madden, Karweit, Livermon & Dolan, 1990) and Clay (1993), and its main objective is to reduce the number of dropouts in early reading from 7.5 per cent to 1 per cent. An important aspect of this programme, as in 'Success for All', developed by Slavin and colleagues, is tutorial instruction for pupils who lag behind.

In more local school support institutes improvement projects take place, like in Delft, where an outcome-oriented strategy is used based on effectiveness thinking (Van Gendt, 1993). However, in school improvement projects based on educational effectiveness, the evaluation of pupil outcomes should be an important criterion. Most improvement projects in the Netherlands, however, do not meet that criterion. The projects refer to school effectiveness studies, but do not contain information on pupil achievement.

Sometimes the results of school effectiveness studies are used in a particular way, especially when we take into account the inconclusive results of Dutch studies with respect to effective school correlates of most American or British studies. In some school support institutes these factors are used to make quality inferences about schools. In Rotterdam, schools showing the characteristics of effective schools can obtain 50 per cent more support time for their school improvement activities.

There are two currently on-going school improvement programmes in which the school effectiveness knowledge base is the main guiding principle in shaping improvement-oriented actions. The first is the National School Improvement Project, an extension of the Friesland-project referred to above, in which 28 primary schools participate. The aims of this project are:

- to implement an achievement-oriented school policy, focused on specific objectives related to technical reading;
- to increase the evaluative potential of schools (i.e. stimulate the use of pupil monitoring systems and assess the content covered during lessons).

Apart from these school-level objectives, the following sub-objectives at teacher level were specified:

- the introduction of a systematic planning approach to technical reading;
- teacher training aimed at optimizing effective learning time and direct instruction;
- specific training in the didactics of technical reading (Houtveen, Booy, De Jong & Van de Grift, 1996).

The project was evaluated over a three-year period using a quasi-experimental research design. The evaluation results indicated that teachers had made substantial progress in the practice of efficient use of time and direct instruction approaches. At grade 1 level project schools scored significantly higher, on average, than control schools on a technical reading test. By grade four level, however, this significant difference had disappeared. After this first evaluation follow-up programmes have started for mathematics and reading comprehension.

A second on-going school improvement project is in the city of Rotterdam and is aimed at increasing the opportunities of disadvantaged learners. This was launched in schools with large percentages of ethnic minority pupils and is aimed at improving mathematics and language achievement. The programme is based on the 'classical' five-factor model of school effectiveness (strong educational leadership, high expectations of pupils' progress, basic skills emphasis, a safe and orderly climate and frequent monitoring of pupils' achievement). The use of 'direct instruction', geared to efficient classroom management increasing net learning time and frequent diagnostic testing appear to be the cornerstones of the programme. Existing textbooks and methods are enforced by means of a more detailed pre-structuring of subject matter and an intensive and direct form of teacher counselling (so called classroom consultation). The first evaluation results are positive, both with respect to improved teacher behaviour and improved learning achievement (Hogendijk & Wolfgram, 1995).

9.2.4 Educational effectiveness research in the framework of EPA-evaluation

The national Educational Priority Policy (EPA) programme is not a large-scale school improvement project but provides extra resources and support to schools in areas with large numbers of ethnic minority and low SES pupils. A programme of evaluation is attached to this in which achievement in language and reading is tested regularly and background characteristics of pupils, schools and classrooms are measured. The school effectiveness literature has strongly influenced the choice of malleable school and classroom/teaching variables to be measured so that the evaluation results are quite relevant for this line of empirical educational research.

Sontag (1997) looked for effects in grade 1 of primary school in a study involving 28 schools, 35 teachers and 250 pupils. Pupils were tested twice for non-verbal intelligence and passive vocabulary knowledge. School-level variables included in the study were: staff consensus, teacher expectations and educational leadership. At classroom level classroom climate, frequency of performance evaluation, emphasis on basic skills and age composition of classes was measured. Multilevel analyses with test scores adjusted for SES, ethnicity, gender and pre-test scores indicated that staff consensus was the only variable that had a significant positive association with achievement. The authors conclude that high staff consensus may contribute to a more favourable climate in school as it leaves teachers more time and energy for educational activities.

Studies aimed at the higher grades of primary school were constructed with respect to achievement data collected in 1988, 1990 and 1992 (Van der Werf, 1995). Multilevel analyses were carried out to determine whether schools differed, after controlling for pupils' background characteristics, such as socio-economic status, ethnicity and aptitude. The between-school variance ranged from 6 to 16 per cent depending on the year of measurement and subject matter (with greater variance for mathematics than for language). The patterns of association of school and classroom characteristics with the criterion variables did not convincingly support the factors known from school effectiveness literature. For the 1988 data 'incidental' positive associations were found for whole-class instruction, the use of minimum objectives and homework, with the amount of homework showing the relatively largest effect. 'Incidental' in this sense means that effects were found only for a particular category of schools and not for all categories of schools, and only for one, instead of all (two) subject areas.

More in-depth study of schools with a majority of ethnic minority pupils indicated that the more effective schools created better opportunity to learn and effective learning time (Van der Werf, 1995). More effective schools also appeared to have a more positive classroom climate, placed a stronger emphasis on reading comprehension and on basic skills.

At lower secondary level it was found that the margins to improve the achievement of disadvantaged groups were much smaller than at primary level. School variables that appeared to matter at this level were achievement-oriented policy and pupil guidance policy. The most effective instructional variables were emphasis on basic skills and amount of homework. For ethnic minority pupils high expectations and high academic standards appeared to be particularly effective (Van der Werf, 1995, 91).

From the overview of improvement projects on the one hand and educational effectiveness research conducted within the evaluation framework of the national Educational Priority Policy programme on the other, it can be concluded that targeted educational and instructional interventions show better results than more general, resources-oriented, stimulation programmes, where actual educational improvement is more or less left to the discretion of individual schools or community-based groups of schools.

9.3 Prospects and new directions

9.3.1 Introduction

In two ways Dutch educational effectiveness research is now seeking to enlarge its disciplinary basis, while addressing a more explicit confrontation with constructivist approaches to learning and instruction on the one hand, and looking for a further exploitation of concepts and methods from micro-economic theory and research on the other. These two new approaches are now briefly outlined.

9.3.2 Structured independence: the effectiveness of new learning arrangements

The general approach of a newly proposed research programme is to combine the knowledge bases and research paradigms from two internationally acknowledged traditions, i.e. educational effectiveness and constructivism. It seems promising to start out with the strong points of each tradition. The research questions for the programme will address theoretical gaps, i.e. the issues which the traditions have not yet addressed or only in a rudimentary way (see figure 1), as well as new and more integrated concepts built on both traditions.

The research traditions of effectiveness and constructivism show several differences, including:
- relationships between variables studied;
- number of levels studied;
- types of schools studied;
- measurement methods.

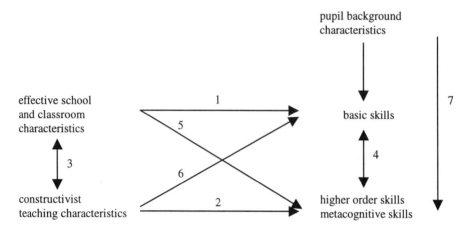

Figure 1. Effectiveness and constructivism

Educational effectiveness theory and research pay attention to the relationship between effective school and classroom characteristics and basic skills, corrected for pupil background influences (arrow 1). Recent theory and research points at the importance to study several levels of the educational system, i.e. educational context, schools, classrooms/teachers and pupils, and most studies now refer to two or three levels. Effectiveness research has mainly concentrated on primary and secondary schools and uses traditional methods to measure basic skills (standardized paper and pencil tests). It also mainly uses survey and case study methods, while experiments are somewhat rare.

Constructivism focuses on teaching and learning processes that lead to the development of higher order skills and metacognitive skills (arrow 2). The multilevel approach of effectiveness is not often applied in constructivist research. Many studies still concentrate on pupil level only. Some studies address pupil level and classroom level, while school and context level are hardly addressed at all. Constructivist studies address tertiary education relatively often. Constructivism has used more diverse measurement methods than effectiveness research to study learning processes and outcomes, such as thinking aloud and retrospective analysis of learning processes. Constructivist research mainly consists of laboratory experimental studies, while studies in regular school settings are rather rare.

Research questions

A first set of research questions relate to the *theoretical concepts* that lie behind the research traditions. The educational effectiveness paradigm and constructivism are often described as opposed to each other and as competing on various dimensions, such as teacher repertoires, instruction, classroom organization, tasks and types of outcomes. Although the educational effectiveness paradigm and constructivism certainly differ in their positions on some of these dimensions, it is not possible to use the outer ends of the dimensions for an adequate characterization. On taking a closer look the idea of a dichotomy is not so appealing. Both traditions for example make clear statements about their position on certain dimensions but not on others, which makes a strict theoretical comparison virtually impossible. The instructional approaches of both traditions are better characterized by means of profiles. These can show more accurately which position a tradition takes on the dimensions which actually are a part of the tradition at stake, and allow for the possibility that insights from educational effectiveness and constructivism may be integrated into new approaches for teaching and learning.

The means-to-end instrumental orientation is helpful in further clarifying this issue. Constructivism has been described in terms of 'new goals and new means', the new goals being higher order skills and metacognitive skills whereas independent, active or self-directed learning with teachers as coaches are seen as innovative means to reach these goals. In the effectiveness research tradition, structured, direct or expository instruction has repeatedly been shown as yielding better results in basic skills. In both traditions 'structuring' or 'scaffolding' learning tasks has been described as a continuum, rather than a dichotomy (Veenman, 1992; De Jong & Van Joolingen, 1996). The degree of structure in learning and instruction appears to be a key variable in a further exploration of optimizing learning and assessing effectiveness. The main research questions for the programme that can be derived from the theoretical basis of both traditions are:
- what differences and similarities exist in the two research traditions;

- what new approaches can be built on the integration of concepts from both traditions?

A second set of questions for the research programme is generated by the arrows 3, 4, 5, 6 and 7 in figure 1. The arrows depict the *conceptual gaps* that still exist in the domain of both traditions. These questions, which refer to relationships between independent variables, dependent variables, and between independent and dependent variables from both traditions have received little attention in either tradition. For example:

- what school-level characteristics are meaningful for constructivist and mixed approaches of teaching?
- to what extent do basic skills, higher order skills and metacognitive skills influence each other?
- what are the effects of effective classroom and school characteristics on higher order skills and metacognitive skills of pupils (corrected for pupil background)?
- what are the effects of constructivist characteristics of teaching on basic skills of pupils (corrected for pupil background)?

An innovative element of a research programme that tries to integrate both traditions, for example, would be to examine constructivist approaches more consequently for their effectiveness. Such a confrontation would not only have theoretical but also practical relevance. For example it would lead to a critical study of the new teaching and learning approaches that draw heavily on constructivist ideas and are currently being implemented in Dutch upper secondary schools.

Context	Input 'given' entrance conditions	Teacher repertoires (skills, attitudes, roles)	Technology Throughput				Aims (type of outcomes)
			instruction	learning	classroom organization	tasks	
school as professional bureaucracy instructional leadership	low aptitudes	teacher, 'structuror'	direct	reactive receptive	whole class individual	highly structured	basic skills academic
school as adhocracy, learning organization facilitative leadership	high aptitudes	facilitator	open	active productive discovery learning	groups	real life problems	higher order processes 'real life' knowledge social skills

Figure 2. Degree of structure in instructional technology conditional upon entrance conditions and goals

A third set of research questions concerns the *scope* of both traditions. The effectiveness tradition seems the better starting point because its scope has always been broader in several senses than the constructivist one. One aspect of the attempt to integrate the traditions is a multilevel comprehensive mapping of the research domain, distinguishing the levels of individual learners, groups of learners, teachers and school context (figure 2). Figure 2 uses the basic context-input-process-output framework common in educational effectiveness research to depict this comprehensive view. The basic framework consists of several continua reflecting technology and throughput. Pupil entrance conditions and teacher roles are input, while school organization and management is seen as a contextual condition (figure 2).

Figure 2 does not depict a structure of variables for separate research projects, but it can be used to extract a range of experimental conditions. It should be noted that the paradigm of aptitude treatment interaction research is included in figure 2, allowing for the possibility that structured approaches may achieve stronger effects on low aptitude pupils. By starting from the framework of effectiveness research, research questions are broadened to include several educational levels. In addition questions may be studied in different groups of pupils, teachers, types of schools and school subjects. For example:
- to what extent does the school influence teaching approaches and their effects on pupils, under which conditions are schools able to implement educational effectiveness, constructivist and mixed approaches successfully at classroom level?
- what skills do teachers need to implement educational effectiveness, constructivist and mixed approaches successfully at classroom level?
- what learning materials and equipment do teachers need to implement educational effectiveness, constructivist and mixed approaches successfully at classroom level?
- what skills do pupils need to profit sufficiently from effectiveness, constructivist and mixed approaches? Which approaches are most successful for different types of pupils (differences concern aptitude, learning style, etc.)?
- to what extent are findings comparable across primary, secondary and tertiary education?
- to what extent are findings comparable across school subjects?

Methodological issues

Overall comparability of conditions, common dependent measures and the 'ghosts' of small effect sizes in a 'sea' of noise and complexity are three methodological problems that should be faced. The alleged problem of non-comparability because the aims of constructivism differ from the educational effectiveness tradition can be circumvented by using both traditional, subject-matter oriented tests and more general skills oriented measurements for all conditions to be compared. It is also assumed that there will very likely be a common core in the learning objectives of constructivism and educational effectiveness.

A restriction of range in experimental conditions is a plague of comparative educational research. The difficulties encountered with the aptitude-treatment research programme (Cronbach & Snow, 1977) is a case in point. The 'no effect' syndrome should be dealt with in each and every part of the research programme. The following principles should be considered:

- maximization of differences between conditions (e.g. outliers);
- checking the implementation of conditions;
- providing for sufficient units of analysis to yield acceptable levels of statistical power;
- disattenuation of explanatory variables (i.e. adjusting for unreliability);
- applying multilevel techniques when variables are defined at different levels and units are nested.

Structure of the research programme

In the first phase of the research programme, activities will focus on *fundamental* research which deals with the first set of research questions mentioned above. The aim of this phase is to analyze the differences between both traditions and to construct integrated approaches for teaching in several areas of learning (basic skills, higher order skills, metacognitive skills) based on a conceptual analysis of both traditions. In the second phase of the research programme, activities will concentrate on the second and third set of questions. In this phase fundamental studies will be joined by *applied* studies, especially where the scope of research is at stake. During the full research programme *foundational* studies will be programmed which will focus especially on the measurement of the dependent variables, the design of research studies and the analysis of multilevel data.

9.3.3   School effectiveness modeling and micro-economic theory

Another route to be followed results from combining economic approaches to education, more specifically micro-economic theory and the educational effectiveness tradition. Micro-economic theory has been described as 'the theory of optimal choice among alternative possibilities' (Correa, 1995, 410). Optimal choice is equivalent to maximizing the well being of the agent making it. Taking into account certain limitations or 'constraints', this type of behaviour is also called rational behaviour. The micro-economic theory of education studies the rational behaviour of persons acting in the roles of teachers, pupils, principals or parents. Identification of the determinants of well-being of these actors, the specific constraints they face, and establishing the links between the determinants of their well-being and their constraints is known as specifying the 'utility function' of the agents playing a specific role (ibid, 410).

For example, in the theory of 'human capital' a pupil is considered an investor, investing time and tuition costs. "The income received as a result of this education is the benefit the pupil tries to maximize in order to maximize her well-being" (ibid, 412). In the case of a manager well being is seen as directly related to the 'profits' of the organization, where profits are seen as equal to the difference between revenues and incomes. Revenues are described in terms of the monetary value of output produced. Determining the relationship between inputs invested in the work processes and the outputs produced is known as the production function.

Typically education production functions describe education outputs (e.g. results on an achievement test) as a linear function of time and monetary investments, taking into account innate abilities of pupils (cf. Hanushek, 1979; Monk, 1992).

Research traditions in education, labelled 'educational effectiveness', 'school effectiveness' and 'educational productivity', are quite close to the basic characteristics of the homo economicus model. The distinction between school effectiveness and school efficiency, as already outlined by Cheng (table 2), however, shows some of the 'blind spots' in state of the art school effectiveness research as indeed the commonly used designs of programme evaluation in education.

Table 2. Distinction between school effectiveness and school efficiency (Cheng, 1993, 4)

	Nature of school output	
	in school / just after schooling short-term effects Internal (e.g. learning behaviour, skills obtained)	on the society level long-term effects external (e.g. social mobility, earning, productivity)
Nature of school input		
non-monetary (e.g. teachers, teaching methods, books)	school's technical effectiveness	school's societal effectiveness
monetary (e.g. cost of books, salary, opportunity costs)	school's technical efficiency (internal economic effectiveness)	school's societal efficiency (external economic effectiveness)

Educational effectiveness studies have typically concentrated on what Cheng calls "school's technical efficiency". Effectiveness studies and programme evaluations in education are notorious for an almost total lack of cost consciousness. A recent exception in Dutch educational policy is the issue of reducing class-size in primary education (Bosker, 1997).

Apart from setting right this limitation, an even more important objective of the ensuing research programme is to make greater use of the theoretical implications of micro-economic theory in studying educational effectiveness. This certainly does not imply solely focusing on monetary outputs. In micro-economic theory the utility function can depend on *any* kind of output the actor tries to maximize and *any* kind of input he/she is willing to invest.

Further structuring the field

Integrating micro-economic theory and the modeling of empirical school effectiveness covers a broad field, if only because of the many branches of micro-economic theory. Those aspects that seem to be the most interesting and feasible for the purposes of this theme are subsumed under three headings.

Accommodating for 'blind spots'

The 2nd, 3rd and 4th quadrant of Cheng's distinctions depicted in table 2 show as several blind spots in educational effectiveness research. To accommodate these shortcomings in future studies specific elements can be derived from the distinction into cost-effectiveness, cost-benefit and cost-utility (cf. Levin, 1988) as:

- careful accounting of costs of education and training (examples exist mainly for corporate training situations, e.g. Van Sandick & Schaap-Neuteboom, 1993; Witziers, 1996);
- expressing education effects (i.e. acquired learning gain) in monetary terms; see Witziers (1996) for a review of direct and indirect methods for this;
- measuring societal outcomes like 'on-the-job' results and 'progress in education careers' is almost a prerequisite for the previous item.

Although outputs are measured in the previous instances directly or indirectly in monetary terms, a second approach might be found to produce meaningful cut-off scores to value the outcomes of schools. This requires using methods to set standards (norms) in evaluation studies, as well as studies on equating the various kinds of outputs.

Theory driven studies

Analyzing joint utility functions of pupils, teachers and school managers may offer new inroads for empirical effectiveness studies. An interesting possibility offered by this approach is the recognition of trade-offs in the efforts that (for example) pupils and teachers are willing to make. Applications concern assigning teachers to classes (cf. Monk, 1992), readiness of teachers and principals to implement computer applications in education (cf. Scheerens, Moonen & Van Praag, 1997), and the division of teachers' attention over individual pupils and the whole class (cf. Maas, 1992).

Constraints on effective management of (school-)organizations are of central interest in the so-called new institutional economics. Eggertsson (1990) summarizes the main characteristic of this "extension of micro-economics", as he calls it, as follows:

1. ... the authors tend to make explicit attempts to model the constraints of rules and contracts that govern exchange, and the idealized structure of property rights is used primarily as a benchmark;

2.   ... the neoclassical assumptions of full information and costless exchange have been relaxed, and the consequences of positive transaction costs are examined;

3.   ... apart from quantity and price, also qualitative variations in goods and services are considered.

New institutional economics includes 'institutional' aspects of public choice theory, as described by Niskanen (1971), phenomena like x-efficiency (Liebenstein, 1978) and opportunistic behaviour (Furubotn & Richter, 1992), the constraining impact of institutional norms and 'transaction costs' (all those costs connected with the creation of change in an organization, and the running of the organization, e.g. coordination costs etc.).

Key-processes
Feedback of adequate information on performance can be seen as an important prerequisite of managerial behaviour aimed at optimizing outputs. Therefore assessment and evaluation and use of this information by such actors as principals, teachers and pupils are interesting processes for more in-depth study. Contents of application can be organizational learning (improvement perspective), or external control either by higher administrative levels (accountability) or education consumers (stimulating market forces).

Setting standards so that optimum motivating conditions are created for all pupils has also been studied as a central means of enhancing effectiveness (e.g. Clauset & Gaynor, 1982; De Vos, 1989; De Vos, 1998).

Monk (1992) draws attention to the optimum matching of good teachers and good/weak pupils.

Finally, ways of using renumeration as a means to motivate teachers to perform effectively could also be kept on the research agenda. Although such approaches - merit pay being the most straightforward - have been criticized for being impractical and unfeasible, modified forms are being contemplated in several countries. Obviously there is a link between adequate teacher performance and fairness in reward systems.

9.4   Conclusions

It is clear from the preceding paragraphs that educational effectiveness is an important topic in education. It combines different earlier separated research strands like teacher effectiveness, learning and instruction and school organization. This development took place after an initial phase when research was dominated by school organizational research questions. Since 1985 educational effectiveness has been an important programme in Dutch educational research. Especially after 1990 theoretical positions were developed and research to test specific areas of these positions has taken place. In different areas progress has been made, like in the elaboration of a theoretical position related to theories on learning, organization, and the methodology of effectiveness research (multilevel modeling). Specific components such as opportunity to learn, stability issues, and the impact of departmental level in schools were studied intensively and successfully.

In the overview of past research recommendations were made and some of these still hold.

- It is still advocated to design research projects that specifically validate the educational effectiveness models.
- Evaluation studies can be used more strongly as a further possibility for empirically validating educational effectiveness models, and they can also contribute to the further development of these models.
- Studies are still needed which highlight specific important components of educational effectiveness, such as the size of effects and the stability of effects.
- The operationalization and instrumentation of variables can be improved, preferably embedded in longitudinal and experimental studies.
- Theoretical orientations that turned out to be fruitful for educational effectiveness took place in the areas of learning and instruction and school organization. Recently new developments are taking place in these areas. Independent and less structured forms of learning and instruction are emphasized and these also refer to one of the main criticisms of educational effectiveness research in the past. In school organization theoretical orientations received more attention. In addition less structured organizational models are being studied, such as restructuring approaches

and chaos theory. Combining those new theoretical orientations with educational effectiveness research can promote the already fruitful combination of different paradigms;.

- A further extension of the educational effectiveness approach points to the combination with monetary and non-monetary inputs for education, i.e. the economic view on education. In the past a distinction was often made between effectiveness and efficiency, pointing to the fact that efficiency is an important viewpoint to make rational decisions between alternatives. Combining effectiveness and economic viewpoints can result in a more elaborated evaluation and measurement of the outcomes of education and the way those outcomes are achieved through inputs and processes.

- An ongoing discussion in educational effectiveness is the relationship between the stability of effectiveness and educational change, i.e. the improvement of education. In the recent past some issues came up related to this topic:
  - the relationship between the knowledge base of educational effectiveness and its use in strategies for improvement;
  - the relevance of notions such as consistency, constancy, cohesion and control;
  - the importance of the school mission in sustained school improvement.

- The methodological developments in the past mainly concerned multilevel causal modeling, but maybe we need more complex modeling in effectiveness and efficiency studies. It seems useful for instance to look at threshold levels of effective characteristics (levels where the effectiveness of a characteristic might turn into its opposite) and system dynamic models. The development of such models to study the relationships between effective school factors and outcomes in a process of educational change is one of the major tasks in the near future of effectiveness research.

9.5   References

Bosker, R.J. (1997). Het einde van de klassenstrijd? *Pedagogische Studiën,* 74(3), 210-227.
Brookover, W., Beady, C., Flood, P., Schweitzer, J., & Wisenbaker, J. (1979). *School social systems and pupil achievement: Schools can make a difference.* New York: Bergin.
Cheng, Y.C. (1993). *Conceptualization and measurement of school effectiveness: An organizational perspective.* Paper presented at AERA annual meeting, Atlanta, GA.

Clauset, K.H., & Gaynor, A.K. (1982). A systems perspective on effective schools. *Educational Leadership,* 40(3), 54-59.

Clay, M. (1993). *An observation survey of early literacy achievement.* Auckland: Heinemann Education.

Correa, H. (1995). *The microeconomic theory of education* [Special issue]. *International Journal of Educational Research,* 23(5).

Cotton, K. (1995). *Effective schooling practices: A research synthesis.* 1995 Update. School Improvement Research Series. Northwest Regional Educational Laboratory.

Creemers, B.P.M. (1994). *The effective classroom.* London: Cassell.

Creemers, B.P.M., & Knuver, J.W.M. (1989). the Netherlands. In B.P.M. Creemers, T. Peters & D. Reynolds (Eds.), *School Effectiveness and School Improvement. Proceedings of the Second International Congress, Rotterdam* (pp. 79-82). Lisse: Swets & Zeitlinger.

Creemers, B.P.M., & Lugthart, E. (1989). School effectiveness and improvement in the Netherlands. In D. Reynolds, B.P.M. Creemers & T. Peters (Eds.), *School Effectiveness and Improvement. Proceedings of the First International Congress, London* (pp. 89-103). Groningen/Cardiff: RION/University of Wales.

Cronbach, L.J., & Snow, R.E. (1977). *Aptitudes and instructional methods: a handbook for research on interactions.* New York: Irvington Publishers.

Doolaard, S. (1999). *Schools in Change or Schools in Chains?* Enschede: University of Twente.

Eggertsson, T. (1990). *Economic behavior and institutions.* Cambridge: Cambridge University Press.

Furubotn, E.G., & Richter, R. (1992). *The new institutional economics: a collection of articles from the journal of institutional and theoretical economics.* Tübingen: Mohr.

Gendt, W. van (1993). Resultaat gericht werken in OVG Delft. Denken begint met meten. *Stimulans,* 11, 8-10.

Hanushek, E.A. (1979). Conceptual and empirical issues in the estimation of educational production functions. *Journal of Human Resources,* 14, 351-388.

Heyl, E. (1996). *Het docentennetwerk.* Enschede: University of Twente.

Hogendijk, W., & Wolfgram, P. (1995). *KEA halverwege.* Rotterdam: CED.

Houtveen, Th., & Osinga, N. (1995, January). *The Dutch National Project School Improvement.* Paper presented at the International Congress on School Effectiveness and Improvement, Leeuwarden, the Netherlands.

Houtveen, A.A.M., Booy, N., Jong, R. de, & Grift, W. van de (1996). *Effecten van adaptief onderwijs.* Evaluatie van het Landelijk Project Schoolverbetering.

Jong, T. de, & Joolingen, W.R. van (1996). *Discovery learning with computer simulations of conceptual domains.* Enschede: University of Twente.

Knuver, J.W.M., & Brandsma, H.P. (1993). Cognitive and affective outcomes in school effectiveness research. *School Effectiveness and School Improvement,* 4, 189-204.

Lam, J.F. (1996). *Tijd en kwaliteit in het basisonderwijs.* Enschede: Universiteit Twente.

Levin, H.M. (1988). Cost-effectiveness and educational policy. *Educational Evaluation and Policy Analysis,* 10, 51-70.

Levine, D.U., & Lezotte, L.W. (1990). *Unusually effective schools: A review and analysis of research and practice.* Madison: National Center for Effective Schools Research and Development.

Liebenstein, H. (1978). On the basic proposition of x-efficiency theory. *American Economic Review Proceedings,* 68, 328-334.

Maas, C.J.M. (1992). *Probleemleerlingen in het basisonderwijs.* Utrecht: Rijksuniversiteit Utrecht, Interuniversitair Centrum voor Methodenontwikkeling en Theorievorming in de Sociologie (ICS).

Monk, D.H. (1992). *Micro-economics of school productions.* Paper for the Economics of Education Section of the International Encyclopedia of Education.

Niskanen, W.A. (1971). *Bureaucracy and representative government.* Chicago: Aldine, Atherton.

Rutter, M., Maughan, B., Mortimore, P., & Ouston, J. (1979). *Fifteen thousand hours.* London: Open Books.

Sammons, P., Hillman, J., & Mortimore, P. (1995). *Key characteristics of effective schools: A review of school effectiveness research.* London: OFSTED.

Sandick, A.S. van, & Schaap-Neuteboom, A.M. (1993). *Rendement van een bedrijfsopleiding: Een instrument voor het bepalen van het financiële rendement van trainingen.* Groningen: Rijksuniversiteit Groningen.

Scheerens, J. (1992). *Effective schooling: Research, theory and practice.* London: Cassell.

Scheerens, J., & Bosker, R. (1997). *The foundations of educational effectiveness.* Oxford: Pergamon.

Scheerens, J., & Creemers, B.P.M. (1989). Conceptualizing school effectiveness. *International Journal of Educational Research,* 13, 691-706.

Scheerens, J., & Creemers, B.P.M. (1996). School effectiveness in the Netherlands; the modest influence of a research programme. *School Effectiveness and School Improvement,* 7, 181-195.

Scheerens, J., Moonen, J.C.M.M., & Praag, B.M.S. van (1997). *Micro-economische theorie en instrumentele onderwijstheorie.* Subsidie-aanvraag SGW.

Slavin, R.E., Madden, N.A., Karweit, N.L., Livermon, B.J., & Dolan, L. (1990). Success for All: First-year outcomes of a comprehensive plan for reforming urban education. *American Educational Research Journal,* 27(2), 255-279.

Sontag, L. (1997). *Vormgeving en effecten van onderwijs aan vier- tot zevenjarige leerlingen.* Amsterdam: Thesis Publishers.

Veenman, S. (1992). Effectieve instructie volgens het directe instructiemodel. *Pedagogische Studiën,* 69, 242-269.

Velden, L.F.J. van der (1996). *Context, visie, aanpak en effectiviteit.* Groningen: GION.

Ven, H. van de (1994). *Effectief leren lezen, ondersteuningsprogramma.* Tilburg: Catholic University of Brabant.

Vos, H. de (1989). A rational-choice explanation of composition effects in educational research. *Rationality and Society,* 1, 220-239.

Vos, H. de (1998). *Educational effects: a simulation-based analysis.* Enschede: University of Twente.

Werf, M.P.C. van der (1995). *The Educational Priority Policy in the Netherlands: Content, implementation and outcomes.* The Hague: SVO.

Witziers, B. (1996). Kosten-batenanalyse: een inleiding. In P. Schramade (Ed.), *Handboek effectief opleiden* (pp. 3.1/2.01-3.1/2.20). The Hague: DELWEL.

10. THE FUTURE AGENDA OF STUDIES INTO THE EFFECTIVENESS OF SCHOOLS

David Reynolds[1] & Charles Teddlie[2]
[1]*Department of Education, University of Durham, UK*
[2]*College of Education, Louisiana State University, Baton Rouge, USA*

This chapter briefly summarizes some of the common findings in and some of the major criticisms of school effectiveness research. Eleven 'cutting edge' areas are identified where it is argued that the future of the discipline lies in terms of a research agenda to continue disciplinary advance. These areas are: the need to use multiple outcome measures; the need to use the third, relational dimension of school; the need to expand the study of context variables; the need to analyze range within schools and classrooms; the need to study the possibly additive nature of school and family effects; the need to explore the interface between levels of schooling; the need to study naturally occurring experiments; the need to expand variation at the school level; the need to study school failure or dysfunctionality; the need to use multilevel structural models, the need to recognize the salience of issues concerning curriculum and assessment.

10.1 Introduction

Many authors have speculated upon the future of school effectiveness research (e.g. Good & Brophy, 1986; Mortimore, 1991; Reynolds, 1992; Scheerens & Bosker, 1997; Teddlie & Stringfield, 1993) over the past decade. However, due to rapid developments in the field, both in terms of methodology and in substantive findings, the areas identified in need of further research ten years ago or even five years ago are either no longer relevant, or have been significantly reconceptualized.

This chapter contains a summary of eleven issues that we have identified as being on the 'cutting edge' of school effectiveness research as we approach the twenty-first century. These issues emerged as we reviewed the entire body of the worlds' research findings for a soon to be published book, *The International Handbook of School Effectiveness Research* (Teddlie & Reynolds, in press). Some of these issues are simply embodiments of repetitive themes in the literature (e.g. the need for multiple outcome measures to judge school effects and the importance of context issues), while others have only emerged in the past one or two years (e.g. the study of the relational aspects of schooling or the study of the possibly additive effects of school and family).

Before examining each of these issues, we will briefly review some of the criticisms of school effectiveness research and speculate on the general health of the field.

10.2   The current criticisms of school effectiveness research

It has been somewhat fashionable in certain educational circles to criticize school effectiveness research, with assaults being launched on the earliest work (e.g. Acton, 1980; Cuttance, 1982; Goldstein, 1980; Musgrove, 1981; Ralph & Fennessey, 1983; Rowan, 1984; Rowan, Bossert & Dwyer, 1983) and through to the present (e.g. Elliott, 1996). Part of the reasons for these criticisms have been political, part methodological and part theoretical.

School effectiveness research will always be politically controversial, since it concerns 'the nature and purposes of schooling' (e.g. Elliott, 1996), but it is interesting that school effectiveness research has been criticized politically on contradictory grounds. For instance, much of the scathing early criticism of effective schools research in the United States (e.g. Ralph & Fennessey, 1983; Rowan, 1984) concerned the researchers' embrace of well defined political goals (i.e. equity in schooling outcomes for the disadvantaged and ethnic minorities), which critics believed blocked the researchers' use of appropriate scientific research methods. Critics believed that these effective schools' researchers were liberal reformers more interested in improving the lot of the children of the poor than in conducting good science.

In the United Kingdom, on the other hand, much recent criticism (e.g. Elliott, 1996) of school effectiveness research has come from 'progressive' educators. These critics portray school effectiveness research as being underpinned by an ideology of social control and school effectiveness researchers as having an overly 'mechanistic' view of the organization of educational processes. Critics from the United Kingdom perceive school effectiveness research as giving credence and legitimization to a conservative ideology. As Elliott stated:

> 'The findings of school effectiveness research have indeed been music in the ears of politicians and government officials. Currently, for example, they are being used to politically justify a refusal to respond to teachers' anxieties about the increasing size of the classes that they teach, the use of traditional teaching methods, such as whole class instruction, and a tendency to blame headteachers for 'failing schools' on the grounds that they lack a capacity for strong leadership.' (1996, 199)

Political criticism is probably always going to be a part of the literature associated with school effectiveness research. It seems safe to conclude that as long as the researchers in the field are accused at the same time of supporting *both* conservative *and* liberal causes, these criticisms can be accepted as simply an unwarranted part of the territory in which we work.

Methodological criticisms have been a part of school effectiveness research since the original Coleman and Plowden Reports. Much of the history of school effectiveness research has been a reaction to these methodological criticisms. With the advent of methodological advances, particularly multilevel modeling, many of these criticisms have now become muted. In fact, a sign of the health of the field is that we now have a set of generally agreed prescriptions for conducting methodologically correct studies, including the following:

- school effects studies should be designed to tap sufficient of the 'natural variance' in school and classroom characteristics;
- school effects studies should have units of analysis (child, class, school) that allow for data analysis with sufficient discriminative power;
- school effects studies should use adequate operationalization and measurement of the school and classroom process variables, preferably including direct observations of process variables, and a mixture of quantitative and qualitative approaches;
- school effects studies should use adequate techniques for data analysis, which involves multilevel models in most cases;
- school effects studies should use longitudinal cohort based data, collected on individual children;

- school effects studies should adequately adjust outcome measures for any intake differences between schools.

School effectiveness research has also been criticized as having little or no theoretical basis. This criticism still has some validity, but there are present indications that researchers and theoreticians are busily working to address this perennial problem and appear to be making some headway, at least in terms of the development of heuristic midrange theories, and in the illumination of some of the possible theoretical explanations of the relationship between various school and classroom factors by interrogating existing studies with the predictions of 'meta' or 'grand' theories such as contingency theory or public choice theory (e.g. Scheerens & Bosker, 1997).

10.3   'Cutting edge' areas

We now move beyond issues of criticisms, and responses, to our eleven 'cutting edge' areas where we would argue the future of the discipline lies in terms of a research agenda to continue disciplinary advance:
- the need to use multiple outcome measures;
- the need to use the third, relational dimension of school;
- the need to expand the study of context variables;
- the need to analyze range within schools and classrooms;
- the need to study the possibly additive nature of school and family effects;
- the need to explore the interface between levels in schooling;
- the need to study naturally occurring experiments;
- the need to expand variation at the school level;
- the need to study school failure/dysfunctionality;
- the need to utilize multilevel path analysis;
- the need to recognize the salience of issues concerning curriculum and assessment.

10.3.1 The need for multiple outcomes measures in school effectiveness research

This issue has been discussed by many since the 1970's (e.g. Good & Brophy, 1986; Levine & Lezotte, 1990; Rutter, 1983; Rutter, Maughan, Mortimore, Ouston & Smith, 1979; Sammons, Mortimore & Thomas, 1996), with most commenting that multiple criteria for school effectiveness are needed. Critics have noted that schools may *not* have consistent effects across different criteria, and that to use one criterion (typically academic achievement) is not adequate for ascertaining the true effectiveness status of a school. It is also now widely recognized that multiple outcomes force the development of more sensitive explanations than are likely with restricted measures, since the pattern of why school and teacher factors are associated with some outcomes but not others (as in Mortimore, Sammons, Stoll, Lewis & Ecob, 1988 for example) is exactly the kind of scientific dissonance that is needed for creative theorizing.

Within the past decade, researchers have been making progress in this area as follows:
1. More sophisticated studies of consistency across different achievement scores have emerged, especially from the United States (e.g. Crone, Lang, Franklin & Hallbrook, 1994; Crone, Lang, Teddlie & Franklin, 1995; Lang, 1991; Lang, Teddlie & Oescher, 1992; Teddlie, Lang & Oescher, 1995). These studies have utilized more statistically appropriate measures of consistency across achievement scores (e.g. kappa coefficients), have compared consistency ratings generated by composite and by component scores, and have compared consistency ratings across very different types of academic achievement tests (e.g. criterion referenced tests versus norm referenced tests, or different public examination boards in the United Kingdom, Fitz-Gibbon, 1996).
2. Studies from the United Kingdom have continued to compare different criteria for school effectiveness beyond academic achievement scores. These comparisons have included academic versus affective/social outcomes, different measures of attitudes, different measures of behaviour and different measures of self-concept (Sammons, Mortimore & Thomas, 1996).
3. Recent research utilizing composite academic achievement scores has yielded higher estimates of consistency, thus indicating the value of constructing such scores (e.g. Crone, Lang, Franklin & Hallbrook, 1994;

Crone, Lang, Teddlie & Franklin, 1995). Additionally, Kochan, Tashakkori and Teddlie (1996) have explored the use of composite scores measuring student participation rates (including student attendance, dropout and suspension data) at the high school level in the USA. Results from a comparison of two composite school effectiveness indices from this study (one based on academic achievement scores and the other on student participation rates) indicated moderate agreement between them (Kochan, Tashakkori & Teddlie, 1996).

4. Teddlie and Stringfield (1993) utilized a matrix approach to classifying schools in a longitudinal study of school effects. In this study, seven different indicators of school effectiveness (two concerning academic achievement, four behavioural and one attitudinal) were compared to determine the current effectiveness status of matched pairs of schools that were being studied longitudinally. The resulting classification of school effectiveness status was multidimensional, involving achievements, and behavioural and attitudinal school effectiveness indicators.

These results point the way toward designing school effectiveness research that utilizes multiple criteria in the determination of school effectiveness status. Guidelines as to 'good practice' include the following:

- Use varied measures of the effectiveness of schooling, including academic achievement, attitudes (toward self, and towards others), and behaviour;
- Use measures that are sensitive to the mission of schools in the 21st century. For instance, measures of perceived racism may be important indicators of the effectiveness of schooling in some contexts (e.g. Fitz-Gibbon, 1996). Equal opportunities concerns are important in schools in many countries, yet equal opportunities orientated behaviours and attitudes are rarely used to assess school effectiveness. 'Learning to learn' or 'knowledge acquisition' skills are widely argued to be essential in the information age, yet achievement tests utilized continue to emphasize student ability to recapitulate existing knowledge;
- Use composite variables where possible, since they present a better overall picture of a school's effectiveness;
- Use where possible multidimensional matrices to assess the effectiveness of schools;

- Use measures of student behaviour wherever possible, since it is behaviours that are likely to be crucial in determining the nature of the future society that young people inhabit.

10.3.2   The need for study of the third dimension of schooling - relationship patterns

A new area of study has emerged in school effectiveness research over the past few years: the study of the relationship patterns that exist within staff groups and within student groups. This relational component constitutes the third dimension of schooling, joining the more frequently studied organizational and cultural components (Reynolds, 1992). There are three reasons why the relational component of schooling has *not* been featured much in school effectiveness research until now.

First of all, the relational patterns of faculties and teachers is difficult to measure, since questionnaires and interviews regarding school relationships may constitute 'reactive' instruments susceptible to socially desirable responses (e.g. Webb, Campbell, Schwartz, Sechrest & Grove, 1981). By contrast, sociograms are relatively non-reactive instruments designed to measure the social structure of a group and to assess the social status of each individual in the group (e.g. Borg and Gall, 1989; Moreno, 1953). The study of Teddlie and Kochan (1991) was the first within school effectiveness research to use sociograms to assess the types of relationships that exist among faculty members, although of course many researchers have used sociograms to measure student peer relationships in classes and schools (e.g. Asher & Dodge, 1986; Tyne & Geary, 1980), including individuals working within the school effectiveness research paradigm (e.g. Reynolds, 1976; Reynolds, Sullivan & Murgatroyd, 1987). It is also important to note that in many cultures (such as probably the Netherlands, Scandinavia and the countries of the Pacific Rim) it would be regarded as an unwarranted intrusion into aspects of teachers' lives to even ask them the sorts of questions that are needed to evoke analyzable data (e.g. 'Which three of your colleagues would you approach for help if you had a professional problem?').

Secondly, the interpersonal relations of teachers and of students have been difficult to conceptualize and analyze due to the complexity of the interactions within such social groups. The analytic technique that has been used in the handful of studies in the area is network analysis, utilizing data gleaned from the administration of sociograms to staff members. Social network analysis is a relatively new field, dating from the work of Moreno and expanding in the late 1970's and early 1980's (e.g. Rogers & Kincaid, 1980) that appears to provide the requisite analytical and modeling tools for analyzing school generated sociograms. The recent work of Durland (e.g. Durland, 1996; Durland & Teddlie, 1996) is the first in school effectiveness research to utilize network analysis to model and analyze data from sociograms administered to faculty members in schools.

And thirdly, there is a common perception that interpersonal relations within a school, especially among staff members, are very difficult to change, so researchers in the school improvement area have not been particularly interested in studying these patterns of relationships until recently.

The recent realization of the importance of the relational dimension, especially in the case of interpersonal relations among staff members (Reynolds, 1991; Reynolds & Packer, 1992; Reynolds, 1996), has been due to the following:

Empirical work in the United States noted above (e.g. Durland, 1996; Durland & Teddlie, 1996; Teddlie & Kochan, 1991) that has successfully linked the effectiveness levels of schools with their different patterns of interpersonal relations among staff members;

More speculative work done both in the school effectiveness and school improvement traditions in the United Kingdom and the United States that has linked ineffective schools with the presence of dysfunctional relations among staff members (e.g. Reynolds & Packer, 1992; Myers, 1995; Stoll, 1995; Stoll, Myers & Reynolds, 1996; Stoll & Fink, 1996; Teddlie and Stringfield, 1993). Reynolds (1996) has characterized these 'grossly dysfunctional relationships' in such schools as follows:

'The presence of numerous personality clashes, feuds, personal agendas and fractured interpersonal relationships within the staff group, which operate .... to make rational decision-making a very difficult process.' (154)

These dysfunctional relationships arise through the unique social-psychological history of the school (Teddlie & Stringfield, 1993) and have a tendency to continue unless drastic changes (planned or not) occur. Often these relationships manifest themselves in the generation of sharply delineated subcultures (Stoll & Fink, 1996) or cliques within the school;

Some of those in the school improvement tradition have found that the existence of relational 'shadows' or 'ghosts' of the past have had a considerable influence in affecting the progress of attempts at staff professional development (Hopkins, Ainscow & West, 1994).

Recent interesting work in this field has been done by Durland and Teddlie (1996), who posit the Centrality-Cohesiveness Model of Differentially Effective Schools. This model postulates that differentially effective schools can be distinguished by how cohesive the faculty is (measured in network analysis as network density) and how central the principal (or surrogate) is within the organization (measured by group centralization, or betweenness centralization in network analysis terminology).

Sociograms generated by network analysis can be utilized to detect the presence of cliques, such as those that occur in dysfunctional schools. Durland and Teddlie (1996) have presented some suggestive preliminary results utilizing network analysis to analyze the differences between effective (described as 'well webbed') and ineffective (characterized by cliques and/or 'stringy' structures) schools, but this area of research is obviously still in its infancy.

If relational patterns do relate to effectiveness levels, then clearly they require more intensive study, particularly since school improvement is likely to have to influence these factors as well as school organization and culture if schools are to be changed.

Further research in this area could develop in several ways:

- More work needs to be done on more refined descriptions of effective and ineffective schools in terms of sociometric indices and sociograms. Hopefully, this work will lead us to sets of prototypical sociometric indices and sociograms for differentially effective schools;
- Longitudinal studies of sociometric indices and sociograms should prove useful in describing how social relations change over time (e.g. setting the sociograms 'in motion' over time) and whether or not those changes are associated with changes in effectiveness status;
- Sociometric indices and sociograms should also be developed for students within classrooms. These data may be considered as additional

school effectiveness indicators, if one assumes that effective schools should be fostering positive relationships among students. It may also be that there are different *student* relational patterns in more effective classes and schools than in less effective.

10.3.3   The need to expand the study of context variables

The introduction of context variables into school effectiveness research has had a large impact on all three strands within the field (school effects, effective schools, school improvement). The consideration of contextual variation in school effectiveness research has also led to increased sophistication in theory development (e.g. Creemers & Scheerens, 1994; Scheerens, 1992, 1993; Scheerens & Creemers, 1989; Slater & Teddlie, 1992; Wimpelberg, Teddlie & Stringfield, 1989) as theorists have explicitly taken into account the impact that different levels of a context variable can have on school effects and processes associated with them. These contextually 'sensitive' theories of school effectiveness have incorporated tenets of contingency theory (e.g. Mintzberg, 1979; Owens, 1987) as a framework from which to interpret results from school effectiveness research.

Contingency theory purports to explain why certain school effectiveness variables 'travel' across levels of context, while others do not. For instance, the failure of the well known principal leadership effect on student achievement in the Netherlands (e.g. Van de Grift, 1989, 1990) is a good illustration of a school effectiveness variable that did not 'travel' from one country to another due to the differences in country contexts.

The study of context in school effectiveness research is also beginning to have an impact on theories of school improvement, because school improvers realize now that there aren't 'silver bullets' that always lead to school improvement. Instead, contextually sensitive models for school improvement with 'multiple levers' have emerged as studies have demonstrated that what works to change processes can vary to a large degree by context factors such as SES of catchment area, school effectiveness level or schools' improvement 'trend lines'.

While the impact of context variables in school effectiveness research is now well established, there are several research areas where additional work would be useful:

- The variation in context should be expanded by the enhanced use of 'nation' as a context variable. However, the enhanced range of educational factors and cultural contexts that this produces may be potentially damaging if study leads to the simplistic, direct import of 'what works' without analysis of cultural differences;
- Researchers should enhance the variation in context factors where possible. Considering international studies, it would be very beneficial to have more developing societies in comparative studies of school effectiveness research. It would be interesting to determine the magnitude of school effects for these countries compared to first world countries using a common methodology, and it would be also interesting to expand further our knowledge of the 'context specificity' of effectiveness factors (Reynolds & Farrell, 1996);
- Other new context variables should be added to school effectiveness research designs. For instance, the region of a country could have a large impact in some countries. In the United States, for instance, it could be argued that school effects and the processes associated with them may be quite different in the Northeast, the Midwest, the South, and the West. In the United Kingdom, there are considerable historical differences and cultural differences between regions (Reynolds, 1989), such as the tradition of sons following their fathers into mining or industrial employment in the North East, compared with the Welsh tradition of encouraging the 'escape' of children from the prospects of such employment, both of which differential contextual responses to disadvantage could be argued to have considerable implications for 'what works' within schools. Another example concerns grade level: pre-school and college could be added as additional levels of this context variable;
- In general, as the study of context in school effectiveness research matures, there should be more levels of the context variables and more range across the variables.

10.3.4   The need to analyze consistency within schools and classrooms

There are some interesting hints in the recent literature that the *range* or variation in school and teacher factors may be important determinants of outcomes and effectiveness additionally to the *average* levels scored on the factors themselves. The Louisiana School Effectiveness Studies noted the enhanced consistency evident in effective schools and in their teachers within lesson behaviours (Teddlie & Stringfield, 1993), as did the study of Crone and Teddlie (1995) (see table 1). Scheerens and Bosker (1997) also review the evidence on this topic.

Table 1. Comparison of variance in scores on teacher behaviour for effective versus ineffective schools

Teachers in effective schools (n=30)

variable	lowest score	highest score	range	coefficient of variation
time-on-task (interactive)	.15	.85	.71	31.22
time-on-task (overall)	.55	.90	.36	10.39
management	2.37	5.00	2.64	11.78
teacher's instruction scale 1	2.74	4.61	1.88	12.28
teacher's instruction scale 2	2.75	4.88	2.14	12.42
classroom climate scale 1	2.60	4.90	2.31	12.71
classroom climate scale 2	2.33	5.00	2.68	17.88

Teachers in ineffective schools (n=30)

variable	lowest score	highest score	range	coefficient of variation
time-on-task (interactive)	.08	.75	.68	34.45
time-on-task (overall)	.48	.96	.49	19.01
management	2.10	4.60	2.51	18.86
teacher's instruction scale 1	1.28	4.30	3.03	23.74
teacher's instruction scale 2	1.38	4.38	3.01	22.04
classroom climate scale 1	2.30	4.80	2.51	16.97
classroom climate scale 2	1.50	4.67	3.18	22.07

Note: The coefficient of variation is computed by dividing the standard deviation by the mean and multiplying by 100. From: Crone and Teddlie, 1995.

The International School Effectiveness Research Project (ISERP) of Creemers. Reynolds, Stringfield and Teddlie (1996) also found both that successful and educationally effective countries possessed a more homogeneous set of teachers and schools, and that effective schools in all of the nine countries participating evidenced predictability and consistency in their organizational processes both over time and between organizational members at a point in time. Interesting speculations about consistency, constancy and cohesion, and the power of these factors to socially control young people have been offered by Creemers (1994) and Reynolds (1996). In a similar way, Murphy (1992) has talked about the symbolic, cultural and organizational 'tightness' of effective school organizations and, by implication, the looseness and wide range within ineffective organizations.

And from school improvement has come a recognition that reliability or fidelity of implementation (i.e. consistency) is necessary to ensure improved educational outcomes from school improvement programmes. Indeed, the growing recognition that school improvement can generate enhanced inconsistency (and lower potential effectiveness) because the educational ceiling of competent persons/schools improve much faster than the floor of less competent persons/schools, seems to be a powerful 'face valid' explanation for the consistently disappointing effects of school improvement that has been unconcerned with 'inconsistency', viewing it as a necessary part of teacher professional development (Reynolds, Creemers, Hopkins, Stoll & Bollen, 1996).

Such ideas are not surprising - the literature upon family socialization has always indicated parental consistency in rule enforcement as of crucial importance to healthy child development, and erratic and inconsistent discipline, rule enforcement and goal setting has long been seen as a cause of disturbed and dysfunctional individual behaviour (Rutter, 1980). It is arguable, though, that the influence of the range of school and teacher factors may have become more important of late, since many of the more historically consistent influences upon child development such as the family, the community, the mass media and the wider society have all become more heterogeneous and varied. The historical possibility is that inconsistent schooling, with a wide range in teacher behaviours, goals and means, might have been historically outweighed in any possible negative influences by consistency emanating from non-educational sources. Now, however, the consistency of families seems to have been reduced by social changes of the last 30 years.

All this suggests that we need further research to establish the importance of 'range', 'consistency' and 'inconsistency' in such areas as:

- teacher behaviours in lessons, looking at differences between teachers at a point in time, and at individual teacher consistency over time;
- the goals of education as perceived and practiced by school members;
- consistency in the relationship between classroom factors, school factors, district level factors and societal factors.

Ensuring that school effectiveness research always presents the standard deviations for all variables (and other measures of variation), as well as the more conventionally used means, would seem to be axiomatic if these speculations are to be further developed.

10.3.5   The need to study the possibly additive nature of   school and family

There are now a number of datasets across a variety of national contexts that suggest that family background and school quality may be related, with consequent considerable importance both for children affected and for educational policy in general. Work in Sweden by Grosin (1992) and in the United States by Teddlie (1996) shows that even after one has controlled out the effects of individual pupil background factors and/or achievement levels, there is a tendency for schools in low SES areas to do worse than one would have predicted and for schools in middle class areas to do better. Particularly marked is the existence of a group of schools 'below the regression line' in disadvantaged communities, even though such schools have often been the source of additional financial resources to help them improve and even though they have often attracted considerable attention from educational reformers.

What may be happening, then, is that school and home have additive effects, a possibility also suggested in an intriguing study of male delinquency by Farrington (1980), in which schools acted to increase the levels of delinquency when the prediction was already for a high rate, and to lower it below prediction when that prediction was for a low rate. From within recent writing on dysfunctional schools noted earlier (Reynolds, 1991, 1996; Stoll, Myers & Reynolds, 1996) has also come an appreciation of the depth of problems that schools in this category can face, an appreciation now increasingly shared by those school improvers who are attempting to unravel the complexities of such schools (Hopkins, 1996).

The 'additive' idea is an important one, since it might explain that most persistent finding of all post-war educational reform attempts - that social class inequality in access to educational qualifications has been largely unchanged by educational 'improvement' on both quantity and quality dimensions. It also integrates the two literatures which have appeared to be at cross purposes, much to the detriment of the mutual understanding of the scholars working in the two fields - that from the sociology of education which stresses the influence of social structure, and that from school effectiveness which stresses the independent effects of schools. Schools do make a difference in this formulation, but that difference acts to reinforce pre-existing differences in the structure of society.

We still need to know, of course, why there is this tendency for the less effective schools to be in more disadvantaged areas. Differential quality in schools' teacher supply may be a factor, given the likelihood of a greater number of applications for jobs being in schools in advantaged areas. The 'drift' of good people to more socially advantaged settings, offering expanding job prospects because of population growth and a less stressful environment, may also be a factor, as may be the tendency for high stress situations such as the education of the disadvantaged to find 'flaws' and 'weaknesses' in organizational arrangements and personnel that would not occur in the absence of the 'stressors' that are associated with disadvantage.

10.3.6   The need to explore the interface between levels in schooling

The recent popularity of multilevel methodology has clearly created a need for reconceptualization of the process data that have historically been collected, since the use of the individual, class, school and potentially outside school factors (such as District or even possibly country) has clearly created multiple levels where formerly in the early years of school effectiveness research there was only one (a group of pupils generating a school mean).

At present, we have very little understanding of the 'interactions' or 'transactions' between levels, either at the more commonly used focus of classrooms nested in schools (class/school) or the more rarely used schools nested in Districts (school/District), although Scheerens and Bosker (1997) have begun to explore this issue. The growing recognition of the importance of 'range' or variation noted above propels us urgently in this direction also, given that the management interface between school and classroom generates enormous variation in classroom effectiveness in some settings, but not in others (e.g. Teddlie & Stringfield, 1993).

What might the focus of investigation be, for example, of the classroom/school interface? Possible areas of interest might include:

- the selection of teachers;
- monitoring of the teachers' performance by the principal (at the school level);
- the schools' use of mechanisms to ensure homogeneity of teachers' goal orientation;
- the use made of performance data to detect 'unusual' or 'outlier' teacher performance;
- the constancy of personnel at the two levels, and the relational patterns between them.

Other interactions take place at other levels, with perhaps the interaction between the school and the District level being of considerable importance. Areas of interest here include:

- school variation in what is evoked from District level advisers, inspectors and personnel;
- district differential allocation of staff to different schools (in the case of schools in the United States where this is a possibility).

The pupil/class interface would also be an interesting one to explore further, with interesting areas here including:

- the extent to which there are well managed transitions between teachers across grades/years;
- the coordination of various distinctive pupil level programmes for children with special needs perhaps, or for children of high ability.

10.3.7   The need to study naturally occurring experiments

All societies, and perhaps especially Anglo-Saxon ones, currently show considerable experimentation with their educational systems, involving both national macro level policy changes and more micro level classroom and school changes in organization, curriculum, governance, assessment and much else. Experimental studies have, of course, considerable advantages for the study of school effectiveness, with the methodological 'gold standard' (Fitz-Gibbon, 1996) being the random allocation of some educational factor to a 'treatment' group of children and the use of other children as an untouched 'control'. However, various considerations have greatly held back the utilization of experiments, namely: ethical problems concerning the difficulty of denying any control group the factors that were being given to some children in the 'treatment' group, and contamination between the experimental and the control groups if the random allocation is within a school, or if the schools being used are geographically close together in a District.

The use, then, of experiments of nature could be of considerable potential use within the field since this involves the utilization of *already existing* experiments to generate knowledge, with schools or classes or children that are being given educational factors being studied by contrast with those similar schools or classes or children that are not being given the educational novelties. If the groups compared are similar in the background factors that may affect educational outcomes, then any differences in educational outcomes can be attributed to the effects of educational factors. This method has the benefit of avoiding (by the separating out of home and school effects) the problems of multicollinearity that often exist in school effectiveness research and which have bedeviled the field since its inception, given the well researched tendency for more able children to be educated in more highly performing schools. Inevitably the study of experiments of nature is likely to involve a long term and often cohort based design, given the tendency of the experiments to be long term themselves.

However, the problems involved in utilization of this methodology of educational research cannot be overlooked either. Experiments of nature are sometimes themselves changed over time, and are sometimes taking place where *multiple* factors are changing, as is the case currently with educational reform in Britain that involves teacher training, school organization, school curriculum and teaching methods. Attempting to unravel the effects of some of the component parts of the experiment from the general effects of the experiments may be difficult, and in the long term the problem of multicolinearity may return, given that the already advantaged students from already advantaged homes often seem able to find the schools that are showing the most promise in their utilization of new programmes. However, the considerable advantages offered by experiments of nature to generate a more rigorous and robust knowledge base in school effectiveness research seem to heavily outweigh any disadvantages. We would hope that school effectiveness researchers would be increasingly drawn to the 'quasi experiment', particularly since virtually all countries are conducting multiple experiments of nature at the present time and are thereby providing multiple opportunities for study (e.g. Cook & Campbell, 1979).

10.3.8   The need to expand variation at the school level

The accumulated research knowledge is strongly suggestive of the view that the 'class' level or 'learning' level is a more powerful influence over children's levels of development and their rate of development than the 'school' level, which is in turn a more powerful level than that of the District or Local Education Authority. Until the development of various forms of multilevel methodology, variance at the classroom level was 'hidden' by the exclusive use of school level 'averages'. Now the classroom variance within schools is clearly exposed. As Stringfield (1994) rather nicely puts it, 'Children don't learn at the Principal's knee - they learn in classrooms', although if one examined school effectiveness research historically one would see much greater concentration upon the Principal's knee than the classroom context. The teacher and classroom are the 'proximal variables'. It is important, though, to retain a focus on the school and to continue and develop the study of the school. The school is the unit of policy analysis and of policy intervention. Schools have their own effects separate from those of classrooms or Departments. School influence at the level of 'culture' or 'ethos' is more than the influence of the summation of their component parts, as Rutter, Maughan, Mortimore, Ouston and Smith (1979) originally noted.

Part of the reason for the inability of researchers to show much 'strength' or 'power' at school level has been that they have been operating with highly constricted variance in the 'school' factor itself, since samples have been taken from within countries and cultures that already possess schools which are quite similar because of the influence of national traditions. As an example, United Kingdom schools for the primary age range vary from the smallest of perhaps 15 pupils to the largest of perhaps 750 pupils, so within the United Kingdom sampling will generate a certain range. However, in Taiwan the smallest schools (in the rural areas) are of restricted size of perhaps 60, whilst the largest is perhaps of 8000 pupils. Sampling cross culturally and across national boundaries would therefore be likely to generate much greater variation than sampling within a country.

Classroom variation is unlikely to increase as much as school variation if sampling were to be cross national. To take size as a factor, class sizes within the United Kingdom perhaps range from 17/18 up to a maximum of 40. Sampling across the globe would only increase the variation probably to 12/13 at the lower end and perhaps to 60/70 in some developing societies at the top end. The hugely enhanced range, and likely enhanced explanatory power, of the school, if one deliberately seeks to maximize its range rather than minimize it by within nation sampling, is also likely to be found in terms of school *quality* factors, not just *quantity* factors. As an example, within Britain there would be a degree of variation in the leadership styles of headteachers, ranging from the moderately lateral or involving/participatory, to the moderately centralized and dominating. Looking outside the United Kingdom context, one could see apparently totally autocratic, non-participatory leadership in Pacific Rim societies such as Taiwan, and also apparently virtually totally 'lateral' decision making within the primary schools of Denmark, where school policy is generated by teachers.

We would argue, then, that the existing estimates as to the relatively small size of school effects (Scheerens & Bosker, 1997) are an artifact of researchers unwillingness to explore the full range of variation on the 'school variable'. Cross national research would expand variation on the school level by much more than on the classroom level - since classrooms are more alike internationally than are schools - and is essential if a more valid picture of school/classroom influence is to be generated, although there will clearly be a need for contextual issues to be taken account in any discussions and analyses.

10.3.9   The need to study school failure/dysfunctionality

School effectiveness research has historically taken a very different disciplinary route to that of many other 'applied' disciplines such as medicine and dentistry, in that is has studied schools that are 'well' or effective, rather than those that are 'sick' or ineffective. Indeed, with notable exceptions in school effectiveness research (Reynolds, 1996; Stoll & Myers, 1997) and in school improvement research, (Sarason, 1982), the dominant paradigm has been to study those schools already effective or 'well' and to simply propose the adoption of the characteristics of the former organizations as the goal for the less effective. In medicine, by contrast, research and study focuses upon the sick person and on their symptoms, the causes of their sickness and on the needed interventions that may be appropriate to generate health. The study of medicine does not attempt to combat illness through the study of good health, as does school effectiveness: it studies illness to combat illness.

It is, of course, easy to see why school effectiveness has studied the already 'well', or effective, schools. The failure of the experiments of social engineering in the 1970's (Reynolds, Sullivan & Murgatroyd, 1987), combined with the research and advocacy that suggested that schools make no difference (Coleman, Campbell, Hobson, McPartland, Mood, Weinfeld & York, 1966; Jencks, 1975; Bernstein, 1968), led to a defensiveness within the field of school effectiveness and to an unwillingness to explore the 'trailing edge' of 'sick' schools for fear of giving the educational system an even poorer public image. Access to sick schools additionally has always been more difficult than to well or effective schools, given the well known tendency of such ineffective schools to want to isolate themselves from potential sources of criticism from the world outside. The routine involvements of professional life in education have also tended to be between the good schools and the researchers, who tend to prefer to involve themselves in the successful schools rather than to put up with the toxicity, problems and organizational trauma that is the day to day life of the ineffective school.

The problems for school effectiveness research because it has concentrated upon the effective rather than the ineffective schools are numerous. Because the effective schools have already become effective, we do not know what factors *made* them effective over time. There may be whole areas of schooling which are central to educational life in non-effective schools that simply cannot be seen in effective schools, such as staff groups that possess 'cliques' or interpersonal conflict between staff members for example. To propose dropping into the context of the ineffective school those factors that exist in the effective school may be to generate simply unreachable goals for the ineffective school, since the distance between the practice of one setting from the practice of the other may be too great to be easily bridged.

If school effectiveness research were to reorientate itself towards the study of the sick, then a number of likely events would follow. Given that these schools are likely to increasingly be the site for numerous interventions to improve them, then there will be naturally occurring experiments going on that are much more rare in the 'steady state' effective schools. The study of sickness usually necessitates a clinical audit to see which aspects of the patient are abnormal - an educational audit can perform the same function, which of course is not necessary in an effective school because there is no concern about organizational functioning.

We believe that school effectiveness research has been fundamentally misguided in its belief that the way to understand and combat sickness is through the study of the already well. The sooner that the discipline reorientates itself to the study of sickness, ineffectiveness, dysfunctionality and failure the better, since focus will inevitably shift to the utility of the various interventions that may be possible in such settings. In such a way, the discipline will acquire a much needed more applied orientation.

10.3.10   Curriculum and assessment

It is obvious from all literature reviews (Scheerens & Bosker, 1997; Reynolds & Cuttance, 1992) that the study of curricular variation within and between schools has not been a focus over the last three decades of school effectiveness research. The explanations for this are simple:

- the orientation of researchers has been towards a behavioural, technicist approach in which the 'vessel' of the school is studied rather than the 'contents';
- school effectiveness research has often possessed a conservative political orientation in which schooling was seen as a 'good', which school effectiveness research was to encourage more children to take up. In such a formulation any evaluation of the 'most effective curriculum' in terms of desired knowledge produced was superfluous, and less important than cascading existing knowledge to more children;
- school effectiveness research was in many ways a reaction against those educationalists who generated a discourse within educational research that concentrated upon discussion of value judgements about 'what ought to be' and 'what ought to be the goals of education'. School effectiveness research therefore accepted existing goals, accepted the pattern of existing curricular knowledge that was to orientate children towards those goals and concentrated upon discussion as to the most appropriate school organizational means that were appropriate to achieving them;
- school effectiveness research has been well aware of the immense difficulties involved in measuring the variable 'curriculum'. Time allocated to curricular knowledge in general has not been difficult to measure, likewise the time allocation to different subject groups (see for example the results of international surveys reported in Reynolds and

Farrell, 1996). However, attempts to move further and develop typologies of curriculum content and organization, along continua such as 'open/closed', 'traditional/new', or 'culturally relevant/culturally elitist' have resulted in the expenditure of considerable effort for very little reward! Indeed, perhaps the best known attempt to organize and analyze curriculum as *knowledge*, that of Bernstein (1968), was systematically destroyed by the work of King (1983) who noted that there were in reality only perhaps a tenth of relationships between curricular variables that were in the direction predicted by Bernstein's theory of classification and framing.

Whilst the neglect of curricular issues is not surprising, there is now a possibility that such neglect may be damaging the field. Partly this is because the reluctance to think about curricular issues cuts the field off from the very widespread discussions now in progress about the most appropriate bodies of knowledge that should be in the schools of a 'post modern age' or an 'information economy and society'. Also, the reluctance to discuss curriculum matters and participate in the debates about whether 'new' bodies of knowledge may be more effective than the 'old' ones encourages the discipline to continue with what can only be labelled as a strikingly traditional range of outcomes, rather than diversify towards new, and more broadly conceptualized, ones. As an example, metacognitive skills are currently receiving a considerable amount of attention, in which learning is seen as an active process in which students construct knowledge and skills by working with the content (Resnick & Resnick, 1992). The new metacognitive theories differ considerably from the traditional views that are on offer historically within school effectiveness research, in which teacher instruction generates the possibility of a student mastering the task, with the knowledge being mainly declarative (how it works) and procedural (how to do it). With metacognitive theorizing the focus is more upon conditional knowledge (how to decide what to do and when to do it). The old model of instruction that school effectiveness research represents aims mainly at the direct transfer and the reproduction of existing knowledge as it is defined by schools and teachers in curricula, while the new model of instruction takes the learning of strategies by students as the centre of attention. These new models see a consequent need to change the role of the teacher, since the student being responsible for his or her own learning means that the teacher is no longer the person who instructs but is rather the person who now teaches the techniques and strategies that students need to use to construct their own knowledge.

School effectiveness research and its conservative curricular and outcome orientation is therefore not engaging with, and learning from, the new paradigms in the field of learning and instruction. Additionally, it is not learning from or debating with those who argue for a new range of social or affective outcomes to be introduced that are relevant to the highly complex, fast moving world of the 1990's (see Stoll & Fink, 1996), in which personal affective qualities become of greater importance because knowledge itself is easily accessible through information technology.

The school effectiveness research of the present may, because of its reluctance to debate the issues of values that are incorporated in discussions of the curriculum, and because of its reluctance to countenance new outcome measures that are appropriate to the future rather than to the past, be in danger of being left behind by those who are actively exploring these issues. Will the new outcomes that an information age requires, such as 'students having the capacity to handle and access and construct information', be generated by the schools that are 'effective' in the school effectiveness literature? Will the schools successful in generating conventional academic excellence through their predictability, cohesion, consistency and strong structure be the schools to generate the new social outcomes of 'coping' and 'psychosocial resilience' that are needed for today's youth? We fear the answers to both these questions may be 'no'.

10.3.11   Multilevel structural equation modeling

The great success of multilevel modeling has been largely due to the fact that such models more adequately depict the process of schooling, as we currently envision it, than does regression analysis. It is possible that multilevel structural equation modeling (SEM) will eclipse multilevel modeling in the future for the same reason. Several authors (e.g. Hallinger & Heck, 1996; Scheerens & Bosker, 1997) have speculated that the effect of the school on the student is indirect, largely through the mediating level of the class. Recent advances in multilevel structural equation modeling make it possible to model statistically the indirect effects of school variables on student achievement using the multilevel approach. Given the tremendous enthusiasm that has been associated with multilevel modeling among many in school effectiveness research, the emergence of multilevel structural equation modeling is likely to generate much high quality theoretical and statistical work over the next few years.

10.4   Conclusions: the end of the beginning

There is no doubt that school effectiveness research has achieved a great deal in the last two decades. Knowledge has been advanced considerably in the areas such as the size of school effects, their consistency across outcome measures, their stability over time, and particularly in the area of the effective school level processes that generate 'gain' on academic and social outcomes. Also, the professional apparatus of normal science has been established with the journal *School Effectiveness and School Improvement* and the establishment of the professional association, The International Congress for School Effectiveness and Improvement (ICSEI).

Some of the reasons for the discipline being on a steep curve are indeed to do with ICSEI itself. Unlike many educational associations which are composed of persons from a restricted range of countries, ICSEI's international scope from the beginning meant that there was considerable potential in people learning from the knowledge bases of people from other societies with whom professional and personal contacts were made. Also, the merger of the interests of school effectiveness and school improvement within the emerging discipline led to an interesting education for members of both paradigms, as they became aware of the divergent perspectives offered by the 'other paradigm'.

Further reasons for what is generally seen as a very steep intellectual curve include the disciplines 'problem orientation', which seems to be particularly associated with successful disciplinary development in the case of beginning disciplines because of the restricted and tight focus that it brings and because the 'taken for granted' of the problem orientation restricts metaphysical speculation.

It may be, though, that for further intellectual advance to take place, a number of different potentiators are now necessary, since the factors associated with a discipline's advancement are likely to be different in its medium term to those which potentiate advancement when it is newly established. Factors of importance currently may be:

- interaction with cognate disciplines such as those noted in our eleven cutting edge directions above, such as cognitive psychology, human relations, social psychology, comparative education, sociology of education, and teacher/instructional effectiveness;
- additionally, there may be utility as we noted above in adapting the medical model to see if its focus upon the remediation of sickness, its distinction between presenting symptoms and the 'real' problems and its clinical distinctions between 'core' conditions that need treatment and 'peripheral' problems that will respond if the 'core' problems are addressed, are useful approaches for school effectiveness research to take.

If in addition to the factors above school effectiveness research can also expand its definitions of outcomes and adopt a more pluralistic attitude and values base, instead of the problem orientation that 'takes' problems as governmental and societal determined rather than rendering them as problematic, then further disciplinary advance can be predicted. No discipline has been on a steeper intellectual curve over the last ten years than school effectiveness research, and there is no reason why that should not continue.

10.5   References

Acton, T.A. (1980). Educational criteria of success: Some problems in the work of Rutter, Maughan, Mortimore and Ouston. *Educational Researcher, 22*(3), 163-173.

Asher, S.R., & Dodge, K.A. (1986). Identifying children who are rejected by their peers. *Developmental Psychology, 22*(4), 444-449.

Bernstein, B (1968). Education cannot compensate for society. *New Society, 387*, 344-347.

Borg, M., & Gall, W. (1989). *Educational Research. (Fifth Edition).* New York: Longman.

Coleman, J.S., Campbell, E., Hobson, C., McPartland, J., Mood, A., Weinfeld, R., & York, R. (1966). *Equality of educational opportunity.* Washington, DC: Government Printing Office.

Cook, T.D., & Campbell, D.T. (1979). *Quasiexperimentation: Design and analysis issues for field settings.* Boston: Houghton Mifflin Company.

Creemers, B.P.M. (1994). *The Effective Classroom.* London: Cassell.

Creemers, B.P.M., & Scheerens, J. (1994). Developments in the educational effectiveness research programme. In R.J. Bosker, B.P.M. Creemers, & J. Scheerens (Eds.), *Conceptual and methodological advances in educational effectiveness research.* Special issue of *International Journal of Educational Research, 21*(2), 125-140.

Creemers, B.P.M., Reynolds, D., Stringfield, S., & Teddlie, C. (1996). *World Class Schools: Some Further Findings.* Paper presented at the annual meeting of the American Educational Research Association, New York, NY.

Crone, L.J., Lang, M.H., Franklin, B., & Halbrook, A. (1994). Composite versus component scores: Consistency of school effectiveness classification. *Applied Measurement in Education,* 7(4), 303-321.

Crone, L.J., & Teddlie, C. (1995). Further examination of teacher behavior in differentially effective schools: Selection and socialisation processes. *Journal of Classroom Interaction,* 30(1), 1-9.

Crone, L.J., Lang, M.H., Teddlie, C., & Franklin, B. (1995). Achievement measures of school effectiveness: Comparison of model stability across years. *Applied Measurement in Education,* 8(4), 365-377.

Cuttance, P. (1982). Reflections on the Rutter ethos: The professional researchers' response to Fifteen thousand hours: Secondary schools and their effects on children. *Urban Education,* 16(4), 483-492.

Durland, M.M., & Teddlie, C. (1996). *A network analysis of the structural dimensions of principal leadership in differentially effective schools.* Paper presented at the annual meeting of the American Educational Research Association, New York, NY.

Durland, M.M. (1996). *The application of network analysis to the study of differentially effective schools.* Unpublished doctoral dissertation, Louisiana State University, Baton Rouge, LA.

Elliott, J. (1996). School effectiveness research and its critics: Alternative visions of schooling. *Cambridge Journal of Education,* 26(2).

Farrington, D. (1980). Truancy, delinquency, the home and the school. In L. Herson & I. Berg (Eds.), *Out of School.* Chichester: John Wiley.

Fitz-Gibbon, C.T. (1996). *Monitoring Education: Indicators, Quality and Effectiveness.* London, New York: Cassell.

Goldstein, H. (1980). Critical notice - *'Fifteen Thousand Hours'* by Rutter et al. *Journal of Child Psychology and Psychiatry,* 21(4), 364-366.

Good, T.L., & Brophy, J.E. (1986). School effects. In M. Wittrock (Ed.), *Third Handbook of Research on Teaching* (pp.328-375). New York: Macmillan.

Grift, W. van de (1989). Self perceptions of educational leadership and mean pupil achievements. In D. Reynolds, B.P.M. Creemers, & T. Peters (Eds.), *School effectiveness and improvement: Selected proceedings of the first international congress for school effectiveness* (pp. 227-242). Groningen, Netherlands: RION.

Grift, W. van de (1990). Educational leadership and academic achievement in secondary education. *School Effectiveness and School Improvement,* 1(1), 26-40.

Grosin, L. (1992). *School Effectiveness Research as a Point of Departure for School Evaluation.* Paper presented at the conference on Theory and Practice of School Based Evaluation, Lillehammer: Norway.

Hallinger, P., & Heck, R.H. (1996). Reassessing the principal's role in school effectiveness: A review of the empirical research, 1980-1995. *Educational Administration Quarterly,* 32(1), 5-44.

Hopkins, D., Ainscow, M., & West, M. (1994). *School Improvement in an Era of Change.* London: Cassell.

Hopkins, D. (1996). Towards a theory for school improvement. In J. Gray, D. Reynolds & C. Fitz-Gibbon (Eds.), *Merging Traditions: The Future of Resarch on School Effectiveness and School Improvement* (pp.30-50). London: Cassell.

Jencks. C. (1975). *Inequality*. Harmondsworth: Penguin Books.

King, R. (1983). *The Sociology of School Organisation*. London: Methuen.

Kochan, S.E., Tashakkori, A., & Teddlie, C. (1996). *You can't judge a high school by test data alone: Constructing an alternative indicator of secondary school effectiveness*. Paper presented at the annual meeting of the American Educational Research Association, New York, NY.

Lang, M.H. (1991). *Effective school status: A methodological study of classification consistency*. Unpublished doctoral dissertation, Louisiana State University, Baton Rouge.

Lang, M.H., Teddlie, C., & Oescher, J. (1992). *The effect that varying the test mode had on school effectiveness ratings*. Paper presented at the annual meeting of the American Educational Research Association, San Francisco.

Levine, D.U., & Lezotte, L.W. (1990). *Unusually effective schools: A review and analysis of research and practice*. Madison, WI: The National Center for Effective Schools Research and Development.

Mintzberg, H. (1979). *The structuring of organisations*. Englewood Cliffs, NJ: Prentice Hall.

Moreno, J.L. (1953). *Who will survive?* New York: Beacon.

Mortimore, P., Sammons, P., Stoll, L., Lewis, D., & Ecob, R. (1988). *School Matters: The Junior Years*. Somerset, Open Books (Reprinted in 1995 by Paul Chapman: London).

Mortimore, P. (1991). School effectiveness research: Which way at the crossroads? *School Effectiveness and School Improvement*, 2(3) 213-229.

Murphy, J. (1992). School Effectiveness and School Restructuring: Contributions to Educational Improvement. *School Effectiveness and School Improvement*, 3(2), 90-109.

Musgrove, F. (1981). *School and the social order*. Chichester: Wiley.

Myers, K. (1995). *School Improvement in Practice: Schools Make a Difference Project*. London: Falmer Press.

Owens, R.G. (1987). *Organisational behaviour in education (3rd ed.)* Englewood Cliffs, NJ: Prentice Hall.

Ralph, J.H., & Fennessey, J. (1983). Science or reform: some questions about the effective schools model. *Phi Delta Kappa*, 64(10), 689-694.

Resnick, L.B., & Resnick, D.P. (1992). Assessing the thinking curriculum. In B.R. Gifford & M.C. O'Connor (Eds.), *Changing assessment: Alternative views of aptitude, achievement and instruction* (pp. 37-75). Boston, MA: Kluwer Academic Publishers.

Reynolds, D. (1976). The delinquent school. In P. Woods (Ed.), *The process of schooling* (pp. 217-229).London: Routledge and Kegan Paul.

Reynolds, D., Sullivan, M., & Murgatroyd, S.J. (1987). *The Comprehensive Experiment*. Lewes: Falmer Press.

Reynolds, D. (1989). 'The Great Welsh Education Debate, 1980-1990'. *History of Education*, 19(3), 251-260.

Reynolds, D. (1991). Changing Ineffective Schools. In M. Ainscow (Ed.), *Effective Schools for All* (pp. 92-105). London: David Fulton.

Reynolds, D. (1992). School effectiveness and school improvement in the 1990s. In D. Reynolds & P. Cuttance (Eds.), *School Effectiveness* (pp.171-187). London: Cassell.

Reynolds, D., & Cuttance, P. (Eds.) (1992). *School Effectiveness: Research, Policy and Practice*. London: Cassell.

Reynolds, D. (1992). School effectiveness and school improvement: An updated review of the British literature. In D. Reynolds & P. Cuttance (Eds.), *School effectiveness: Research, policy and practice* (pp. 1-24). London: Cassell.

Reynolds, D., & Packer, A. (1992). School effectiveness and school improvement in the 1990's. In D. Reynolds & P. Cuttance (Eds.), *School Effectiveness* (pp. 171-187). London: Cassell.

Reynolds, D., Creemers, B.P.M., Hopkins, D., Stoll, L., & Bollen, R. (1996). *Making Good Schools.* London: Routledge.

Reynolds, D. (1996). Turning around ineffective schools: some evidence and some speculations. In J. Gray, D. Reynolds, C. Fitz-Gibbon & D. Jesson (Eds.), *Merging Traditions* (pp. 150-164). London: Cassell.

Reynolds, D., & Farrell, S. (1996). *Worlds Apart? - A Review of International Studies of Educational Achievement Involving England.* London: HMSO for OFSTED.

Rogers, E.M., & Kincaid, D. L. (1980). *Communication networks: Toward a new paradigm for research.* New York: Macmillan.

Rowan, B., Bossert, S.T., & Dwyer, D.C. (1983). Research on effective schools: A cautionary note. *Educational Researcher,* 12(4), 24-31.

Rowan, B. (1984). Shamanistic rituals in effective schools. *Issues in Education,* 2, 76-87.

Rutter, M., Maughan, B., Mortimore, P., & Ouston, J., & Smith, A. (1979). *Fifteen thousand hours: Secondary schools and their effects on children.* London: Open Books and Boston, MA: Harvard University Press.

Rutter, M. (1980). *Changing Youth in a Changing Society.* Oxford: Nuffield Provincial Hospitals Trust.

Rutter, M. (1983). School effects on pupil progress - findings and policy implications. *Child Development,* 54(1), 1–29.

Sammons, P., Mortimore, P., & Thomas, S. (1996). Do schools perform consistently across outcomes and areas? In J. Gray, D. Reynolds, C. Fitz-Gibbon, & D. Jesson (Eds.), *Merging traditions: The future of research on school effectiveness and school improvement.* (pp. 3-29). London: Cassell.

Sarason, S. (1982). *The Culture of the School and the Problem of Educational Change.* Boston: Allyn & Bacon.

Scheerens, J., & Creemers, B.P.M. (1989). Conceptualising school effectiveness. *International Journal of Educational Research,* 13, 689-706.

Scheerens, J. (1992). *Effective schooling: Research, theory and practice.* London: Cassell.

Scheerens, J. (1993). Basic school effectiveness research: Items for a research agenda. *School Effectiveness and School Improvement,* 4(1), 17-36.

Scheerens, J., & Bosker, R. (1997). *The Foundations of Educational Effectiveness.* Oxford: Pergamon Press.

Slater, R.O., & Teddlie, C. (1992). Toward a theory of school effectiveness and leadership. *School Effectiveness and School Improvement,* 3(4), 247-257.

Stoll, L. (1995). *The complexity and challenge of ineffective schools.* Paper presented at the European Conference on Educational Research Association, Bath, UK.

Stoll, L., & Fink, D. (1996). *Changing our schools.* Buckingham: Open University Press.

Stoll, L., Myers, K., & Reynolds, D. (1996). *Understanding ineffectiveness.* Paper presented at the annual meeting of the American Educational Research Association, New York.

Stoll, L., & Myers, K. (1997). *No Quick Fixes: Perspectives on Schools In Difficulty*. Lewes: Falmer Press.

Stringfield, S. (1994). A model of elementary school effects. In D. Reynolds, B.P.M. Creemers, P.S. Nesselrodt, E.C. Schaffer, S. Stringfield & C. Teddlie (Eds.), *Advances in School Effectiveness Research and Practice* (pp. 153-188). London: Pergamon.

Teddlie, C., & Kochan, S. (1991). *Evaluation of a troubled high school: Methods, results, and implications.* Paper presented at the annual meeting of the American Education Research Association, Chicago, IL.

Teddlie, C., & Stringfield, S. (1993). *Schools make a difference: Lessons learned from a 10-year study of school effects*. New York: Teachers College Press.

Teddlie, C., Lang, M. H., & Oescher, J. (1995). The masking of the delivery of educational services to lower achieving students. *Urban Education,* 30(2), 125-149.

Teddlie, C. (1996). *School Effectiveness Indices: East Baton Rough Parish Public Schools, Academic Years 1991-92, 1992-93, 1993-94.* Baton Rough, LA: Louisiana State University, College of Education.

Teddlie, C., & Reynolds, D. (in press). *The International Handbook of School Effectiveness Research*. Lewes: Falmer Press.

Tyne, T.F., & Geary, W. (1980). Patterns of acceptance-rejection among male-female elementary school students. *Child Study Journal,* 10, 179-190.

Webb, E.J., Campbell, D.T., Schwartz, R.D., Sechrest, L., & Grove, J.B. (1981). *Nonreactive measures in the social sciences*. Boston, MA: Houghton Mifflin.

Wimpelberg, R., Teddlie, C., & Stringfield, S. (1989). Sensitivity to context: The past and future of effective schools research. *Educational Administration Quarterly,* 25(1), 82-107.

Index

A

ability level, 129
academic standards, 207
accommodation, 17, 28
accountability, 2, 62, 112, 138, 143, 219
achievement, 1, 6, 7, 38, 53, 54, 55, 58,
    59, 63, 87, 89, 90, 97, 98, 99, 101,
    102, 103, 104, 105, 106, 107, 108,
    111, 115, 119, 121, 122, 123, 124,
    125, 131, 132, 134, 135, 136, 137,
    138, 139, 141, 143, 146, 162, 166,
    168, 175, 185, 187, 188, 199, 203,
    204, 206, 207, 216, 227, 228, 232,
    236, 246
achievement orientation, 199, 203
action plan, 51, 137, 140, 142, 144, 145,
    146, 147, 150, 155, 156, 158, 161,
    162, 165, 167, 191
adaptive education, 72, 74, 76, 77, 81, 84
adaptive instruction, 6, 65, 69, 75, 76, 81,
    111, 123, 129, 130, 188
adolescent, 170, 171, 172, 173, 174, 175,
    177, 179, 181, 188, 191, 192, 195
adult education, 23, 28
aptitude-treatment, 215
assessment, 8, 63, 72, 73, 75, 76, 84, 87,
    88, 89, 107, 108, 149, 162, 174, 187,
    188, 189, 193, 203, 219, 223, 226,
    239, 243
attitudes, 7, 73, 77, 87, 106, 146, 155,
    167, 168, 169, 170, 185, 212, 227, 228
autonomy, 1, 2, 5, 9, 12, 13, 14, 15, 16,
    21, 64, 92, 164
autonomy of schools, 13, 15

B

basic skills, 166, 206, 207, 209, 210, 211,
    212, 215
bilingual education, 63

C

capacities, 96, 119, 173
Carroll model, 106
catchment area, 233
chaos theory, 221
class size, 3, 4, 6, 89, 90, 91, 92, 93, 94,
    95, 96, 97, 98, 99, 101, 102, 103, 104,
    105, 106, 107, 108, 109, 110, 111,
    112, 190, 192, 225, 241
classroom climate, 107, 198, 203, 206,
    207, 234
classroom management, 107, 206
clusters, 5, 69, 70, 71, 72, 73, 74, 77, 78,
    79, 80, 82, 83, 84
cohesion, 116, 123, 127, 128, 146, 166,
    203, 221, 235, 245
cohort, 4, 52, 53, 80, 101, 102, 120, 121,
    124, 125, 126, 127, 131, 132, 133,
    134, 135, 136, 137, 138, 226, 239
combating educational disadvantages, 29
common core curriculum, 6, 113, 114
comparative studies, 73, 79, 202, 233
compensatory education programmes, 35
consistency, 8, 145, 146, 148, 154, 155,
    157, 159, 163, 181, 202, 221, 227,
    228, 234, 235, 236, 245, 246
constancy, 146, 221, 235, 238
constructivism, 179, 208, 209, 210, 211,
    214, 215

F

G

H

I